Beyond the Mainframe

For the other Conor – the planet must now support two of us.

Beyond the Mainframe

A guide to open computer systems

CONOR SEXTON

Butterworth-Heinemann Ltd
Linacre House, Jordan Hill, Oxford OX2 8DP

℞ A member of the Reed Elsevier plc group

OXFORD LONDON   BOSTON
MUNICH NEW DELHI SINGAPORE SYDNEY
TOKYO TORONTO WELLINGTON

First published 1995

© Conor Sexton 1995

British Library Cataloguing in Publication Data
A catalogue record for this book is available from the British Library

ISBN 0 7506 1902 3

Produced by Graham Douglas, Bath

Printed in Great Britain
by Scotprint Ltd, Musselburgh

Contents

Part 3   Standards for Interconnection and   143
Interoperability

Preface

This book started life in 1992. The motivation was real, if not completely clear at the time. My experiences in commercial computing and development of system software indicated a need for a text dealing firstly with the technologies of open and client–server computer systems and secondly acting as a kind of compendium of clear definitions and explanations of those technologies. The whole thing should go into the technology to a level deep enough to be useful while not so deep as to lose the main intended audience, the intelligent non-specialist user or manager of computer systems.

A number of excellent books on open systems and client–server have been written; with a few exceptions they seem too abstract and dense for this kind of readership. Also, topics such as IBM PCs, Windows 95, pipelining in RISC microprocessors, and LU6.2 communications are not automatic choices for inclusion in open systems texts, which tend to concentrate on things like the POSIX standards. But they are real and affect everyday business, so they are included here, along with many other subjects which might not be considered part of 'pure' open systems.

An important influence on this book is the rise of client–server technologies, often implemented with open systems. Here is a related subject needing explanation and clarification.

If this book has one objective, it is clarity, both of expression and in demystifying open systems and client–server. It has been influenced by seminars I have presented in association with IBM, Philips Austria GmbH and Siemens Nixdorf Information Systems: probing questions from real people are better than all the abstract thought in the world.

The title, *Beyond the Mainframe*, was chosen only shortly before publication. The initial intention was to use the current subtitle as the main title but *Beyond the Mainframe* seemed more likely to attract the kind of general readership for which the book is intended. It is not intended to indicate that the mainframe computer is a thing of the past – it is not, being used increasingly as a so-called data warehouse or enterprise server – but rather to recognise the more general shift to smaller, distributed systems.

By way of acknowledgement, I should mention the assistance and (not always just moral) support of Peter MacNamara, formerly of Philips, and Brian Cahill of Siemens Nixdorf.

Mike Cash, my Publisher at Butterworth-Heinemann, deserves my thanks for his amused tolerance in accepting several lengthy delays before finally receiving a completed draft.

Conor Sexton
Dublin, Summer 1995

General introduction

The objective of *Beyond the Mainframe* is to describe clearly the component technologies of open and client–server computer systems and networks. It is intended to be accessible to non-specialist readers including:

▸ Managers responsible for procurement of computer systems or management of them when they have been procured

▸ Managers directly, indirectly or not at all involved with computers who want to know the terminology and the main principles, as an aid to working with their colleagues

▸ Those in education, either giving or receiving; probable courses where this book will be relevant include Computer Science, Informatics and Business Studies

▸ Sales, pre-sale and post-sale staff working for computer manufacturers, resellers and other system vendors

▸ The educated general reader

This book contains only three chapters, which are rather large. The alternative was about twenty small ones; I feel that the presentation herein is more coherent, based as it is on the distinction of portability from interoperability, of the system from the network.

Part 1 looks at why we need open systems and client–server anyway. At the end, it gives a summary of necessary standards, which are described in Parts 2 and 3. Each of the three Parts has its own Introduction. It is enough here to point out that Part 2 describes computers as stand-alone entities and that Part 3 deals with networking them. The formats of both Part 2 and Part 3 are based loosely on the OSI Reference Model considered from Layer 1 (the hardware) up to Layer 7 (application software). While a book of this size cannot be exhaustive either in breadth of topics treated or in the depth of their consideration, I hope that not too much is omitted that is important. A large Glossary is given in Appendix A. It does not attempt to be a dictionary of computing terms but presents concise definitions and explanations of many proper nouns and acronyms used in everyday computing.

Part 1

The Need for Standards in Computing

Introduction: definition of terms

Beyond the Mainframe is about open systems and the many technical and business subjects which surround the concept. It also tries to show how open systems are important in the implementation of client–server computer networks. There are as many definitions of the term open systems as there are computer systems which claim actually to be 'open'. It is possible to hold that the IBM-compatible PC is an open system because its use is so widespread. Others will claim that openness is characterised by the UNIX operating system because it is not tied to any particular type of computer equipment. Some say that 'the computer is the network' and that communications technologies define openness.

This book will straight away settle on a definition of open systems with which some people may disagree in detail but which is difficult to dispute in general. Open computer systems, where 'computer system' includes communications and networks, have the following characteristics:

- ▸ Portability
- ▸ Scalability
- ▸ Connectivity
- ▸ Interoperability

to a greater degree than do closed systems.

Portability means that a computer program can be transferred unchanged from an arbitrary computer system A to a (probably completely different) computer system B and will work properly on B. A fully portable program therefore might be moved from an IBM 3090 mainframe to a completely different type of system running the UNIX operating system, and be expected to work without change.

Scalability means that a computer program will work with acceptable performance across a range of computer systems of different sizes and power.

Connectivity implies that open computer systems can be physically connected and that communication is possible between them.

Interoperability means that it is possible for open computer systems to work together: a user of computer system A can use the resources of computer system B or remotely run a program on computer system B, perhaps without being aware that the two systems may be hundreds of miles apart.

Portability implies scalability, and interoperability requires connectivity. We can therefore say that the openness of a computer system is defined by the degree of its software portability and interoperability with other systems. If a computer system is so devised that:

- ► Its programs are portable to widely-used systems

- ► It can interoperate with widely-used systems

- ► It conforms to internationally-accepted standards defining portability and interoperability

then it can be called an open system.

As defined in Part 3, a client–server system is an arrangement of networked computing devices which uses distributed intelligence to treat both the server (often a minicomputer or mainframe) and the clients (usually PCs or workstations) as intelligent programmable devices, thus exploiting the full computing power of both. Many components of a client–server system use open systems technologies.

The rest of this book explores what open systems and client–server are about, dealing on the way with a number of fascinating related technologies.

The benefits of compatible equipment

'Compatible' is one of the computer industry's more overused terms. Its meaning, on the face of it, is quite clear; one dictionary definition is 'of equipment which can be used in combination'. And yet the world of computers succeeds in muddying these otherwise clear waters. The meaning of IBM-compatible (especially), VGA-compatible, PostScript-compatible, and others, will cause disputes even among people technically qualified to know what is meant, and confusion in the minds of most others.

Before we consider exclusively the world of computer systems let us look at what compatibility means in a wider context.

There are many industries whose viability would be seriously prejudiced if the equipment produced by their various manufacturers were not compatible.

One of the oldest examples is the railway industry. For a railway network to be viable economically and indeed to make any sense at all, the thickness of the tracks used and the distance (or gauge) separating them must be standardised. As is the case with so many things which originated in the 19th century, the standard which was in the end adopted is a British one: a gauge of four feet, seven and one-half inches was internationally adopted (with some dissent from Russia, which later paid a military price for it). Why 55 ½ inches was thought a satisfactory measure is of no consequence; what is important is that it was widely agreed to.

Other important examples of compatibility in the transport industry include the design of internal-combustion and Diesel engines; fuel types; placement of controls in cars; and agreement (at least on a national basis) to drive on one side of the road or the other. In the military area, incompatibility can have catastrophic consequences. The NATO alliance expended much effort in the 1970s and 1980s in ensuring standardisation of the equipment used by its member countries. These efforts ranged from large-scale purchase of identical aircraft by several states to ensuring that the diameters of the nozzles of refuelling pipes were made uniform.

Standard equipment can accelerate recovery from natural disaster. After the 1993 flooding in the Midwest of the U.S.A., supplies of electricity were usually quickly restored by the utility companies because of standardisation of equipment used in damaged substations.

It seems obvious and natural that all fax machines appear able to send messages to all others and be understood; that the audio cassette cartridge introduced by Philips in 1963 is a universal standard; and that nearly all video cassette tapes and VCRs conform with the VHS standard.

Consider the last of these examples. Beginning in the late 1970s, three separate technologies were developed for video-cassette recording:

VHS, Betamax and the Philips V2000 system. The industry ended up standardising on VHS, notwithstanding the fact that the other two systems are held to be, in many respects, technically superior. The impetus behind the standardisation was a market-driven, not a technological, one: consumers would not tolerate two or more incompatible recording formats and the industry accepted the absolute need to settle on one.

Manufacturers of equipment may try to protect their market share by making the equipment incompatible with that of any other manufacturer. Sometimes, as in the video case, the market will not tolerate this. In other fields, there is a gain for the supplier of incompatible equipment, but the gain is usually short-term.

When automatic teller machines (ATMs) were first widely introduced, competing banks and other financial institutions deliberately made their systems incompatible with all others. The banks' networks were not linked: to get money, you had to go to an ATM of your own bank. This approach was clearly restrictive and tended to annoy the consumer, who generally just wanted money and did not very much care whose ATM it came out of.

As experience grew and networking technologies improved banks increasingly linked their ATM networks and made access to their machines available to customers of other financial institutions. It was found that cross-use of different banks' ATMs tended to balance out when a large number of consumers was involved and – most importantly – overall use of the ATM systems increased.

So it is with computers. The early (and in some cases, still current) policy of computer-system suppliers was to make their machines purposely incompatible, unable to run the software of other vendors and unable to intercommunicate. The resulting proprietary lock-in seemed to guarantee continuing high revenues and margins for these suppliers but those marketing open systems benefit from an increase in size of the overall market.

Standardisation of simple railway, fax and videotape systems was almost unthinkingly demanded by consumers. In the case of computer systems, however, things have been different. Computers, communications and software are complex and it is only in recent times that they have become reliable and cheap enough to be regarded as commodity items, with corresponding increases in the standardisation, or openness of systems.

The move towards open computer systems depends on a core set of the services provided, particularly by operating systems and communications subsystems, conforming with international standards. To meet the needs of a particular application an open system supplier may design in extra functionality incompatible with that of other vendors. The system remains open provided the core services still conform with the standards.

In the world of the late 1990s and the early 21st century, consumers will see no more reason to tolerate gratuitous incompatibilities between computer systems than do users of fax machines now. The greatest force driving standardisation will be intolerance on the part of consumers of needless differences between the products of different suppliers.

Widespread availability of open computer systems and software will have the effect of increasing the size of the market for them, in the same way as the acceptance of the IBM PC as a standard has caused those systems to proliferate. It is with the technologies involved in rendering computer systems open that this book is concerned.

Problems of compatibility in computing

Although moves toward standardisation of computer systems and their software are accelerating, most programmers and users of computers still accept the existence of a myriad of incompatibilities between the equipment and software of different vendors. It is the purpose of this section briefly to explain the problems caused by these incompatibilities for users and purchasers of computer systems and to give some background to the importance currently accorded the movement toward open, standardised systems and software.

The incompatibilities range from (at the lowest level) variations in cabling and magnetic storage media to (at the highest) differences which affect the end-user's efficiency and productivity. They can be summarised as follows:

▶ Incompatible equipment including cables, storage media and peripheral devices

- ► Different file formats: files readable on one system cannot be read by another

- ► Various terminal display standards: display units cannot be moved between systems

- ► Non-portable software

- ► Inconsistent and non-standard programming languages

- ► Differing communication protocols: one system cannot communicate and share information with another

- ► Non-standard procedures for managing and administering different systems

- ► Usability problems: programs to do a given job (a word-processor, for example) differ enough between systems to make transfer by a non-specialist user difficult or impossible

After a certain investment of time, a user of a given system can become productive and efficient. It is when the user, or programs and data required by the user, must move to a new system that difficulties and extra costs are incurred.

The cost of incompatibility

When computer equipment or end-user programs are introduced or replaced the direct costs – the capital costs of the hardware and software – are those most often considered. The indirect costs, however, may be much greater:

- ► Re-cabling buildings

- ► Training system operators and administrators

- ► Training end-users in the new procedures necessary to do their work

- ► Converting and moving old data files to the new system

- ► The loss of the investment which was made by users, operators and others in becoming proficient in use of the old system

- ► Reduced productivity and increased frustration on the part of users of the new system

Anyone who has ever been faced with an unfamiliar computer system is aware of the obstacles in the path of doing even the simplest of tasks.

We have a new system, a word-processing program, a laser printer and a lot of cables. There is a requirement to enter and print a one-page letter. Feeling a little adventurous, we hook everything together, hoping that the cables we have used are the right ones and, further, that they are connected to the right sockets in the computer, monitor and printer.

We switch everything on and, yes, there are results. Perhaps the computer even starts properly and, after a few minutes, a login prompt or a screen full of graphic icons is visible. Using accumulated experience, we start the word-processor, enter our letter and go to print it.

It refuses to print. The little green light doesn't come on; there are no satisfactory sounds of paper moving and printer whirring. Is it the cable? Should it be a null-modem or a Centronics? There are three identical 9-pin plugs and two 25s on the back of the computer. Which is for the printer? What is the connection on the back of the printer marked Auxiliary? Maybe the word-processor somehow isn't set up to print? Any equation of four variables takes time to solve. One gets used to solving them. But the experience seems to be the same every next time a new system is involved. After much effort, the page is printed and immediately a red light appears on the printer panel alongside a message complaining about the paper size being wrong.

It just printed, didn't it? How can it be wrong? Do I have to program the printer to know page sizes or the word-processor – or both?

Many users give up at the start of a sequence like this, call their customer representative and, of course, the object of the exercise, the letter being produced, is not accomplished. The persistent user-turned-service-engineer will succeed but at the end will notice that a rather small fraction of the effort expended was directed to the productive end of getting the letter out. If the user has an accounting sense, he or she may wonder who or what is paying for the three hours it has taken to accomplish a ten-minute task.

At every point of the learning-curve of adopting a new computer system, there is a harassed user or operator suffering similar bewilderment. When a productive goal is to be accomplished, there is a strong sense of 'starting from two steps behind' – of having to do a lot of preparatory work irrelevant to the end goal in order to realise that goal. After all the capital acquisition is done and the sales representatives have departed, frustration and waste of time are the major costs of incompatibility. One of the major objectives of open systems and standardisation is to remove this cost.

Data transfer

One of the main considerations in changing computer system is that of transferring the data files which were in use on the old system and which may contain several years' accumulated information.

The exercise is usually not simple. Broadly, there are three ways of getting the data from one system to the other:

- ▶ Transfer by compatible magnetic media: tapes or disks
- ▶ Transfer by communications link
- ▶ Manual re-entry

The last option in a surprising proportion of cases is the most effective. The effort required, along with the certainty of error, seems to render it prohibitive in cost. It may not seem so bad when set against the less obvious costs of the alternatives:

- ▶ Ensuring that the old and new systems have physically compatible disk or tape devices. Most do not and there are even differences in format between different kinds of IBM PC
- ▶ Setting up a communication link between the systems, involving compatible cabling and driver software at each end. If the old and new systems are different enough, it may be impossible to do a direct transfer: a third system such as an IBM PC may be necessary as a communications 'common-denominator'
- ▶ When the data is eventually transferred, converting it to the (inevitably different) format required by the application program on the new system. The converter will be a program which may not exist and may not be simple to write. Conversion may also cause some of the original formatting information (consider underlining in a word-processor document) to be lost which must later be re-entered

The greater the disparity in age between the old and the new systems the more likely that the manual re-entry route will be the one adopted. On the other extreme, transfer of word-processor documents between modern systems will likely be quite simple, with conversion programs supplied for the purpose.

Porting and rewriting software

In the same way as the data files referred to above, programs may need to be transferred from an old system to a new one. The process is referred to as (trans)porting software. Software which can be ported with little or no change is called portable. The technical issues which define and influence portability of software are complex and far-reaching, involving considerations of operating systems and programming languages. Standards for software portability, together with standards allowing computer systems to interoperate, define open systems.

Once again, the greater the disparity in age and type between the new and the old systems, the more likely it is that software will have to be transferred by completely rewriting it. For example, an application program written in the 1960s in assembler specifically for an IBM mainframe computer is unlikely to be in any way portable to a modern workstation or network system and will almost certainly have to be rewritten.

If it is rewritten, care should be taken that the owner of the software is not once again locked in to a non-portable system which will in the future be expensive to change.

At the other extreme, a program written in a standardised computer language for a modern computer system is very likely to be capable of being ported with little or no change.

Because of the huge costs of porting and rewriting software, great emphasis is now being placed by major software developers on producing programs which are easily portable between popular computing environments.

Lack of horizontal software

In another classification, computer software comes in two types: horizontal and vertical.

Horizontal software is that which is not specifically directed at any particular application or industrial sector but is potentially usable by many. A word-processing program is an excellent example.

Vertical software is that which is for a specific application: a good example is a bill-of-material program in a suite of manufacturing software.

Usually, for historical reasons, horizontal software is more portable than vertical software.

The computer companies which came to prominence in the 1950s – IBM, Univac (later Sperry Univac, now part of Unisys), Honeywell and others – did so by selling large mainframe computers to other enterprises which needed for specific purposes the computing power offered by these machines. Examples include manufacturing, airline reservation, aerospace applications and large-scale databases. This vertical software, written for mainframes to meet the specific application requirements of individual clients, was inherently non-portable.

With the advent of microcomputers, supporting standard operating systems and programming languages, which are within the reach of individuals and small companies, there has been an explosion in the availability of horizontal software packages including word-processing, spreadsheet, personal-finance and simple database programs. These have mostly been written in standardised programming languages to run under the control of standard operating systems such as MS-DOS and UNIX and, compared to the mainframe assembly language program, are very easy to port between modern computer systems.

If it is not easy to port software to a given type of computer system then vendors of horizontal software are deterred from doing so on the grounds of cost. Users of the system will either have to forego popular and useful horizontal software or incur the expense of acquiring a system capable of running it.

Trapped investment

Until the appearance of the microcomputer and the new standardised operating systems, computer manufacturers were able to lock customers into a single-supplier purchasing policy by supplying computer equipment which would run only the software specifically written for it. The customer then had two major reasons not to change this proprietary system:

▸ The cost of replacing equipment and rewriting software

▸ The cost of abandoning the technical expertise built up in operation of the proprietary system

In a single-supplier relationship, pricing by that supplier is unlikely to be competitive. Also, the costs of expertise and development of software for proprietary computer systems are invariably higher than the equivalent costs in a standardised environment.

Difficulty in connecting systems and networks

The advent of IBM PCs and the UNIX operating system (both are more fully described later) has made it less difficult than heretofore to interconnect computer systems and networks.

Before the PC and UNIX were available to act as the glue between the computers and networks of different suppliers, it was very difficult to connect proprietary systems – for example IBM and Digital Equipment Corporation networks – so that they could communicate and share data.

IBM's network strategy is System Network Architecture (SNA), extended since the mid-1980s with Advanced Program to Program Communications (APPC) and Advanced Peer-to-Peer Networking (APPN). The protocol suites naturally favour IBM computers and other equipment as elements (called nodes) within the network. Digital Equipment Corporation's network environment is called DECnet; it equally is biased toward Digital Equipment's VAX line of computer systems. Both have been adopted as *de facto* standards by other companies specialising in network products such as gateways, which allow interconnection of dissimilar networks.

The more modern standardised PC and UNIX systems can readily be organised in networks. Equipment and software, including gateways, bridges, routers and repeaters, are available which allow these networks to be connected to each other as well as to the proprietary networks of the more traditional computer suppliers.

As the computer infrastructure of a large enterprise develops over time, it usually results in the implementation of a number of incompatible networks which must then be interconnected as something of an afterthought. Although the equipment and software are available to achieve this, it is still a challenge for large computer users to organise their various systems cohesively in networks to the benefit of business.

Conversion costs: future-proof software

The costs of converting software to run on an incompatible system are very high. One of the factors which determines whether a computer system is or is not open is the portability of its software. Although to convert application programs from an older, non-standard, system to an open system may be expensive, there is then some assurance that the cost of moving the software to the next replacement system will be very much less.

Hardware and software complexity

As software applications grow increasingly complex, the need to be able port at least large parts of them unchanged is growing more pressing.

Development of computer hardware has led that of software in its use of modularity, the Black Box concept. If a part malfunctions, a service engineer (or, on small systems, the user) replaces the faulty electronic component at the board level. No understanding is needed of what went wrong; the inherent complexity of the equipment and its operation are ignored.

Of necessity, the same trend is now becoming apparent with software: it should be possible to move a large body of software between different systems unchanged, without having to know how it works (the internals), and to have a high degree of assurance that the software will work as well on the destination system as it does on the original.

The sheer complexity of modern software systems (even PC operating systems now run to 3 million lines of code) and the expense of making changes to it demand this portability.

Also, to recoup the enormous costs of the development of such complex systems, their suppliers find it necessary to sell as many copies as possible – typically 500,000 copies to break even in the mass PC market.

While it is possible for software suppliers to survive by servicing only the huge PC market, that market is very competitive with tight margins of profit. It gives a supplier new markets if its software is easily portable without change to other standardised (open) systems.

Background to open systems

Basics of computing

The degree of a system's openness is defined by the ease with which its programs may be ported to other systems and how readily it interoperates with them. In the jargon, a computer system, its operating system software, utilities and application programs are collectively often referred to as a computing *platform*.

Development of the electronic computer, software and communications began in the 1940s. Many technical advances since have made current efforts at standardisation possible.

This section gives a summarised history of the development of computer technology. This additionally serves to introduce and explain many terms and concepts which appear often in computer literature and later in this book. Many of these terms mean nothing to the uninitiated and, even to those who are very computer-literate, may be ill-understood. Consider *architecture, application program interface (API), host, client–server* and *cache* as examples. These and very many other terms, which at least originally had precise meanings, tend to be used without explanation; different understandings of them come into being and their true meanings are lost through slack usage. It is one of the purposes of this book to explain clearly the meaning of a large number of terms which are more usually allowed to mystify the user.

The fundamental technology of digital computers has remained unchanged since the 1940s. Computers are built according to the so-called von Neumann architecture (the *stored-program computer*) which has the following general characteristics:

▸ A *processor* that executes program instructions and *memory* in which a program and its data are stored

▸ A memory that is as large and as fast as possible and may be accessed randomly

▸ When executed, programs are first loaded into memory from an external storage device, in most cases nowadays a magnetic disk

▸ Under control of an operator or a controlling program (an *operating system*), a program instruction is fetched from memory into the processor and executed. This is done repeatedly (the *fetch–execute* cycle) until the program's instructions are exhausted

▸ Because the program's instructions as well as its data reside in memory the instructions themselves may be modified to indicate the next instruction to be executed. In modern computers this sequencing is usually controlled by a *program counter*, a *register* (high-speed memory area) which records the address in memory of the next instruction. Altering the contents of the program counter during execution of the program makes iterations (loops) possible

Although, in the period since John von Neumann's 1945 design, there have been innumerable refinements to computers and software, modern machines are essentially nothing more than very much smaller, faster and cheaper developments of their early counterparts. Computers remain devices which blindly carry out instructions in a predetermined sequence at very high speeds – routinely ten million basic operations, such as addition or subtraction, per second.

The earliest computers had memory made up of banks of valves, each recording an on/off (one/zero) status. The valves were later to be replaced by magnetic core memories, transistors and semiconductors – leading to today's *silicon chip* – but the function of their replacements is unchanged. The benefits of smaller components include saving of space, reduction in electrical power used (and waste heat generated), and improved reliability.

The earliest computers had no control programs or operating systems and were programmed manually using physical cable interconnections. The computers were automatic; the instructions executed in sequence until exhausted and the operator would know the program was finished when the lights on the computer's front panel went out.

In any technological field, efforts toward standardisation start when the following conditions are met:

▸ When the component technology is mastered and is no longer confined to the research laboratory

▸ When the technology is used for productive purposes in real life

▸ When the technology becomes sufficiently inexpensive to start generating commodities

▸ When the products of the technology are market-driven by consumer demand

The technology of computer systems and software has very recently come to satisfy these criteria. It is sometimes said that computers are now in the position in their evolutionary path which the Ford Model T occupied in the development of automobiles in the 1920s: they can for the first time be mass-produced and sold to a mass market. The development and standardisation of computer systems and software can be considered under the headings of the major component parts. These are:

▸ The computer hardware

▸ The control program or operating system

▸ Communications and networking facilities

▸ Languages in which programs are written for the computer

▸ The interface presented by the computer system to the people using it

The remainder of this section briefly considers the past and present of computers under each of these classifications in turn.

Computer hardware

Modern computer systems have their genesis in the military necessity of the Second World War. The earliest applications of the stored-program computer model originated by von Neumann were Colossus, developed in Britain (1943) and ENIAC (Electronic Numeric Integrator And Calculator), operational in the U.S.A. from 1946.

Colossus was a special-purpose computer designed to break the German Enigma rotor cipher. This was thought by the German military to be for all practical purposes unbreakable, relying as it did on enormous numbers of permutations in the scrambling of plain text transmitted. In fact, with the aid of Colossus, the German cipher was broken throughout the war; many of the research activities related to Colossus are still classified in the U.K.

ENIAC was designed mainly for computing artillery fire-control tables but also had general-purpose capabilities and proved more important to the future development of computer systems than any other early design. It contained 19,000 vacuum tubes, could perform 5,000 arithmetic operations per second and consumed no less than 200 KW of power. Each run of the machine had to be programmed by changing plugged connections. This process could take several days and was only worthwhile doing if the resulting run carried out significant processing.

The first truly commercial computer was the UNIVAC (Universal Automatic Computer), designed by Eckert and Mauchly and delivered first (1951) to the United States Census Bureau. The machine incorporated more than 5,000 vacuum tubes and could do 500 multiplications per second. A single unit of information was the *binary digit* (bit), representing the one/zero on/off state of a vacuum tube. The UNIVAC had a *word* (a group of bits which has a specific *memory address*) length of 45 bits; each word could represent an 11-digit decimal number or 6 alphabetic characters.

Apart from consideration of some terminology, the further development of computers through the 1950s up to the mid-1960s is not very important for the modern reader. It is said that development of the technology has proceeded in a number of *generations*, based on the nature of electronic devices used in successive systems. The first generation is characterised by use of vacuum tubes; the second replaced these with transistors; the third used groups of transistors in *integrated circuits*;

and the (less-generally accepted) fourth generation employs enormous numbers of transistors implemented with semiconductors in wafers of silicon called chips.

In all cases, the basic component is a device capable of recording a one/zero value. Large numbers of these devices are then used in combination to implement very complex circuits. These circuits in turn control a computer's operation and allow it to represent data and execute programs, sequences of instructions which carry out processing operations on that data.

A computer's power has traditionally been measured by its *word-length* and, more recently by the width of its *data path*, the number of bits which can be transferred in parallel along a *data bus* (a parallel set of electrical connections) between the computer's processor and the main memory. Since the mid-1960s, word-length has come to be calculated in multiples of eight bits. The eight-bit unit is called the *byte* and is nowadays almost always the smallest data unit which for which there is an individual address in the computer's memory. It is said that the byte is the smallest *addressable* memory unit. Because it has eight bits, each byte can be used to store up to 256 different combinations of settings. Some or all of these 256 combinations are used in modern systems to record numeric, alphabetic and special characters.

A given combination of bit settings is arbitrarily assigned a meaning, say the lower-case letter 'b'. A *code-table* of meanings is built which accommodates all or most of the characters required for use in processing. Any number of code tables is possible, but two have become predominant: the EBCDIC (Extended Binary Coded Decimal Interchange Code) largely used in IBM systems; and ASCII (American Standard Code for Information Interchange) used by most other computers. In EBCDIC, the letter 'b' is represented as the bit sequence 10000010. The ASCII representation of 'b' is 01100010. The code table used for programs and data has implications for program portability (how readily a program can be moved between different computers) of which we shall see more later. Use of such sequences promotes use of the *octal* (numeric base 8) and *hexadecimal* (base 16) number systems, in contrast to decimal, which is hardly ever used by modern computers to represent their data.

The UNIVAC is the quintessential first-generation computer. A good example of a second-generation transistor based machine is the IBM

1400 series, dating from about 1959. But it is the IBM System/360, announced in April 1964, which was the first of the third-generation computers and has dominated development of the computer industry ever since.

The 360 used the eight-bit byte and a 32-bit word length. It introduced the OS/360 operating system which allowed orderly scheduling of batch jobs. Later versions of the operating system supported *interactive* use – *ad-hoc* question-and-answer computing sessions conducted by individual users. OS/360 introduced a comprehensive *instruction set*: a large number of low-level instruction formats which could be combined in *assembly language* programs.

These instructions were in turn implemented by *microprogramming*. A microprogram is essentially a subsidiary set of commands, substituted for an instruction when it is used, which work directly with the machine's register, memory and other hardware. The full set of microprograms used to implement a computer's instruction set is sometimes referred to as the machine's *firmware*. The effect of microprogramming was to separate the system's hardware design from the instruction set which used the hardware. If an error appeared in the design, it was only necessary to change the firmware, not the actual circuits. Also, the instruction set itself could more easily be altered, with further implications for program portability. After System/360, microprogramming was widely accepted and used in competing designs.

The 360 also introduced *indirect addressing*. A *base register* contained a memory address to which was added an *offset* specified by a program instruction. The resulting address was the location of the required data in memory. The indirect addressing scheme simplified the circuits necessary to do decoding of addresses.

Finally, the 360 introduced *I/O channels*: independent input-output processors to handle transfer of data between memory and peripheral devices such as magnetic tapes and disks. As well as offloading from the main processor the job of processing input-output operations, the channel approach also allowed IBM to sell the same peripheral equipment to all its System/360 customers, regardless of the system model in question.

This in turn points up the fact that the System/360 was in fact a range of systems. A program which ran on any member of the range, whether relatively low- or high-powered, would also run unchanged on any other system in the range. This characteristic defines the term scalability. The 360 was one of the first scalable computers. Scalability would later also be offered in the VAX line produced by Digital Equipment Corporation and the IBM PC.

The System/360 established itself in the 1960s as a standard centralised *mainframe* computer. Facilities for data communication were rudimentary. The user's programs were brought to the computer at the data centre; computing power was not brought to the user.

As electronic technology progressed, smaller systems appeared which could compete in processing power. These came to be known under the collective description *minicomputer*. One of the first examples of the minicomputer was Digital Equipment's PDP-1 in 1965. This started a line of systems which ended with the PDP-11 and indirectly continued with the very successful VAX range of minicomputers predominant in the late 1970s and 1980s. During the same period, the *microcomputer* was introduced: a low-powered personal machine with all the essential characteristics of the larger computers. The first leader in the production of microcomputers was Apple Computer of California. IBM came late to the market, in 1981, with the first Personal Computer. The IBM PC quickly established itself as a *de facto* standard, with the Apple alternative remaining.

During the 1980s, the mainframe came to be regarded as a corporate computing system, the minicomputer as departmental and the PC as personal. In the 1990s, especially with the advent of the *workstation* – very powerful PCs and other special-purpose desktop computers – these distinctions are now blurred. Mainframes and minicomputers are in decline. Some would say that the minicomputer as a class has disappeared altogether. Most effort is now being devoted to the integration, by means of networking, of the types of computers which remain.

All computer systems have an *architecture*. Architecture is one of the most abused words in computing, perhaps because it is difficult to define and because there are different meanings for the term depending on the standpoint of the person defining it. From the programmer's point of view, a computer system's architecture is characterised by the attributes of the system as they affect software design and development for it. If two computers have the same architecture, then a given program will run on both unchanged, although perhaps at different speeds.

Attributes which define a system's architecture are:

- ▸ Processor
- ▸ Storage
- ▸ Input/Output and communications

Basic computer structure

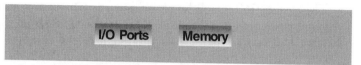

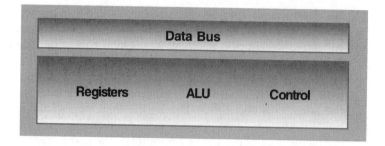

A computer's processor comprises the *control unit*, which governs the system's operation and the *arithmetic and logic unit* (ALU) which does the actual computation and processing. Computation is carried out by means of programs written to use the processor's instruction set, which may in turn be implemented by a system of microprogramming. The processor may be a *complex instruction set computer (CISC)* such as the Digital Equipment Corporation VAX or a *reduced instruction set computer (RISC)* like the newer IBM RS6000. A computer may use more than one processor, which introduces the concept of *parallelism* – the computer may be able to carry out more than one task simultaneously rather than *concurrently* (rapidly switched in and out of execution), which is the case with single-processor systems.

A computer's *processor architecture* is defined by the nature of the processor's instruction set, registers, data bus and the extent to which it is capable of parallelism. The characteristics of a system's memory, I/O and communications capabilities are relevant but less important aspects of its overall *hardware architecture*. Processor architecture determines whether software is portable and is of central importance to open systems.

Operating systems

As far as the computer user is concerned, the operating system is a program which runs all the time, allocates the system's resources among competing users and allows programs to run apparently simultaneously while ensuring that they do not damage each other, the operating system or the data stored on the computer.

This definition is valid for systems which allow many programs to run concurrently. In respect of the earliest computers and, indeed, MS-DOS as it runs on IBM PCs, it is overly complex.

Up to the mid-1960s, most computers did not have operating systems. Programs were started by the user, who used arrangements of switches and plugs to control its execution. When a program finished another one could be started. Control of the system in this way by the user had a number of disadvantages:

▸ Every user had to know in detail how the computer and its programs operated

▸ Programs ran sequentially and inefficiently

▸ Sharing of system resources was inefficient

▸ Facilities which are taken for granted today, such as hierarchical *file systems* and *memory protection*, were absent

In the 1950s, the first *monitors* appeared: simple programs perpetually resident in the computer's memory which improved the efficiency of scheduling of sequential tasks (programs in execution). These early operating systems were loaded into a memory by means of a technique called *bootstrapping* or *initial program load (IPL)*. The system was 'booted' using data supplied on a small number of punched cards. Using this data, the CPU and I/O devices were commanded to read more data, thus loading the operating system 'by the bootstraps'.

The inefficiencies of sequential execution of programs were mitigated by using overlapped I/O: input-output operations could take place independently of the program which started them. The best-known application of I/O overlapping is the print operation called *spooling* (*simultaneous peripheral operations on-line*). Using spooling a program can direct a file or data to print. An independent print-manager program controlled by the operating system schedules the print job in a queue for later execution and the user program which started that job can continue executing. The main drawback of overlapped I/O is that programs using it are made more complex: they have to be able to communicate with other programs in order to know the status of the I/O operations.

In the 1960s, *timesharing* and *multiprogramming* operating systems were introduced. Both allow many tasks to run concurrently but with a difference. Timesharing systems have a single memory space for tasks which are swapped in and out to a secondary storage device such as disk after a predetermined *timeslice*. Such systems are also said to be capable of *multitasking*. In a multiprogramming scheme, several separate memory areas are reserved for execution of concurrent programs. The original UNIX operating system introduced in 1969 supported timesharing; OS/360 adopted the multiprogramming approach.

With operating systems resident in the same memory as the programs they controlled, memory protection schemes were needed to ensure that programs did not occupy each other's memory or encroach on the operating system itself.

A drawback of both timesharing and multiprogramming operating systems is that all programs being executed must be fully resident in contiguous memory. Therefore, the size of programs and data which can run concurrently is limited by the physical size of memory. In early computers, with their small amounts of RAM, this was a serious problem. To address the problem the first *virtual memory* schemes were devised in the 1950s. Operating systems which implement virtual memory use the technique of *paging*. This allows application programs to run apparently in a contiguous memory space, but in fact using memory demanded in pages (*demand paging*) from the operating system. Addresses used by these programs (*virtual addresses*) are *memory mapped* to *physical addresses* within the paged memory.

Virtual memory management allows the operating system to run application programs which give the appearance of running in one area in memory but which may in fact be paged all over memory and for which pages of memory may be obtained from peripheral devices, usually magnetic disks. The overall effect of virtual memory is that the number and size of programs which can run under the control of an operating system is, in principle, unlimited by the size of the computer's physical memory. However, other limitations, such as competition for peripheral devices and the slow speed of paging, place practical limits on the number of programs which can execute even using virtual memory.

Nowadays almost all computers and operating systems except basic personal computers use some scheme of virtual memory. Virtual memory was introduced to widespread use by the IBM System/370 – a direct derivative of the S/360 – in 1972, and has been used by all successor operating systems including MVS and VM. All operating systems provide most of the following facilities in varying degrees:

▶ *Concurrent program execution:* many programs can run apparently at the same time, with the operating system separating the programs using memory protection

▶ *Resource allocation and resolution of deadlock:* the system's peripheral devices and other resources are allocated to programs by the operating system. The situation where program A is waiting for a resource being used by program B, which is in turn waiting for program A, is called *deadlock* and is resolved by all modern operating systems

▶ *Processor scheduling:* any of various schemes which try to ensure that application programs get an equitable share of execution and peripheral resources. One typical scheduling method is *round-robin scheduling*, employed by the UNIX operating system

▶ *Memory management:* for programs in execution

▶ *Filesystems:* logical groupings (usually hierarchical) of files which aid programs and users in their retrieval

▶ *Distributed systems:* including distributed filesystems, many computer systems connected by network with the facilities that a program can be run on computer B from computer A and that the filesystem and resources of another system, say computer C, can be used directly from computer A or computer B

▶ *Multiprocessing:* the facility provided by some operating systems to spread the execution of its programs over several processors. The job of scheduling many programs running on several processors is much more difficult than traditional *uniprocessor* scheduling. Only a few more modern operating systems currently support multiprocessing

Whether a program will run on a given computer system depends on whether it is in the *executable format* required by the host operating system and underlying CPU and whether it can use the facilities provided by the operating system, included those listed above. The nature of a computer's processor and operating system defines the portability part of open systems for that system.

To say (as is often said) that a program 'runs under DOS but not under UNIX' means that the program has been built in the executable format required by DOS and that it only makes requests on DOS which DOS can understand. Neither the executable format nor the requests are suitable for or understood by UNIX and the program is said therefore to be not portable between DOS and UNIX.

Popular modern operating systems include the following:

- ▸ **MS-DOS** and the nearly identical PC-DOS: control operation of nearly all of the world's personal computers. It was released with the first PC in 1981 and has more recently been extended by Microsoft Windows. Windows is not an operating system in its own right but allows multiple programs to be run in up to 16MB of memory under the control of DOS

- ▸ *System 7:* the operating system of the Apple Macintosh, was the leader in providing a sophisticated *graphical user interface* (GUI)

- ▸ *UNIX:* a multiuser, multitasking, timesharing operating system. It predates all the above operating systems, comes in dozens of versions and thus runs on all types of computer. It made its name as a good platform for programmers doing software development. It is the basis of all current efforts at standardisation of open systems

- ▸ *OS/2:* IBM's competition for DOS/Windows and Windows NT, an excellent technical achievement providing full multitasking on a single-user computer, along with a sophisticated GUI

- ▸ *Windows NT:* a new operating system produced by Microsoft which is a direct competitor for OS/2 and UNIX. It provides full multitasking, the Windows GUI and the ability to run on several different types of processor

- ▸ *OpenVMS:* (formerly just VMS) the operating system of Digital Equipment Corp.'s VAX family of minicomputers and mainframes. It is a timesharing, multiuser system which also provides facilities for execution of *batch* (sequential execution, not interactive) and *real-time* (performing time-critical operations) programs as well as advanced *transaction processing* and multiprocessing

▶ **IBM mainframe operating systems:** started with OS/360, developed alongside the mainframes derived from the System/360 through OS/370 into today's MVS and VM operating systems. These are powerful mainframe operating systems although their user-interfaces and ease-of-use are dated

▶ **New operating systems:** these include UnixWare, a derivative of UNIX integrated with Novell networking software and promoted by Novell Inc.; Windows 95 (Chicago, or Windows 4.0), the successor for DOS/Windows; Taligent, an *object-oriented* operating system developed by the company of the same name and promoted by IBM and Apple Corp.

Almost all these operating systems provide facilities for interconnection and interoperation with the others. Programs are in varying degrees portable between them. The operating systems are therefore in varying degrees open, with UNIX commonly accepted as being the most open of them all.

Communications and networking

Operating systems and the processors which underlie them determine portability of programs between systems; the extent to which systems can interoperate is determined by the facilities for communications and networking which they provide.

Early computer systems provided no facilities for communication. The first links between computers were simple *point-to-point* connections, over which data was transferred according to simple transmission rules called *protocols*. These protocols include so-called *character protocols* including Binary Synchronous and the 3270 protocols, the latter governing the operation of terminal devices in IBM SNA networks. They also include *bit protocols* such as *High-Level Data-Link Control (HDLC)* and *Link Access Protocol Balanced (LAP-B)* which underpin the *X.25* network protocol. A variation of HDLC is used by SNA for low-level transmission of data frames.

Apart from point-to-point connections, there are two main types of networks, the *Local Area Network (LAN)* and the *Wide-Area Network (WAN)*.

Networked PCs are usually organised in LANs within a small geographical area, with no PC separated from another on the same network by a distance of more than about one kilometre. Using LANs, all connected users have access to the resources of the network, with effortless file transfer and remote execution of programs.

Computers on a LAN – usually PCs with DOS but possibly also machines running UNIX, OS/2 or Windows NT – most often are physically connected to each other by means of a coaxial cable. Data is transferred over the cable between the networked computers. The transmission rules under which the data is sent usually conform to one of two standards: *Ethernet* or *Token Ring*. Both Ethernet and Token Ring specify rules which ensure reliable transmission of data over the medium connecting the computers.

Although the cable, and sometimes the network, is often referred to simply as Ethernet or Token Ring, this is inaccurate. Ethernet and Token Ring only define low-level transmission rules; higher-level network software determines the appearance of the network to the user. Such network software includes the Novell NetWare and LAN Manager suites, supplied respectively by Novell Inc. and Microsoft.

Wide Area Networks (WANs) are usually implemented using slower long-distance connections over a *Public Switched Data Network (PSDN)*, with transmission governed by the rules of protocols such as X.25, X.75 and Frame Relay. X.25 and X.75 are among the standards which collectively define the *seven-layer Reference Model for Open Systems Interconnection (OSI)* defined by the International Standards Organisation (ISO).

In 1977, the International Standards Organisation (ISO) adopted the OSI Reference Model. This model defines most aspects of interconnection and networking of computer systems and networks in terms of a model of seven layers. It is left until Part 3 to explain the OSI model and other aspects of computer communications in any detail. It is enough here to remark that the OSI model defines hardware, electrical and software aspects of connectivity as a layered structure extending from the lowest to the highest, where the software defining each layer only interacts with the layers immediately above and below. This layering results in clearly defined interfaces between software modules with consequent flexibility and reliability.

The lowest layer of the OSI model is the Physical layer; this defines the physical and electrical characteristics of the medium (perhaps cable, radio or fibre-optic link) which carries the data to be communicated. The highest layer is the Application layer which describes rules governing the operation of application programs which use the lower OSI levels to converse with other systems.

The following diagram depicts the seven layers in the context of two separate computers, the *client* and the *server*.

Client and Server
using OSI
Reference Model

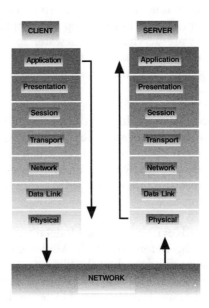

The two computers are connected by a network. An application program, such as a stock enquiry program, runs on the client. Another application program, probably a *database management system* (DBMS) for the stock items runs on the server. The user of the enquiry program can make a request on the database. The enquiry program is at level 7 (Application) on the client side. Requests from it are translated through the lower software, transmitted across the network to the remote server and re-translated into a form understandable to the server's DBMS. The DBMS then transmits its answer to the client by the same process.

The seven layers of the OSI Model are introduced here and explained in Part 3. You should be able to sense what they mean: Physical describes the cable or other communications medium; Data Link, the rules (protocols) for basic data communication over that medium; Network, the rules for routing of data within a computer network; and so on, in ascending order of removal, or *abstraction*, from the computer hardware. X.25 involves a number of protocols up to the Network Layer (Layer 3); Ethernet belongs to Layer 2.

Layers 5 and 6 are increasingly implemented by software referred to collectively as *middleware*. The purpose of middleware is to allow networked systems running diverse transport layer, network and data link communications software to communicate with each other in a manner transparent to the top-layer application software which uses the middleware services. Middleware, for which software products are increasingly becoming available, is one of the most important components in the interconnection of *heterogeneous* (different) networks.

Programs that implement the top layer – which the end-user sees – have only relatively recently been developed. X.400 is a *message handling protocol*, resident at level 7, which uses the facilities provided by software in underlying layers to allow communication by the user at a high (user-friendly) level with a similar software stack on a remote machine.

Standards exist in the OSI Model to govern network communication at all levels. Before the OSI Model came into being, however, two emergent standards had already appeared. The first was IBM's SNA, the second the TCP/IP suite of protocols developed under the aegis of the United States Department of Defense (DoD).

SNA and its extensions, in particular APPC and APPN, are the most widely used protocols used today for reliable wide-area networking. This is largely because of the dominance of IBM in mainframe computer systems. Implementation of open client–server systems is concerned with the ISO Model and its X series of protocols, the TCP/IP suite, and the SNA family. These all allow *peer-to-peer* operation: a network node in peer-to-peer communication with other nodes operates at the same protocol layer as those nodes, and contributes resources to the network while at the same time running autonomously and executing its own application programs.

TCP/IP (*Transmission Control Protocol/Internet Protocol*) is a suite of protocols organised in a network stack similar to that defined by the OSI model. TCP/IP can run either on LANs or WANs and is typically used for local or wide-area connection of computers running the UNIX operating system. However, TCP/IP was developed by DARPA (*Defense Advanced Projects Research Agency*) specifically to allow connection of different types of computer system, not just those running UNIX. As a result, interconnection between TCP/IP networks and PC LANs is common, as is connection from TCP/IP networks to IBM and Digital Equipment Corporation machines.

Although the ISO model is accepted as a formal international standard, TCP/IP is supplied with UNIX and is the *de facto* standard for networking heterogeneous systems. TCP/IP is also the basis of the worldwide *Internet*. This is the largest public computer network in the world. Its name comes from the fact that it is not just a network but that it is an *internetwork* of hundreds or thousands of existing LANs and WANs which incorporate many very different types of computer.

Programming languages

Every computer program is written as a series of instructions which define the logic of the processing to be carried out by the computer. When the instructions are submitted to the computer, it blindly follows them.

The rules according to which programs are written in a given language are collectively referred to as the *syntax* of the language. The extent to which Computer A can understand the syntax of a programming language understandable to Computer B is of central importance to whether a program written in that language is portable between the two systems. Standardisation of programming languages is a very important part of the technology of open systems.

The first computer languages were simply sequences of ones and zeros. To program a given computer, it is supplied with instructions in this form and it processes them. Programs written in this way are called *machine-code* programs and are said to be the first generation of programming languages. Machine code is specific to the computer for which it is written and is not portable to any other type of computer.

Writing programs in machine code is tedious, time-consuming and error-prone. In the 1950s, the second-generation languages called *assembly languages* appeared. These substitute terse mnemonic instructions for the ones and zeros and assembler programs are thus easier for programmers to write than their machine-code equivalents. An example of an IBM 360 assembly instruction for adding two numbers is:

```
AR 1,2
```

This instruction tells the computer to find the numbers contained in registers 1 and 2 and to add them, leaving the result in register 1. Although more convenient than machine code, assembly languages are still specific to the computers for which they are developed and programs written in them are non-portable.

For portable programs to be possible, it is necessary that the languages in which they are written are independent of the architecture of any particular computer. The assembler instruction above depends on the IBM 360's having the AR instruction in its instruction set and registers numbered 1 and 2. The equivalent instruction for, say, a Digital Equipment Corporation VAX is quite different.

The first languages independent of any computer's architecture were the third-generation languages. Examples of these languages are *Common Business-Oriented Language* (COBOL), *Formula Translation* (Fortran), and the C language. The addition would be written in COBOL like this:

```
ADD B TO A
```

and in C thus:

```
A = A + B;
```

A program written in any language of a level higher than machine code (the first generation) must be translated into a form of machine code (executable code) understandable to the system on which it is to be run.

Programs written in assembly language must be processed into executable form by another program called an *assembler*. Programs written in languages such as C, Fortran and COBOL are processed by a *compiler* and *linker* which, in several steps, reduces them to their executable forms.

Compilers for third-generation languages can be devised for computers of many different architectures. There is a good chance, therefore, that a given COBOL or C program will run on any system which has an appropriate compiler. Languages such as COBOL, C, Fortran and Pascal have been standardised and are the cornerstone of program portability, which is itself one of the two main pillars of open systems.

In recent years the *fourth-generation languages* (4GLs) have appeared. These have syntax of a level of abstraction from computer hardware even higher than the 3GLs. An example of the 4GL is *Structured Query Language* (SQL), which is used with database systems. Here is an example of an SQL statement:

```
SELECT Name, Address, Age FROM Employees.
```

This instructs the system to find a table of data called Employees and select records from it on the basis of name, address and age. This type of statement is more powerful than anything found in lower-level languages. It also requires more processing into executable form and is slower to execute than an equivalent series of statements written in a lower-level language. SQL is restricted in use to database programs and is therefore not as flexible as C, COBOL or Fortran.

To summarise, if a program is written in a 3GL or 4GL, it is inherently more portable than assembly or machine code. Portable programs can be supplied on open systems which have the compilers and operating systems necessary to run them.

User interface

An important characteristic of any program is its ease of use. The first programs could only be submitted to computers by specialist operators who, along with programmers, interpreted their results. Later, programs could be input to the computer on punched cards. These were superseded by teletype machines (ttys) and video-display terminal units (VDUs). VDUs are more commonly known as CTRs (cathode ray tubes) or simply 'screens'. Screen and tty devices provide a *command-line interface* (CLI) by means of which the user interacts with the computer. Examples of the CLI include the traditional PC-DOS and UNIX command lines. This is a sample DOS command:

```
C:\> copy file1 file2
```

and here is the UNIX equivalent:

```
$ cp file1 file2
```

'C:\>' and '$' are respectively the DOS and UNIX *command prompts*.

The syntax of commands accepted by the CLI is difficult for non-specialist users to understand and remember. A novice user who does not know the commands is easily baffled by the CLI and usually can do no work at all.

In the late 1970s, research started at the Xerox Palo Alto Research Center (PARC) into graphical interfaces. GUIs allow the user to interact with the computer on an intuitive visual basis, running programs and processing files by means of manipulating graphical objects (*icons*) which appear on the user's screen. Programs written to present their interfaces through a GUI are usually much easier to use then their command-line equivalents. They share a common *look and feel*. For any given task, such as opening a data file, every program behaves like every other. Learning time for users is sharply cut.

The GUI is the current preferred user interface for small and medium-scale computer systems. But programming GUIs is difficult and time-consuming and GUIs in execution require significant system resources. The GUI has also had implications for portability: a program which hitherto could interact with any CLI must now be tailored for a particular GUI, thereby reducing its portability.

Proprietary and open systems

Definition of terms

A computer system can be called open if:

▶ *Software is easily portable* between it and other (open and proprietary) systems

▶ *It is scalable:* its software can be run with acceptable performance on any size of computer

▶ *It is interoperable* with other systems and networks, with the ability to communicate, share resources and share processing with remote systems

Proprietary, or closed, systems lack one or more of these characteristics.

Proprietary hardware and software

Computer hardware can be termed proprietary or closed:

▶ If it cannot readily be connected to and used with other computer equipment

▶ If, in the case of a CPU, it will not run software generated on another system

Many types of peripheral device for example memory, disk drives, device adapters and terminals are highly portable and therefore open. The operating system controlling a computer, as well as its processor and software tools such as compilers, determines whether software is portable to and from that computer. For example, an executable (compiled) program which runs on an IBM mainframe running the MVS operating system is not portable to any other kind of computer system. MVS itself is a proprietary operating system: it runs only on the IBM computer architecture. The UNIX operating system, on the other hand, is relatively open: it runs on many different kinds of computer. Application programs designed to run under UNIX are made portable and open by this fact; they will run on any system which in turn runs UNIX.

Software is closed if it cannot be ported either in binary (executable code) or in source-code form to an open system on which it can be expected to work with little or no change.

The IBM PC and openness

There are more than 100 million PCs in the world. The PC's popularity means that software and hardware can easily be moved to other PCs, but the PC itself remains a closed system. MS-DOS is a proprietary operating system which will run only on the Intel 80X86 microprocessor. Software written to run on the 80X86 processors under MS-DOS are not portable, in either binary or source-code form, to any other system.

Programs designed to interact with the Microsoft Windows GUI are even less portable than other PC programs. Windows programs must use the Windows *application program interface* (API), a large collection of software functions which are needed to display graphical objects on screen and pass messages under the control of Windows.

Although add-on communications software is available, PCs do not as standard support many internationally-recognised communications protocols, including TCP/IP, X.25 and the other protocols within the OSI Reference Model. Networking standards supported in the PC environment – examples are Novell NetWare and Microsoft's LAN Manager – are usually only supported for PCs and are therefore considered closed software.

There is no user consultation or input into the design of PC hardware or operating systems. Much software is not portable (that is, scalable) across the whole PC range. For example, a program written in C to take advantage of the 80386 microprocessor's *linear addressing* architecture will not run on PCs using the earlier 80286 chip.

The IBM-compatible PC, based on the Intel processor architecture is closed and proprietary in the same way as is the IBM mainframe with MVS or the Digital Equipment Corporation VAX with VMS. However, it is also an exception, in that it has become the first computer which has reached commodity status: people buy them in the same way as they buy television sets or electric kettles. This means that there is a huge installed base of PCs which can be connected and between which software can be freely exchanged. Availability of shrink-wrapped binary-compatible application software – completely portable within the PC world – is the principal market advantage of the PC.

UNIX systems are open

In contrast to PCs, computers running the UNIX operating system approach complete openness. Systems running UNIX can have many different types of processors and architectures which may when considered in isolation be proprietary. However, the fact that UNIX runs on what might otherwise be seen as a proprietary system effectively makes it open: application software designed to run on any other computer using UNIX is easily ported to it. UNIX systems also provide software allowing easy connectivity to computers of almost every other type.

The centrepiece of the UNIX operating system, the *kernel*, is a program written almost entirely in the C language. This makes UNIX relatively easily portable to any system supporting a C software development environment. Only a few hundred lines of the kernel code must be rewritten in assembly code to accommodate the hardware dependencies of the different systems to which UNIX is ported.

UNIX utilities and support software are written in C and are therefore also portable to any system on which C programs can be compiled. The operating system has been implemented on systems ranging from low-powered PCs to supercomputer and on the systems of every major supplier.

Application software written for UNIX is mostly coded in standardised languages such as COBOL, C and Fortran and is therefore readily portable to any other UNIX system and to any other computer (including IBM PCs) which have compilers for those languages.

UNIX source code licences were until recently available from UNIX International (UI); ownership of UNIX has now passed to Novell Inc. Availability of source code means that the manufacturer of any type of computer can buy the UNIX source code and port it to that computer. This availability, and the fact that UNIX is largely written in C, is the main reason for its proliferation across so many different computer architectures.

UNIX implements device independence: almost any kind of peripheral device which is electronically compatible can be connected to a UNIX machine and the system software accommodates it in a manner *transparent* (invisible) to application programs.

All the international standard communication protocols have been implemented for UNIX, as well as *de facto* standards such as TCP/IP and the SNA protocols.

UNIX is used widely as a departmental system to act as a gateway between proprietary networks as well as a system to offload processing from mainframes.

UNIX systems implement software portability and scalability and promote system interoperability.

There are some limitations to the openness of systems running UNIX:

- ▶ UNIX has not been fully standardised; there are as many as 200 versions of the operating system. Most of the differences are slight but they are enough to cause some difficulties in software porting

- ▶ The main differences between UNIX versions lie in the *system-call interface*, UNIX's API. The system-call interface comprises over 100 software functions which are used by application programs to get services and resources from UNIX. The slight differences that exist between the APIs of different UNIX versions limit the portability of software between them

- ▶ Because UNIX runs on all types of computers, which have different processors, only source-code portability is generally possible between UNIX systems. Full binary portability is only possible between computers with the same processors, and this is one condition that the IBM-compatible PC does meet

- ▶ It supports several filesystem designs, complicating the transfer of data on magnetic media between UNIX systems and to other environments

With all its limitations UNIX is still the most open of all computing environments and offers the most scope for expansion of markets for application software.

Benefits of standards

The advantages

Standardisation of computer system components – hardware and software – results in black-box simplicity and is a counter to the complexity of today's technology. A user of a UNIX system, for example, can install TCP/IP communications software quite easily and can access other systems without having to know anything of how the software works. As another example of the black box, a C program can be ported between systems; it will work and can be reused without the user having to understand its logic.

Software is portable: once the initial cost of writing it has been absorbed, the effort and cost of moving it to other types of computer are incremental. If software is portable, the size of its market is increased as are, presumably, the revenues from it.

Open computer systems are interoperable: they can be connected, can exchange data and can execute programs on remote computers. This tends to optimise the use of equipment and software, as well as unifying an enterprise's computing resources.

Open systems reduce costs: much less software needs to be rewritten than is the case with proprietary systems. There is a sharply reduced cost of equipment becoming obsolete. For example, if a standard VT220 character-oriented (non-graphic) CRT is superseded by a graphic monitor, it is likely that a use for the VT220 can be found somewhere on the network of open systems where graphic capabilities are not required. By adopting open systems, retraining costs are reduced, as any future replacement will adhere to the same standards. Also, investment in software and hardware is not lost when a component – for example a networked computer running UNIX – is replaced or upgraded.

With open systems, there is no proprietary lock-in. If the user is unhappy with one supplier, it is easy to go to another and get standard hardware and software. This independence of any particular vendor also has the effect of increasing competition and reducing costs.

Software is readily portable between open systems. To port an application program, its code must be moved to the destination system and compiled there into executable form. Because of standardisation of programming languages and operating systems, especially UNIX, this process is usually not very difficult. As an example, suppose a large suite of software, written in standard C and not using Microsoft Windows, is developed on an IBM-compatible PC and that this development took three programmers six months. Moving the software to a UNIX environment would require only that DOS system-calls (API calls) be changed to their UNIX equivalents and perhaps that the code be optimised to take advantage of the multitasking capabilities of UNIX. Doing a straightforward port, without optimisation, would probably take no more than a few days, with enormous savings when compared to the cost of rewriting or converting the code.

Because software is portable between open systems, versions of a given application can be very quickly available for many different types of system. A good example of this is the fact that the DBMS (largely written in C) supplied by Oracle Corp. is available for upwards of 35 versions of UNIX, as well as PCs, VAX/VMS and IBM mainframes. The relative ease of bringing a product to market on a new system is obviously to the advantage of software suppliers.

Although there are some differences between UNIX versions, for a given piece of software, it is quite likely that no change at all will be required to move it from the UNIX system of one supplier to that of another. This is especially true of programs written in languages such as COBOL, which are standardised and which make no direct calls on the UNIX API. This possibility of porting without change reduces the need to maintain multiple versions of a software product, and the associated costs.

Who benefits?

Developers of packaged software are major beneficiaries of the portability made possible by open systems. As technology advances, software is becoming ever more complex, expensive to develop and prone to time overruns in development. Also the acceptance period or market window is shortening making it more important than ever that software is ready before the market moves on. Because of the very large installed base of PCs, software suppliers have tended to concentrate on that market. But competition is tough and margins small. Easy portability to open (UNIX) systems at low cost makes it possible for suppliers to expand the market for their software and more quickly recoup the cost of developing it.

Hardware manufacturers also gain from the move to open systems. Even the largest manufacturers increasingly use standard components sourced from third party suppliers. This reduces their own direct manufacturing costs. Good examples of standard components include disk drives, memory and VDUs. Many manufacturers can no longer sustain the cost of development and support of proprietary equipment. Neither can they support the costs of training and supporting customers of proprietary systems, who anyway expect availability of open, interchangeable products.

The third sector which gains from the introduction of open systems is that of computer-system resellers, also known as *value-added resellers* (VARs). VARs are often small companies and even larger ones do not want to absorb the higher development cost of software for proprietary systems. Instead they want to stock the smallest complete range possible of computer equipment and to have application software capable of running without change across the whole range. Because VARs usually sell into organisations with existing computer installations, it is important for the reseller's products to be able to interoperate with them. With open systems resellers also minimise the costs of training and user technical support.

Lastly, end-users of computers benefit from open systems too. They benefit from competition, and consequent price reductions, between suppliers of open systems. Consider as an example a company requiring a small multi-user system for its stock control system. It can implement it on an 80486-based PC running a standard version of UNIX. The competitive pressures on suppliers of such systems are severe and the cost will be low. End-users also benefit from the fact that the cost of supporting and administering an open system is lower than the equivalent costs for a proprietary installation. The costs are lower because there is wide availability of people trained in use and management of open systems. For support, the user is not restricted to the original supplier; this again introduces competition and reduces costs. Users (especially governments) can demand and get the security of having alternative suppliers. Finally, educational establishments can assimilate open technologies quickly.

The standards required

To realise all these benefits, formal and informal standards are required in a number of areas. Firstly, in the area of software portability:

▶ Languages, for example: C, Micro-Focus COBOL, SQL

▶ Application Program Interfaces (APIs)

▶ Graphical User Interfaces (GUIs)

▶ *Application Binary Interfaces* (ABIs). These are software components available with some versions of UNIX which ensure that a given program will run on all computers of a particular architecture (for example: Intel, Motorola) which also support UNIX

Standards are needed in the area of system interconnection:

▶ Electrical Interfaces

▶ Communications protocols

▶ Network protocols

▶ Network management and user interfaces

For interoperability, building on system interconnection, standards are necessary in these fields:

▶ High-level communications protocols (levels 4 to 7 of the OSI Reference Model)

▶ Shareable filesystems

Disadvantages of standards

Standards in themselves are alleged to have inherent handicaps:

▶ *There are too many standards:* UNIX is the classic example of this assertion; when it seemed as if the operating system might standardise around System V Release 4 (UI), the Open Software Foundation (OSF, including IBM, Hewlett Packard and others)

introduced competition sufficiently different to cause incompatibility. Proliferation of standards is reducing under market pressure. Additionally, competing versions of products like UNIX cause advances in technology which would not occur in more closed environments such as OS/2 or Microsoft Windows.

► *There is a high cost involved in changing to open systems:* This can be true, but it is also true when changing to a proprietary system and unlike such change, once done it is unlikely to recur.

► *Standard systems are slow:* All standards involve an element of compromise which itself precludes optimisation. In an effort to meet the requirements of many users, standard software may be larger and slower than proprietary equivalents. It is reckoned that the ISO-standard C language is about twice the size of the original C. This means that C compilers are now larger and more expensive to develop. UNIX System V Release 4 is a unification of four earlier UNIX variants. Because of pressure from devotees of each of those variants, SVR4 now includes almost all their features and contains much unnecessary duplication and overhead.

► *Standard systems compromise security:* Standard operating systems like UNIX have standard security mechanisms which are well known and are more susceptible to attack than proprietary security strategies. However, most security risks arise because of network access to computer systems. This problem is not peculiar to open systems.

► *Standards change:* They do, but modern standards are designed to be *backward-compatible*. For example, ISO C is designed not to invalidate any but a very few C programs written under the original language definition. The original release of UNIX System V in 1983 guaranteed that programs which ran under that version would also run under every future version of System V.

General status of computing standards

Introduction

Two main classifications of standards are relevant in construction of open systems and client–server computing environments. The first category is of *de jure* (formally defined and agreed, 'by law') international standards and recommendations specified by national and international standards bodies including:

- ▸ The American National Standards Institute (ANSI)
- ▸ The Institute of Electrical and Electronic Engineers (IEEE)
- ▸ The International Telegraph and Telephone Consultative Committee (CCITT)
- ▸ ISO
- ▸ The functions of the CCITT have recently been subsumed by the International Telecommunications Union (ITU-T), an agency of the United Nations. While recognising this, the term CCITT is used in the remainder of this text.

The second set is of *de facto* (adopted 'in fact', usually in response to market pressure) standards endorsed by a number of computer-industry groups and consortia including:

- ▸ Defense Advanced Projects Research Agency (DARPA)
- ▸ Univel (formerly AT&T and UNIX System Laboratories)
- ▸ UNIX International
- ▸ OSF
- ▸ Common Open Systems Environment (COSE)
- ▸ X/Open

In the first group, standards adopted by ANSI, IEEE and, in part, CCITT are ratified by ISO. For the subject areas under consideration in this book, ANSI is mainly concerned with standardisation of programming languages. The IEEE is the originator of the POSIX set of operating system interface standards as well as electrical standards for low-level data communication over LANs. CCITT is concerned with recommendations defining protocols for transmission over WANs.

The second group concentrates on specifying profiles, groups of standards that define the characteristics of operating systems, application software and distributed computing environments in which they are used. The groups and consortia are driven by market demand. The profiles they endorse are usually defined more rapidly than their *de jure* counterparts, often exactly because processes involved in arriving at international *de jure* standards are very slow.

The national and international standards bodies tend to emphasise standards for data communications, connectivity and interoperability, while the industry consortia lean more towards operating systems and application software. Hence, Part 2 following deals extensively with SVID, OSF, X/Open and the others (although the IEEE POSIX standards and the ANSI language standards are included also). Part 3, on the other hand, covers many of the IEEE, CCITT and ISO standards and recommendations for data communications, while not omitting the *de facto* Internet standards.

The broad current status of open computing standards is set out below under the headings of portability, interconnection and interoperability.

Standards for portability

▶ *Standards for Programming Languages:* The most significant language standards are those for C, Fortran, COBOL and the Structured Query Language used for accessing *relational databases*. All were originated by ANSI and were subsequently ratified by ISO. Depending on the comprehensiveness of the particular standard (in the case of C, maximal, for SQL, minimal), software written in these languages is more or less portable between systems of different vendors.

▶ *UNIX System V Interface Definition (SVID):* The SVID is a document which specifies the 'standard' UNIX system-call interface (API). It was introduced by AT&T but is now specified by Univel. Any program conforming to the SVID will run under any version of UNIX System V. Most other UNIX versions claim to be SVID-compliant; this is so because the United States Government demands SVID compliance for all UNIX systems it acquires.

▶ *Portable Operating System Interface (POSIX):* POSIX is a set of standards developed by the Institute of Electrical and Electronic Engineers (IEEE). Its base standard defines a system-call interface much the same as that of the SVID, but it claims independence of the C language and the UNIX operating system. Other POSIX standards define such things as the nature of the command-line processor and security mechanisms.

▶ *X/Open:* An adopted set of standards which includes SVID and POSIX. The X/Open consortium is a group of companies. It does not itself define standards, but adopts those of other bodies to form a coherent standard computing environment. In addition to operating-system standards, it also includes standards for languages and database access.

▸ *The OSF Application Environment Specification (AES):* A POSIX-compatible operating system interface

▸ **COSE:** Common Open Systems Environment is a product announced jointly in 1993 by a number of major computer-system vendors. It is a profile defining standard approaches to the development of GUIs, network software, object-oriented software and software implementing multimedia, among other things.

Standards for interconnection and interoperability

There are so many technologies involved in connecting computer systems and in making them capable of sharing resources and processing power that to set out a piecemeal summary here of the related standards seems pointless. Instead, the diagram (page 47) gives a (by no means complete) summary of *de jure* communications standards. This is more helpful in giving the big picture of required standards for connectivity and interoperability, but there are still a number of widely-used standards, such as TCP/IP, APPN, X Windows and the OSF Distributed Computing Environment (DCE) which are not covered by it. This is because they are *de facto*, as opposed to *de jure*, standards. In Parts 2 and 3, their equivalence with the official standards is explained.

The OSI Reference Model is informally introduced in the section *Background to Open Systems* (see page 15). Broadly, standards defined at layers 1 to 3 are concerned with connectivity – physically connecting devices and passing simple data between them. Layers 4 to 7 define standards for interoperability – making computers exchange data and run each other's programs. In Part 3, many of the standards shown in the diagram, and the significance of the Reference Model layers, are described in more detail.

		ISO Standards		CCITT Recommendations

ISO Standards   **CCITT Recommendations**

7	ISO 8571 File Transfer Access Method ISO 9040/1 Virtual Terminal ISO 9579 Remote Database Access ISO 10026 Distributed Transaction Processing ISO 8831/2 Job Transfer Access & Management ISO 8649 Common Application Service Elements	**Application**	Common Management Information Protocol *(CMIP; ISO 9595/6; CCITT X710, X711)* Inter-Personal Messaging *(IPM; ISO 10021-7; CCITT X420)* Message Handling System *(MHS; ISO 10021-1; CCITT X400)* MHS Message Store (CCITT X.413; ISO 10021-5) EDI Messaging System over X.400 (CCITT X.435) Directory Services (DS; ISO 9594-1; CCITT X.500)
6	Connection-Oriented Presentation Service ISO 8822/3/4/5	**Presentation**	Presentation Service for CCITT Applications X.216, X.226
5	Connection-Oriented Session Service ISO 8326, ISO 8327	**Session**	Session Service Definition for CCITT Applications X.215, X.225
4	Transport Layer Protocol Specification COTS/CLTS ISO 8073 (TP 0-4)	**Transport**	Transport Service Definition for CCITT Applications X.214, X.224
3	Connectionless-Mode Network Service (CLNS) ISO 8473 Connection-Oriented Network Service (CONS) ISO 8208	**Network**	Network Service Definition for CCITT Applications X.213 - X.25
2	Logical Link Control (LLC) ISO 8802.2 (IEEE 802.2)	**Data Link**	Data Link Service Definition for CCITT Applications X.212, X.222
1	Ethernet Token Bus ISO 8802.3 ISO 8802.4 (IEEE 802.3) (IEEE 802.4) Token Ring MAN ISO 8802.5 ISO 8802.6 (IEEE 802.5) (IEEE 802.6)	**Physical**	Physical layer Interface for X.25 X.21, X.21-bis

◄——— **LAN/MAN** ———►◄—— **PSDN** ——►

Summary of OSI and CCITT recommendations

Part 2

Standards for Portability

Introduction

In Part 1, an open system is defined as one having the characteristics of portability and interoperability. This book proceeds on the basis that an open computer system is one which can easily exchange programs (software) with other systems (portability) and which can communicate and share resources with other systems (interoperability). In examining the components which in turn define portability and operability, you will be introduced to most aspects of current computer hardware and software technology. This Part examines the factors which influence and control portability of software between discrete computer systems.

It is possible, although not commonplace, also to consider aspects of portability as a layered hierarchy analogous to the hierarchy defined by the OSI Reference Model. Here is a suggested equivalence, defined as a set of layers, between portability and interoperability:

	Portability	OSI model
Layer 7	User Interface	Application
Layer 6	Applications	Presentation
Layer 5	API	Session
Layer 4	Tools	Transport
Layer 3	Language	Network
Layer 2	Operating System	Data Link
Layer 1	Microprocessor/Hardware	Physical

The analogy with aspects of portability is not perfect and, like all analogies, should not be pushed too far. Its use is in showing the essentially layered organisation of most computer systems and in providing a fairly neat subdivision of topics for further consideration.

At the lowest level is the computer hardware itself. Computer systems built according to the traditional von Neumann design comprise a Central Processing Unit (CPU) and Arithmetic and Logic Unit (ALU), with both connected by a bus to random-access memory (RAM). In modern, especially small, computers, the CPU, and possibly also the ALU, is on the main system microprocessor. The architecture of that microprocessor defines the ways in which the computer receives its data and executes its instructions and is of central importance to all issues of portability affecting that computer. The instructions which a processor can carry out are part of its architecture and are referred to collectively as the processor's instruction set. The reference to hardware, in addition to the microprocessor means all the other components of the computer – including RAM and peripheral devices – other than the processor itself.

At the second level from the lowest is the operating system. The operating system is a complex computer program which controls the operation of the user (application) program (or programs) running on the computer and allocates the resources of the system, including memory and external devices, among those programs. The operating system interacts directly with the hardware, requesting services required by the application programs.

At the next level are the languages used to construct programs which run on the system. Languages range from those of a very low level, referred to as machine code and consisting of sequences of ones and zeros, through symbolic or assembler languages, to high-level languages which ultimately get translated into machine code but, from the programmer's perspective, adopt a more natural-language syntax. It is possible, from programs written in these languages, to make requests of the operating system for services which the operating system in turn gets from the hardware layer. These requests are made through the operating system's system-call interface or, to use a more recent term, API.

Software tools are application programs, usually built with a high-level language, providing an API to programmers, who use the tools to build further specialised application programs. Use of these tools allows reliable construction of application programs. Examples of software tools include database managers, computer-aided software engineering (CASE) programs, application program generators and macro languages such as the *shell command language* associated with the UNIX operating system. Equating software tools with the Transport layer of the Reference Model *is* stretching our analogy a little far, but the overall equivalence is worth any inaccuracy.

The API, or Application Program Interface, is the set of services provided by the operating system which is visible to and usable by the programmer. However, any application program or user-interface program can also provide an API which other programmers can use to make calls on it. For example, a database-handling program may make available to programmers a call to read records from disk. A user-interface program will provide a call for displaying a dialog box on screen. Such calls are collectively part of a program's API. APIs can be thought of as the means by which programs make calls on each other, in a way similar to which the Session layer of the Reference Model allows applications to communicate across a network.

Applications (user-written programs designed to carry out real tasks other than controlling the computer system) are usually written in high-level languages, perhaps using the tools referred to above, certainly using the APIs provided by both the operating system and the *user interface*, by means of which the application interacts with the end-user.

The user interface, in our analogy, is equivalent to the Application layer of the Reference Model. The user interface has traditionally been a command-line, a line on a screen or teletype device, with which the user enters text commands to the computer and receives text replies. In recent years, at least as far as non-expert users are concerned, the command-line interface (CLI) has largely been superseded by the graphical user interface (GUI). The GUI, of which the most pervasive example is Microsoft's Windows program, allows the user to interact with the computer and its applications in an intuitive way by means of graphic objects on screen. The GUI is itself a large application program, which provides an API to allow programmers to write programs which interact with the end-user through the medium of the GUI.

Having briefly defined the framework within which we will consider the subject of portability, and the individual components of that framework, we now proceed to examine each of the layers in more detail.

Microprocessors

Background

Software portability between computer systems is determined by the design of their Central Processing Units. In modern small-to-medium sized computers, the CPU is implemented by a microprocessor.

A microprocessor is a CPU implemented on a single chip. A chip is an electronic component, usually fabricated mainly of silicon, which contains a large number of integrated circuits (ICs). An integrated circuit is an assembly of connected electronic devices which collectively perform a specific task. The devices include transistors, resistors and diodes; the tasks which an IC may perform are numerous and include the example of an electronic adder: a device which electronically finds the sum of two numbers, the values of which are input to the IC as electrical signals.

ICs are in turn based on the invention of the transistor in 1947. Up to that time a *vacuum tube* (valve) was typically used to switch the status of an electronic device between two voltages. In the earliest computers, valves were used to represent the binary digit (bit) with possible states representing one and zero. Valves are large, generate a lot of heat and are inherently unreliable.

The transistor was a significant improvement on the vacuum tube in terms of reduced heat output, smaller size and greater reliability. To represent an on/off status, transistors make use of materials known as *semiconductors*. Semiconductors are materials such as germanium and silicon. These materials are poor conductors of electricity and can be made either to conduct electricity or insulate from it. The transistor rapidly replaced the valve as the fundamental unit of logic circuits and memory devices.

To create an electronic device more complex than a simple on/off switch, transistors can be grouped together in small numbers to form *gates*. Logic gates usually take as their input a number (often two) of electrical signals and produce an electrical result which depends on the inputs. For example, an AND gate will produce a TRUE (electrical 'on') output if both its inputs are also TRUE. There are many other types of gates. Gates can be combined to implement the kind of logical functions which are required in a complex device such as a CPU.

The key to this combination was the invention of the integrated circuit in 1959 by Fairchild and Texas Instruments. The basic devices, including transistors, were etched on a *substrate* of silicon and connected by printing using lithography. The technique gave rise to the term *printed circuit*.

Once it was possible to implement integrated circuits on chips of silicon, it became theoretically possible to implement a complete computer CPU on one silicon chip. This requires a concentration of a large number of circuits on the chip and the initial technology for packaging ICs was insufficient to achieve the required density. The density to which transistors can be packed in an IC is defined as the level of *integration*. ICs of the early 1960s were of so-called *small-scale integration*, including usually less than 100 transistors on a single chip. A table of levels of integration is given below:

Integration	Size in bits
SSI – Small	0–100
MSI – Medium	100–1000
LSI – Large	1000–100000
VLSI – Very Large	100000–1000000

The distinction between the various levels of integration is arbitrary but widely accepted. Devices are also available incorporating even higher integration – up to one billion bits on a single device.

Until the advent of LSI devices, it was only practical to implement small calculators using integrated circuits on silicon chips. The first single-chip CPU was the Intel 4004, first produced in early 1971. It contained 2,100 transistors and had a 4-bit CPU; data was transferred to and from memory four bits at a time. The associated 4001, 4002 and 4003 chips were provided to perform input-output (I/O) operations. The design of the original 4004 is still reflected in the current generations of Intel 80486 and Pentium chips.

Through the 1970s, the 4004 was followed by a succession of improved chips: first the 4040 and then the first 8-bit processors, the 8008, 8080 and 8080A. The 8080 family were the first widely-used microprocessors, their 8-bit addressing scheme for the first time allowing programs to access useful amounts of memory. They implemented 8-bit instructions, 16-bit arithmetic, provided eight high-speed registers, allowed programs to address up to 65,536 bytes of memory and used a stack arrangement which meant that programs could execute subroutines.

The Intel 8080 family

In 1978, the first of the modern generation of Intel microprocessors was released. The 8086 and 8088 are internally identical but the 8088 is externally restricted to an eight-bit data bus. The design of the 8086, which is explained more fully in the next section, uses a scheme of memory segmentation to allow programs running on the processor to address up to 1 megabyte (1MB = 1024×1024, where $1024 = 1$KB) of memory in chunks (segments) of up to 64KB each. The 8086 has no facilities for memory protection, which in effect means that only one program can run on the processor at any given time. These two limitations – 64KB segmentation and the absence of memory protection – have since 1978 profoundly influenced the development of all 8086-based microcomputers and their software.

Performance of the 8086 was improved in 1982 with the release of the 80286, usually referred to simply as the 286 chip, used in the IBM PC AT (for 'advanced technology'). This has 16-bit addressing and, using a 24-bit address bus, allows a memory area of up to 16MB to be used by its programs. It also introduced a scheme of memory protection, which means that multiple programs can be run concurrently (apparently, but not actually, simultaneously), while retaining the unprotected mode of the 8086. The 80286 retains the scheme of memory segmentation used by the 8086, albeit in an expanded form. This means that programs running on the 80286 can only naturally address 64KB of memory, with the programs having to index memory segments to get at the full potential 16MB.

The 80386 (1985) was a radical departure from the design of the 80286, for the first time allowing programs to access a very large area of memory in a non-segmented way. Programs running on the 386 can reach up to 4GB (four gigabytes, or roughly four million million bytes) of RAM. This is done by means of 32-bit addressing (linear addressing) of *flat memory*. By removing the restrictions imposed by the earlier segmentation scheme, the 80386 allows the programs which run on it to be greatly simplified. However, the 80386 was required not to invalidate the programs which ran on the large numbers of 8086 and 80286 computer systems sold before its release and so it provides special modes under which programs for the earlier processors may be run.

The later 80486 (1989) and Pentium (1993) processors retain the 80386 architecture while achieving higher speeds and component density (see table below). They also incorporate, on the same chip, processors for doing floating-point mathematical operations, and use advanced techniques for increasing the speed of executing long sequences of instructions. The following table gives approximate values for speed, packing density and cost of the Intel microprocessors from the 8086 to the Pentium. Speed is approximated in millions of instructions per second (MIPs).

The Intel 80X86 microprocessor family

CPU		Max MIPS	Transistors	Launch Cost	Current Cost
8086	6/78	.75	29,000	$360	N/A
80286	2/82	2.6	134,000	$360	$8
80386	10/85	11.4	275,000	$299	$50
80486	8/89	54.00	1,200,000	$950	$200
Pentium	3/93	112.00	3,100,000	$900	$500

Competing microprocessors

The principal early competition for the Intel microprocessors came from Motorola in the form of the 6800 and later 68000 series of processors. Today, Motorola chips such as the MC68040 compare well in performance with the Intel 80486. The Z80 microprocessor was produced by Zilog in 1976 and was a higher-performance variant of the Intel 8080A. The Z80 was the processor most commonly used until the advent of the IBM Personal Computer (PC), which adopted the Intel 8088 and thereby made a *de-facto* international standard of the 8080 design.

The 6502 microprocessor was developed by MOS Technology and was based in part on the Motorola 6800 but had a simpler design and instruction set. The 6502 gained prominence as the processor adopted for the first microcomputers from Apple Corp., especially the Apple II, and it was also used for a number of other early systems including the BBC micro, Atari XE and the Commodore PET.

The 6800 family, of which the 6802, 6808 and 6809 were variants, was the last series of 8-bit processors produced by Motorola. The 6800 was more powerful than the 8080. Its programs used less memory and executed faster, thanks to powerful addressing modes for processing data efficiently in main memory.

The 16- and 32-bit Motorola processors which are comparable in performance to the Intel 80X86 series are the 68000 family. The MC68000 was released in 1980. It uses a 16-bit data bus to access 32-bit data values. It has a 24-bit address bus which allows 16MB of addressable memory which, importantly, is non-segmented. The MC68010 (1982) supports virtual memory, which allows programs to use more memory than is in fact physically available. Virtual memory is implemented by the processor generating *page faults* when more memory is required, interrupting the instruction currently being executed, *swapping* data in memory to a peripheral device and then restarting the program in a larger area of memory.

The MC68020 (1984) has 32-bit addressing and data handling. Programs running on it can address a 4-gigabyte memory address space, and the 68020 also includes many high-performance features, including *instruction caching* which made it the processor of choice for fast computer systems required to run the UNIX operating system. A 256-bit *cache memory* is provided on the chip in which commonly-executed instructions are temporarily stored and quickly retrieved.

The MC68030 (1989) is faster than the 68020, includes caching for data as well as instructions, and has a built-in memory management unit which manages virtual memory and multitasking: several programs executing concurrently. The MC68040 has enlarged caches, *floating-point* (mathematical) operations included on the chip, and a scheme for speeding up the execution of instructions called *pipelining*. Finally, the MC68040 runs on average four times faster than the 68030.

The original 68000 used linear addressing, introduced in the Intel family with the 80386. The 8086 and 80286 were handicapped by supporting memory segmentation in 64KB chunks and, further, in requiring the programs which run on them to incorporate logic to accommodate the segmentation. Although the 80386 implemented linear addressing, it had to provide a special mode to support programs which ran on its predecessor using segmented memory. Because of this design history, Motorola processors have mainly been used for very high-performance workstations and multiuser computers while the Intel family, having been made a standard as a result of its adoption by IBM, became universal in PCs.

All the processors referred to in this section are examples of what are known as *complex instruction-set computer* (CISC) processors. In recent years, an alternative has appeared: the *reduced instruction-set computer* (RISC) processor, which is in general faster than its CISC equivalent. The differences between RISC and CISC, and the implications of RISC for software portability and open systems are explained below, as are techniques for improving processor performance including pipelining, used for example in the MC68040, and *superscalar* architectures.

Architecture

The performance of a microprocessor is governed by the packing density of its transistors and the *clock speed* of the computer of which the processor is part. The more densely transistors are packed, and the smaller they are, the faster the chip: the transistors can switch state faster and take new inputs more often. The speed at which the processor can switch state determines how fast the clock controlling the chip can be allowed to run. If the processor can switch state 20 million times per second, the chip can run at a clock frequency of 20MHz; 40 million times allows 40MHz, and so on.

As limits are approached in the possible physical density of transistor packing, new techniques are being sought to increase the throughput of microprocessors. These include Reduced Instruction Set Computer (RISC) and pipelining. RISC is an alternative to the traditional CISC (Complex Instruction Set Computer) of which the Intel 80486 and Motorola 68040 are examples.

RISC vs CISC

Every microprocessor has an instruction set and a control unit which processes instructions. Instructions have operands – data – which are stored either in general purpose machine registers or in memory. Register storage and retrieval is much faster than the memory equivalent.

If instructions are allowed to have many memory operands, the job of compiler writers is made easier but the complexity of the processor control unit – and hence the number of components it uses – is increased. This is the case with CISC processors, where the control unit is a complex device within the CPU which is itself microprogrammed to interpret the instructions it receives. Here are some of the characteristics of RISC processors:

- ALU (Arithmetic and Logic Unit) and FPU (Floating-Point Unit) instructions load and store their (fewer) operands from/to registers only

- RISC processors thus do not require microprogrammed control units and their complexity is reduced accordingly

- Many registers: often 32 or more high-speed registers

- RISC processors access memory using separate instructions reserved specifically for loading operands to registers from memory and storing operands from registers to memory. As a result, RISC processors are sometimes called load/store processors

- RISC processors have a low number of instructions in their instruction sets: usually less than 100 as compared to a typical 200–250 for a CISC chip

- All instructions are the same length

- All instructions are executed in a single clock cycle. (This does not take account of the cycles needed for decoding, setup and processing of the instruction's results.) Thus, if a CISC processor takes an average four clock cycles per instruction and its allowable clock speed is 40MHz, its throughput will be 10 million instructions per second (MIPS). The equivalent RISC chip will be four times faster at 40 MIPS

All things being equal, RISC performance is superior to that of CISC, but it is more difficult to write compilers and other utilities for RISC than CISC. The reason is that RISC instructions are less elaborate than their CISC counterparts (hence the higher speed) and combinations of them are required to achieve the same results.

To exploit the speed of a RISC processor, a compiler needs to be optimised for it, that is to generate efficient executable code using the high-speed native RISC instructions. If the code generated by the compiler is not optimised for RISC, complex instructions have to be translated to their RISC equivalents and the compiled application program may not show the performance improvement which might be expected after porting it to a RISC architecture.

Examples of RISC microprocessors include the Motorola 88000 series, the IBM RS6000, the Digital Equipment Corporation Alpha AXP and the PowerPC developed jointly by Apple, IBM and Motorola. The latest

CISC chips, the Intel Pentium and the Motorola MC68060, incorporate many of the techniques of RISC and instruction pipelining to improve their performance. The two RISC microprocessors most likely to have a significant influence on the future of computing are the PowerPC and the DEC Alpha.

PowerPC

Under an agreement reached in 1991, Apple, IBM and Motorola (AIM), jointly began development of the new RISC PowerPC architecture, based on IBM's POWER architecture first used with its RS6000 AIX minicomputers. At the same time, two subsidiary companies were formed: Kaleida, to develop *multimedia* applications; and Taligent, to produce an object-oriented operating system.

The PowerPC is a direct challenge to the dominance of the Intel 80X86 architecture which has existed since the inception of personal computing. The PowerPC is deliberately incompatible with the Intel architecture. One benefit of this is that the PowerPC does not have to be backward-compatible with, for example, the segmented 80286 design and is therefore likely to be faster than any equivalent 80X86 processor.

The PowerPC makes provision for 64-bit addressing as opposed to the now-common 32-bit addressing. As the requirements of application software grow and the capacity of 32-bit memory addressing is approached, 64-bit addressing will be needed to ensure the viability of the architecture. The PowerPC is a superscalar processor; it can *issue* or *dispatch* many instructions at the same time with clear performance benefits.

Although different in design from the Intel processors, the PowerPC can run 80X86 software in an emulation mode. It can also run Microsoft Windows with most popular application programs using the *Windows Application Binary Interface* (WABI) originally produced by Sun Microsystems. A consortium of major system vendors called Power Open and including Apple, IBM and Motorola has been established to define specifications for a version of the UNIX operating system which runs on the PowerPC and for portability of application software between different PowerPC-based UNIX systems.

There are four main variants of the PowerPC microprocessor: MPC601, MPC603, MPC604 and MPC620, of which the first two already exist.

The Apple Power Mac series of computers is based on the MPC601 and offers software compatibility with the Motorola MC680X0 processors which have traditionally been the engine of the Macintosh. IBM's series of Power Personal Systems also uses the MPC601.

The MPC601 has a 32-bit address bus which allows up to 4GB of memory to be accessed. It uses a 64-bit data bus for fast transfer of data between processor and memory. With a *3-issue superscalar* architecture and three independent units for integer, floating-point and *branch-prediction* operations, it can run three instructions at the same time. The MPC601 has a maximum clock speed of 80 MHz and is smaller, faster, cheaper and less power-hungry than the Intel Pentium. The other PowerPC processors feature a number of improvements over the MPC601. The MPC604 is between two and three times faster than its predecessor, while the MPC620 rivals the DEC Alpha in performance.

DEC Alpha

The Alpha chip is the result of a project started by Digital Equipment Corporation in 1988 to design a processor to replace that used in the VAX series. It is a RISC processor with 64-bit addressing which allows it to address 18.4 exabytes (18×10^{18} bytes) of memory. This addressing capacity gives the design an estimated 25-year lifespan during which performance is expected to increase by a factor of 1,000.

The Alpha is independent of any operating system, unlike most previous RISC processors, which were optimised for UNIX. The Alpha is a new RISC design, with no special registers or complex internal instructions. It is reportedly optimised for throughput of data and can achieve clock speeds of over 200MHz with performance of more than 400 MIPS. The Alpha processor is superscalar – it can issue two instructions at the same time – and *superpipelined* – it can perform instructions in seven parts concurrently. The Alpha also provides facilities for being used in a parallel-processing arrangement with other Alpha processors.

The Alpha is designed with an internal layer of abstraction called the Privileged Architecture Library which allows it to run the OpenVMS, UNIX and Windows NT operating systems and does not preclude support for future operating systems. Application programs built for earlier VAX and MIPS processors can run unchanged on the Alpha.

The first Alpha-based personal computer, the DECpc AXP 150, uses the Alpha 21064 with a clock speed of 150MHz. It is up to twice as fast as the fastest Pentium-based system and can run Windows programs in emulation as fast as a 50MHz 80486 PC.

Pipelining

Pipelining is a technique coming into increasing use in the drive to increase the performance of microprocessors. Essentially, it means taking a single instruction, breaking it up and executing the different parts at the same time. If an instruction can be split into four parts and executed concurrently, the performance increase will approach a factor of four.

There are four stages in the execution of an instruction: *fetch*, *decode*, *execute* and *write*. Each of these will typically take about one clock cycle in a RISC system, so an instruction on the face of it will take four clock cycles.

At any instant in time, the processor is only doing one thing and some of its different functions are idle. For example, when the processor is executing an instruction, its fetch, decode and write handlers may be idle.

If the different parts of several instructions are dealt with by the processor in parallel, the result is pipelining and a potential increase in performance of over 100%. The diagram below depicts in simplified form how four four-cycle instructions can be processed through a RISC pipeline in only seven clock cycles instead of the expected 16.

Pipelining only fails where an instruction in the pipeline has to wait for the result of a previous instruction. Occurrences of stall conditions such as this are minimised by good compilers which recognise dependencies between instructions and generate code optimised for the pipelined processor.

Superpipelining goes further by increasing the granularity of division of instructions. Superscalar processors, instead of increasing the granularity, increase the number of pipelines, which then operate in parallel.

A RISC processor pipeline

Fetch	Decode	Execute	Write	Clock
Instruction 1				Cycle 0
Instruction 2	Instruction 1			Cycle 1
Instruction 3	Instruction 2	Instruction 1		Cycle 2
Instruction 4	Instruction 3	Instruction 2	Instruction 1	Cycle 3
	Instruction 4	Instruction 3	Instruction 2	Cycle 4
		Instruction 4	Instruction 3	Cycle 5
			Instruction 4	Cycle 6

Source and binary compatibility

Definitions

Computer A is binary compatible with computer B if an executable program file which runs on A can be transferred unmodified to B where it runs equally well. A compiler and *linkage editor* are used to take source code, probably written in a high-level language, as input and produce as their output the executable program file.

Computer A is source code compatible with Computer B if the source code of a program which runs on A can be transferred unmodified to B, compiled and linked into executable format on B and then run equally well on B as on A.

Fully-compatible IBM PCs are binary compatible. As an example of this, the .EXE file for Lotus 1-2-3 will run on any compatible PC and is often said to be delivered in shrink-wrapped form. PCs are binary compatible because they all use the Intel microprocessor architecture to run their executable programs.

Other systems (for example, UNIX) which have been implemented for many different microprocessor architectures and computer systems cannot generally be binary compatible. Instead, open systems based on UNIX aim for source-code compatibility. Source-code compatibility is a lesser form of compatibility than binary in that an executable program is not itself directly portable between source-code-compatible computers; the source code must be moved between target systems and on each system compiled into its particular executable code format.

Some UNIX systems have introduced Application Binary Interfaces. ABIs ensure binary compatibility for all computer systems running that version of UNIX which also are based on the same microprocessor architecture.

Computer languages

C offers the highest degree of source-code compatibility between all types of computer systems. If a fully conforming ISO C program is compiled and linked in an ISO C environment on computer A, it is guaranteed to compile, link and run successfully on computer B, if B has an equivalent ISO C compile/link environment. With earlier versions of C, the same guarantee could not be made. If any extensions are made to the ISO C syntax, for example to support the 80286 processor architecture or the Microsoft Windows API, then the program is guaranteed to be not source-code compatible with any system other than an exact equivalent.

Languages which have been standardised and in which programs are more or less portable between systems at the source-code level are:

▶ Ada (ISO standard Ada 8652:1987)

▶ ISO C (includes ANSI standard C, reference X3.159-1989; ISO standard 9899:1990)

▶ COBOL-85 (ANSI standard COBOL, reference X3.23-1985; ISO standard 1989:1985)

▶ FORTRAN-77 (ANSI Standard FORTRAN, reference X3.9-1978)

▶ Fortran-90 (ANSI Standard FORTRAN, reference X3.198-1992; ISO standard Fortran 1539:1991(E))

▶ Pascal (ISO Pascal, reference ISO 7185-1983)

▸ Structured Query Language (SQL) (ANSI standards SQL86, reference X3.135-1986, SQL89 and SQL92, which is also known as SQL-2)

Programs written in assembler languages are not portable at all. Where, for a given language, there is both an ANSI and an ISO standard, those standards are usually identical. Often the United States body, ANSI, defines an American standard which is then ratified by ISO as an international standard. This is the case with the identical ANSI C and ISO C standards. As the lesser standard, ANSI C has now been withdrawn in favour of ISO C.

The POSIX standards describe a portable operating system interface in terms of ISO C. If a program written in C conforms to the POSIX specifications, it will run under and be able to use the services of a POSIX-compliant operating system. Broadly speaking, this effectively means that a conforming C program can run under the control of UNIX.

Strictly, POSIX is language-independent: any language can, in principle, be used to define the interface. Such definitions are referred to as *language bindings*. Currently, POSIX language bindings exist for Ada, C and Fortran, so programs written in those languages can run under a POSIX-compliant operating system (i.e: UNIX).

The main goal of these efforts in standardisation of programming languages is to make programs written in them portable across all computer systems which run a POSIX-compliant (i.e: UNIX) operating system.

Application Program Interface (API)

An API is a definition of an interface comprising a number of function specifications which may be called by application programs. The calling programs do not have to know the internal details of the facility for which the API is the interface. Well known APIs include the functions provided by Microsoft Windows for messaging and graphical display, and the Oracle DBMS API which provides database services. All types of computer software entities have APIs.

The list of well known software systems which provide APIs includes the following:

▸ The UNIX operating system kernel: its API is referred to as the system-call interface

▸ The DOS operating system kernel, including such things as system calls and BIOS requests

▸ Microsoft Windows 3.1, via its Software Development Kit (SDK): for example the 'CreateWindow' call

▸ OS/2 Presentation Manager: for example, the 'WinDlgBox' call

▸ The X Windows library used to implement GUIs on UNIX systems

▸ A number of database management systems, including Informix, Ingres Oracle and Sybase

▸ The last program I wrote containing a function to be called by some other program

The term API is often used very loosely. Confusion arises because it is used both in the singular and in the plural to mean different things, for example 'the program calls an API' (where API means a single function) and 'the program uses the Windows API' (where API is a collective term referring to a large set of functions).

As is explained in 'Computer Languages' above, standardisation of languages promotes portability of the programs written using them. APIs also are a determinant of source-code portability; together, standard languages and standard APIs offer the possibility of complete source-code portability between different computer systems. As a practical example, a C program conforming strictly to the ISO standard can be ported unchanged to and will run on every UNIX system presenting a POSIX-compliant API.

Unfortunately, languages and APIs are both often extended by software suppliers to meet particular needs. For example, a Microsoft Windows program containing a 'ShowWindow' API call, or syntax to accommodate the 'near' and 'far' pointers required by the Intel 80286 processor architecture, will not work when ported to any UNIX environment. This is for two reasons: 'ShowWindow' is not part of the POSIX API and 'near' and 'far' are extensions to the standard C language.

Application Binary Interface (ABI)

An ABI is a back-end interface which allows an executable program to be moved between hardware platforms.

AT&T introduced the concept of the ABI in order to allow binary software portability between all UNIX systems using the same processor architecture. Because all IBM-compatible PCs use Intel processors, it is possible to supply shrink-wrapped executable software – examples include Lotus 1-2-3 and Microsoft Word – which will run 'out of the box' on every compatible PC. Traditionally there has only been source-code compatibility, at best, between UNIX systems, which means that to transfer software between systems of different suppliers, the software must be compiled and linked from its source-code form on the destination system.

In an ABI definition, a generic section describes the complete set of services available from an operating system, while a processor-specific part defines precisely how those services are accessed on a particular computer. The processor-specific part must be rewritten for every target computer.

When an ABI has been defined for, say, the Motorola 68030, then a single conforming program should run on *all* systems based on the 68030 processor.

UNIX ABIs have been defined for the Intel 80386, Motorola 680X0, Motorola 88100, MIPS and SPARC microprocessors. Using ABIs, UNIX systems can make their nearest approach to binary compatibility among systems with the same processor architecture. Most importantly, ABIs for the first time allow shrink-wrapped application software to be supplied for UNIX systems of different vendors but with the same processor architecture.

As another way of looking at it, IBM-compatible (Intel-processor-based) PCs in fact have a *de facto* ABI which ensures binary compatibility between systems. Some limitations to PC compatibility are considered in the next section.

The Application
Binary Interface

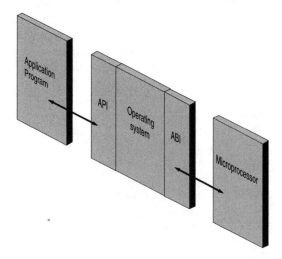

Limitations of the Intel microprocessors

The limitations of the 8086 and 80286 processors and their incompatibility with the 80386 architecture which followed have far-reaching effects on the user's choice of operating system and application software today. To understand the problems, it is necessary to consider each of the processors in turn.

8086/8088

The first PC was designed around the Intel 8086/8088 processors. The 8086 is a 16-bit processor which means that it can address one megabyte (1MB) of memory. The memory space available on the original PC to accommodate DOS and applications supported by it was 1MB. In practice the memory limit was 640KB, the other 360KB being used for services including the Basic Input–Output System (BIOS). At the time, designers did not envisage that PC software applications would ever require more than the 640KB available.

The 8086 can run, under the control of DOS, only one application at a time. Advanced facilities, such as memory protection for multiple applications, common with larger operating systems and more powerful processors, are not available. Additionally, the 16-bit addressing scheme used by the 8086 enforces segmentation of memory into 64KB blocks.

Programs written for the 8086 must run alone in memory and must incorporate logic to handle the segmentation limits. Because of these restrictions, 8086 programs are completely non-portable: they will not run on any other processor without significant change. However, because IBM PCs quickly became popular and were sold widely, this did not pose a particular problem for its users.

80286

Between 1983 and 1985, DOS users and programmers began to be aware of the limitations imposed by the original PC design. Increasingly sophisticated applications were demanding more memory, a graphical user interface and the capability of multitasking with memory protection. To address these needs, IBM introduced the upgraded PC/AT (Advanced Technology) based on the new high-performance Intel 80286 microprocessor.

The 80286-based PC can operate in two modes: real and protected. Real mode is for backward-compatibility with the 8086; DOS and its programs can run unchanged in a 640KB memory space with no memory protection.

80286 protected mode makes it possible for more than one application program to execute concurrently and ensures, by means of a complex memory-protection scheme, that these programs do not interfere with each other.

An 80286 PC can, in principle, run a single DOS program in real mode in the basic 640KB of memory and a number of other programs in extended memory – up to 16MB.

The 80286, like the 8086, uses a 16-bit addressing scheme, so all the memory addressed by it, including the extended memory, is treated as a sequence of 64KB segments. This places an unfortunate overhead on programs written for the 80286, in terms both of complexity in handling segments and in non-portability.

Because DOS is only capable of running programs in real mode, it cannot fully use the power of the extended addressing and memory provided by the 80286. In effect it runs programs using the 80286 as an approximately five-times-faster 8086. More powerful operating systems, such as OS/2 Versions 2 and 3 and Windows NT, are required fully to exploit the 80286 architecture.

80386

The 80386 extends the power of the 80286 by eliminating the 64KB segment architecture and introducing 32-bit memory addressing. This allows linear addressing of up to four gigabytes (four million million bytes, or 4GB) of memory.

An extra processor mode – virtual 8086, or V86 – is also introduced which allows a virtual DOS PC with 640KB of memory to be created for every DOS application required to run on the processor. In summary, the 80386 allows:

▸ One DOS application to be executed in real mode

▸ Several other applications to run in protected mode in a potential 4GB of memory

▸ Several more DOS programs to run as virtual PCs in V86 mode

All these programs can execute concurrently with memory protection. Programs executing with linear addressing in extended memory no longer have to cope with the 64KB segmentation scheme originated by the 8086 and retained by the 80286. The drawback is that code written to use 80386 linear addressing may not be portable backwards to the 80286. Equally, code written for the 80286 may reflect its segmented architecture and cause portability problems when it is moved to 80386.

Microsoft Windows 3.0, released in 1990, runs on an 80386 in 8086 'real mode', 80286 'standard mode' or 80386 'enhanced mode'. Windows 3.1 drops real mode execution and introduces virtual memory and multiple DOS sessions. Windows 3.1 can access 16 MB of physical memory and additional virtual memory.

OS/2 versions 2 and 3 fully use the power of the 80386 and 80486 processors, providing multi-tasking, extended memory up to a potential 4GB, memory protection and an advanced graphical user interface. Microsoft Windows NT and Windows 95 also use the addressing and protection capabilities of the 80386 processor architecture.

Operating systems

MS-DOS

Microsoft's Disk Operating System (MS-DOS) and the almost identical PC-DOS first appeared in 1981 with the release of the IBM PC. DOS is a single-task operating system. DOS and the job it controls must reside in 640K of the 1MB of memory addressed by the basic Intel 8086 microprocessor.

To make DOS appear to be running more than one program at a time, various tricks must be used, such as Terminate and Stay Resident programs (TSRs). Equally, to give DOS more than 640K to work in, tricks must be used. The available memory must be either expanded (into the area between 640K and 1MB) or extended (beyond 1MB using an 80286 or higher processor).

The basic – and, in 1981, only – interface supplied by DOS is a command line to which the user must supply commands with a syntax partly derived from that of UNIX, which preceded DOS by ten years. Together, the memory and single-tasking limitations led to the development of a windowed user interface and the so-called DOS extenders, software which allow programs running on top of DOS to use more than 1MB of memory.

Microsoft Windows

The first version of Microsoft Windows was announced in November, 1983 but not released until two years later. Windows 1.0 had a tiled interface – the whole screen had to be refreshed on every display change – low resolution and unacceptable performance on the PCs of the time.

In May, 1990, Windows 3.0 was introduced and was immediately a runaway success. Windows 3.0 and its successors, Windows 3.1 and Windows for Workgroups, are not operating systems but DOS extenders with a fairly sophisticated GUI. Windows requires the underlying services of DOS as an operating system.

Windows 3.1 has a host of features, but they can be summarised as follows:

- ▸ Graphical User Interface
- ▸ Cooperative Multitasking
- ▸ Dynamic Data Exchange (DDE)
- ▸ Object Linking and Embedding (OLE)

Cooperative multitasking means that more than one job can run concurrently under Windows but that the memory protection features of the 80386 processor are not used and tasks cannot be pre-empted. This means that the Windows is inherently unreliable as a multitasking environment, especially for programs that do their own memory management.

Windows supports three types of interprocess communication:

- ▸ The Clipboard
- ▸ Shared memory in Dynamic Link Libraries (DLLs)
- ▸ Dynamic Data Exchange (DDE)

DDE is implemented using the messaging system built into Windows. Two Windows programs carry on a conversation by posting messages to each other. The programs are known as the client and server, with the client being the program which receives data from the server.

A single Windows program can be both a client to one program and a server to another. This requires two different DDE conversations (and hence message queues). Each conversation on each side communicates via a hidden child window of a parent window. If a program is conducting many conversations, it keeps them separate and distinct by using a hidden window for each. Using OLE, it is possible to embed one Windows program in another so that, for example, a Microsoft Word 6.0 word-processor document can be accessed and manipulated from within the display of a user-written application. The diagram below summarises the characteristics of Microsoft's various Windows products.

Microsoft's
Windows
product family

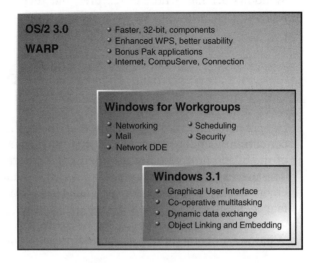

Windows NT

Microsoft Windows NT is a single-user, multi-tasking, multi-threading operating system which uses pre-emptive scheduling and the memory-protection facilities of the 80386 architecture. Windows NT also runs on the Alpha and MIPS machines.

Windows NT presents the user with a graphical interface which is almost exactly the same as the familiar Windows 3.1 interface. The differences are in the new logon procedure and the fact that the hourglass symbol has disappeared – NT is capable of genuine multitasking.

Windows NT runs its tasks as processes, each of which is further divided into one or more threads. A process is the transient memory image of a program in execution. A thread is an independent strand of execution within a process. For example, a word-processing application might run as a single process but perform printing in a special print thread which executes while the user is concurrently editing another document from within the same process. Threads are sometimes called *lightweight processes*.

The internal design of an operating system is either monolithic, layered or a client–server model. DOS is monolithic, UNIX is layered and Windows NT is a combination of the layered and client–server models.

At the bottom of the Windows NT operating system structure is the Executive. The Executive implements services including virtual memory management; object (resource) management; I/O management; filesystems; network drivers; interprocess communication and security. Within the Executive, there are three layers:

▶ *Executive:* carries out the functions listed above

▶ *Kernel:* performs thread scheduling, interrupt handling, exception dispatching and multiprocessor synchronisation

▶ *Hardware Abstraction Layer* (HAL): the bottom-most layer of the Executive; insulates the rest of the system from hardware dependencies. The HAL manipulates the hardware directly, and is the only part of Windows NT which must be rewritten when the operating system is ported

The NT client–server model

Apart from the layered Executive, Windows NT is implemented using the client–server model. The operating system is divided into several processes called servers or *subsystems*, each of which provides a single set of services to clients (application programs or other servers).

Operating system services which are normally part of the kernel are isolated as protected subsystems and accessed using Local Procedure Call (LPC) messaging. This isolation of services into separate entities makes the kernel small – it is called a *microkernel* – and in large part used as a message-switching device. Some advantages of the Windows NT client–server model are:

▶ The base operating system is simplified because it is smaller than it would otherwise be

▶ Isolation of subsystems makes the overall system more reliable

▶ NT lends itself to being implemented on distributed networks, with messages being exchanged between client and server processes on different systems

NT system structure

Broadly, Windows NT is organised in two execution modes: user and kernel mode. Client processes – application programs – run in user mode and make requests on servers, called protected subsystems. Requests are made in the form of messages which are processed by the executive and directed to the appropriate protected subsystem. Each subsystem implements an API on which calls are made to respond to client requests.

NT system
structure

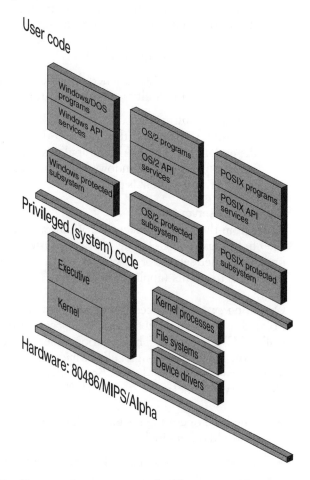

An API call on a subsystem is invoked by means of a message from the executive to the server using the LPC facility, a variant on Remote Procedure Call (RPC), which implements optimised, high-speed message-passing between client and server processes. The server replies by returning a message via the executive to the client.

NT can run any number of servers; those it runs are in two classifications:

► *Integral subsystems:* processes which perform NT operating system functions; they include the security and networking subsystems

► *Environment subsystems:* processes which mimic other operating systems by providing the API, or system call interface, of those operating systems

The most important environment subsystem is the Win32 subsystem which provides the 32-bit Windows API to application programs. Environment subsystems are supplied within Windows NT for DOS/ Windows 3.1 as well as OS/2 and POSIX (UNIX).

DOS and the 16-bit Windows environment (Win16) run in Virtual DOS Machines (VDMs). API calls generated by DOS or Win16 are converted within the VDM to the equivalent Win32 call, which is then sent by message to the Win32 subsystem.

If, say, a UNIX program is run under Windows NT, the system calls it makes are also converted into the Win32 equivalent before being invoked.

Executive services
All messages to and from clients and servers are handled by the Executive, which provides the following services:

► Object manager
► Security Reference monitor
► Process manager
► LPC facility
► Virtual Memory manager
► Kernel
► I/O System
► HAL

Windows NT supports DOS, OS/2, NT and POSIX (UNIX) filesystems. These are respectively: FAT, HPFS, NTFS and either the traditional or fast UNIX filesystems.

Windows NT supports symmetric multiprocessing (SMP), where both the operating system and its threads and processes can be distributed flexibly and evenly across two or more processors. Support for SMP makes NT a good distributed operating system and also promotes robustness and fault-tolerance. Asymmetric multiprocessing (ASMP) is where the operating system runs on one processor and specific threads and processes run on other designated processors. Such implementations are less portable and powerful than SMP.

NT supports internationalisation and diverse character sets using a 16-bit coding scheme called *Unicode*. NT also supports structured exception handling.

Windows 95

Windows 95 is Microsoft's successor to Windows 3.x. The original code name given to the product was Chicago and it has also been referred to as Windows 4.0. Microsoft's intention is that Windows 95 should begin to replace the installed base of Windows 3.x software in 1995. Windows 95 is in many respects a stripped-down 'NT lite'. Its objectives include the following:

- Match or exceed the performance of Windows 3.0 and Windows 3.1 running on a 4MB 80386-based PC

- Present a more intuitive user interface

- Memory protection and multitasking features implemented in Windows NT must be incorporated and must fit in less than 4MB of memory

- Use the Win32 (32-bit NT) API while providing backward compatibility to the Windows 3.x Win16 API

- Provide full DOS program compatibility, including for games, often the most difficult programs to get running in DOS emulation mode

Features provided by Windows 95 which represent improvements over Windows 3.x include:

- Threaded, pre-emptive multitasking; Windows 95 is more reliable than Windows 3.x and handles program crashes better, as well as doing genuine multitasking (as opposed to the simulated multitasking of Windows 3.x)

> ► 32-bit memory addressing, allowing access to up to 4GB of physical memory and virtual memory

> ► Use of a layered device-driver model

> ► Desynchronised input message queue

> ► *Event-driven* scheduling

> ► Long file names

> ► A new partly object-oriented GUI, unifying the functions of the Windows 3.x File Manager, Program Manager and Task Manager

> ► Multiple virtual 8086-based DOS sessions

Windows 95 does not incorporate the NT File System (NTFS), security or scalability features. It eliminates the need for DOS and is thus a true operating system, unlike Windows 3.x. Windows 95 represents a much-improved Windows 3.x, incorporating many of the advantages offered by Windows NT, while fitting on small PCs. Disadvantages include the retention of some internal 16-bit addressing; the need for conversion (*thunking*) of Win32 API calls to their Win16 equivalents; and the tendency for Win16 applications to lock out all others as they are not *re-entrant* (Win16 API functions cannot be called more than once at the same time). Notwithstanding its limitations when compared to Windows NT, Windows 95 is a popular replacement for many of the 50 million-plus copies of Windows 3.0 and 3.1 installed.

OS/2

OS/2 is a single-user, multitasking, multithreading operating system designed to run on IBM or IBM-compatible Personal Computer systems built around the Intel 80386 and 80486 microprocessors. The most widely used version of the operating system is 2.1, as distinct from previous versions 1.0 through 1.3. The current version of OS/2 is OS/2 3.0 (Warp), which supplants version 2.1. The term OS/2 henceforth is intended to mean OS/2 2.1 and OS/2 3.0 collectively, unless otherwise indicated.

OS/2 is an advanced operating system which allows concurrent – apparently simultaneous – execution of many programs. Programs in execution are referred to as threads or tasks. A process comprises one or more threads. The graphic interface presented to the user by OS/2 is the Workplace Shell (WPS). The WPS is an advanced object-oriented GUI which is generally considered superior to the Windows equivalent. WPS, like other graphic programs supported by OS/2, is written to use the API supplied by Presentation Manager (PM) which is similar in many respects to the Windows Win32 API. Windows and PM programs written in C are very similar in form, appearance and techniques used.

OS/2 offers improvements in power and functionality over the DOS and Microsoft Windows environments. It is in many ways equivalent to Windows 95 and approaches the level of Windows NT and UNIX. Many of the features of OS/2 are borrowed directly or indirectly from UNIX. UNIX still has the advantage over OS/2 and all Windows products of being a multi-user as well as a multitasking system. The following diagram summarises the characteristics of the successive versions of OS/2:

Versions of OS/2
since 1987

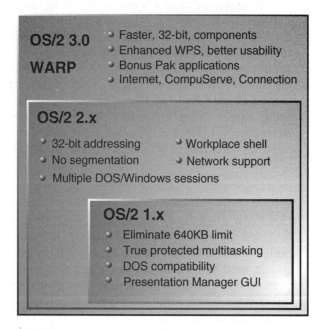

Versions 1.0 through 1.3 of OS/2 were designed to run on the 80286 and higher processors, using its protection features and extended memory but hampered by 64KB segmentation and the fact that only one DOS application could be run. Both Windows 3.0 and 3.1 use 16-bit addressing giving maximum memory availability of 16MB. Both allow V86 mode to be used to run many virtual DOS machines. This is

an advantage over versions 1.X of OS/2, which allow only one DOS application, in real mode, to run. OS/2 Versions 2 and 3 eliminate the disadvantages of OS/2 versions 1.X, taking advantage of the power of the 80386 and 80486 processors, providing multitasking, extended memory up to a potential 4GB, memory protection and an advanced graphical user interface.

OS/2 objectives

OS/2 Version 1.X was designed to meet the following objectives:

▸ Eliminate the 8086 640KB memory limitation and support up to 16MB of physical memory addressed by the 80286 processor

▸ Provide a true multitasking environment with memory protection, allowing multiple applications to run reliably and concurrently

▸ Provide DOS binary compatibility, allowing execution of a single DOS application at a time in 80286 real mode, and promoting DOS-OS/2 migration

▸ Provide a GUI (Presentation Manager was delivered with OS/2 1.1)

OS/2 Version 2.X was designed as an extension, with these additional objectives:

▸ Use all the capabilities of the Intel 80386 and 80486 processors

▸ Provide 32-bit linear addressing and, consequently, a potential 4GB of available memory

▸ Eliminate 64KB memory segmentation, simplifying application software and improving its portability

▸ Use 80386 memory protection, ensuring that programs do not corrupt each other and that, if a program crashes, only that program, and not the whole system, fails

▸ Allow multiple DOS sessions to be run concurrently

▸ Allow fully-compatible Windows sessions to be run, along with unchanged Windows applications, in a protected-memory environment

▸ Provide compatibility with the Windows GUI, and introduce an advanced object-oriented GUI called the Workplace Shell (WPS)

OS/2 features

Major features of OS/2 include the following:

- True multitasking and extended memory

- Ability to run multiple DOS and Windows applications in protected memory

- The Dual-boot and Boot Manager facilities, which allow multiple operating systems to co-exist on the same boot device on which OS/2 is resident. In practice, this means that DOS, OS/2 and UNIX can be started from the same hard disk

- Choice of filesystems. Since 1983, DOS has used the hierarchical File Allocation Table (FAT) filesystem. OS/2 supports this and it is recommended for use on small systems. OS/2 introduces the High-Performance File System, which uses advanced cache techniques to speed filesystem performance on filesystems larger than 50-60MB

- Virtual devices, a concept borrowed from UNIX, which assigns to physical devices file names making the actual mechanisms for accessing those devices transparent to the user

- A large number of built-in applications, including productivity tools such as database, spreadsheet, calendar and calculator

- The REXX procedures language, an interpreted language often used for system-administrative tasks, which is superior to the DOS batch language

- Comprehensive integrated networking support

Common User Access Standard

OS/2 conforms to the IBM System Application Architecture (SAA). SAA consists of three components:

- Common User Access (CUA). Systems conforming to CUA present a Graphical User Interface with the same look and feel for all applications, thereby cutting the time needed by new users to learn them

- Common Programming Interface (CPI). Ensures by means of language standardisation that a program written on any IBM mainframe, midrange or PC system can be recompiled and run correctly on any other member of the family

> ▸ Common Communications Access (CCA). Ensures interoperability, via protocols such as 3270, SNA, APPC and APPN, of mainframes, midrange systems and PCs

OS/2 also provides strong connectivity with open systems based on the UNIX operating system by means of support for the X.25 and TCP/IP communications protocol suites.

UNIX

UNIX is the basis of open systems standards and is a time-sharing, multitasking, multi-user (but not multithreading) operating system which controls the operation of and allocates system resources to programs running on the computer.

UNIX provides a productive software development environment. It offers good connectivity with systems running a number of communications protocols and extensive portability of software among the computers of different vendors.

It is a layered operating system. Its bottom layer is the kernel. In the strictest sense, the kernel which controls executing programs and allocates computer resources, *is* the operating system. Everything else, programs, utilities, files and devices, is separate and outside the operating system. Most definitions of UNIX, however, are not so strict and describe the operating system as being made up of several parts:

> ▸ *Kernel*
>
> ▸ *Filesystem*: an organised hierarchy of files in which user and other data is stored
>
> ▸ *Processes*: programs in execution
>
> ▸ *Shell*: the command processing program which recognises and carries out the user's directives
>
> ▸ Arguably, compilers, editors and other utilities, such as those for copying files and communicating between users and between computers

UNIX structure

Application programs present the user's interface to UNIX and the computer. They include Graphical User Interfaces, word-processing software, CAD/CAM systems and stock-control software. The application may be the nearest encounter a user ever has with UNIX. Application programs communicate with the kernel either through or under the control of the shell and UNIX commands. When an application requires a service from the computer hardware it addresses its request through this layer to the kernel. When the kernel receives such a request, it schedules the request for execution by the computer.

To read information from a disk file, the kernel directs the hardware control module to move the read-heads of the disk unit to the appropriate point on the disk, read the required data and return it to a memory area controlled by the kernel. The data is then copied to a memory area usable by the application program. The user, and the application program, need know nothing of what occurs in the underlying operating system and hardware layers.

Structure of UNIX

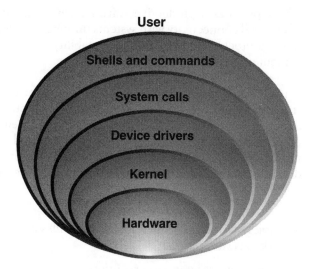

The UNIX kernel essentially has two jobs: to schedule and control processes and to control the UNIX filesystem. When a program is executed on a UNIX system it is first turned into a process, which is an executable image of the program, held in system memory. The process contains all the program's instructions and data, as well as stack space for temporary storage purposes, in a process table. The contents of this table change continuously as the process executes.

When a process requires a service of the kernel, it issues a system call. A system call is the name of a function (written in C) which directs the kernel to carry out some low-level task required by the application. On most versions of UNIX, there are upwards of 100 system calls and the point at which they are invoked is referred to as the system-call interface (or, more recently, API).

An I/O system call, such as 'write', interacts with a *device driver*. The device driver is a program which handles input-output operations for a particular type of device. The kernel contains many device drivers, at least one for every external device supported by the computer. The device driver determines when it is time to write the data to the disk and calls the hardware control level to do so. On completion of the write request, the kernel signals the application process accordingly.

The process control subsystem of the kernel is responsible for the scheduling and synchronisation of the many processes running concurrently under UNIX; for managing memory used by these processes; and for implementing interprocess communication (IPC).

The second main job of the kernel is to control use by processes of the UNIX filesystem. There are many different filesystem types in the latest versions of UNIX.

The UNIX filesystem is hierarchical. Files are uniform in structure – they have no structure – and are used to represent all system resources. The file system control subsystem of the kernel must ensure consistency of the whole file system; correct retrieval of files; file and record locking procedures; and file security.

The layered structure of the UNIX operating system yields a number of benefits:

- ► Application programs are independent of the type of computer system on which they run. All application programs use the uniformly-defined system-call interface, below which the kernel handles low-level requests for computer system resources

- ► Application programs are easily portable between diverse types of computer running UNIX

- ► UNIX itself is portable between systems with relative ease. Only the low levels of the kernel software must be changed to accommodate hardware dependencies; the applications, system calls, shell and filesystem organisation remain the same

- The procedures for accessing files are standard throughout UNIX. Files are used to provide applications with access to all system resources

Objectives of UNIX

The inventors of UNIX wrote a small operating system which embodied a number of clearly-defined design objectives:

- A simple user interface providing services required by users

- A hierarchical file system

- A completely consistent file format, making application programs easier to write

- Files without inherent structure, such as block and record sizes, indexed or relative organisation; they are just a stream of bytes with meaning defined by the software using them

- External devices which are treated as files with the same format as any other files

- Files which need not be allocated disk space; they grow dynamically

- Hardware dependencies are hidden from the user by UNIX promoting software portability

- A multi-user system which allows users to execute several processes concurrently

- Provision of simple software utilities (tools) which may be combined and from which more complex programs may be built

- An operating system written in a high-level language (C), making it easy to modify and move to other computers

- Exclusion of features, such as complex file organisation and access, prevalent in other operating systems

- Easy-to-use for programmers, encouraging high software-development productivity

UNIX was originally designed on the principle that small is beautiful. Unnecessary features were omitted and relegated to external libraries and packages. Over the years, UNIX has grown to the point where this objective is no longer met.

Versions of UNIX

Currently, the two most important broad versions of UNIX are:

▸ *UNIX System V:* This was for many years developed by UNIX System Laboratories (USL), a subsidiary company of AT&T. Univel was established in December 1991 as a joint venture by Novell Inc. and USL. In 1993, Novell acquired USL. Univel now owns and licenses UNIX System V, of which the current version is UNIX System V, Release 4.2 (SVR4.2).

UnixWare, incorporating SVR4.2 and supplied by Univel, is the current official System V. It features full integration of UNIX TCP/IP communications with the Novell NetWare SPX/IPX protocols, allowing easy internetworking of UNIX systems and PC LANs. UnixWare is described further in the section on *Open operating system standards* (page 90) and, in the context of Novell NetWare, in the section *LAN network operating systems*, page 193.

Sun Microsystems' Solaris is partly derived from SVR4.2 but also inherits characteristics from SunOS 4.0, in turn based on BSD 4.X, referred to below.

▸ *OSF/1, licensed by the Open Software Foundation:* An industry consortium of major system vendors, including IBM. It includes parts of IBM's AIX as well as a microkernel based on the Mach operating system supplied by Carnegie-Mellon University

There are many other versions of UNIX, most of which have some commonality with either System V or OSF. They are to be found running on all types of computer systems from the PC AT to the largest supercomputer. Some important versions of UNIX are:

▸ *BSD 4.X:* high-performance versions of UNIX developed since the mid-1970s by the University of California at Berkeley. There have been four major releases of Berkeley Software Distribution (BSD) UNIX, 4.0 through 4.3

▸ *SCO UNIX:* based on System V and supplied by the Santa Cruz Operation

▸ *HP-UX:* based on System V and supplied by Hewlett-Packard

▸ *SunOS:* based on 4.2BSD and supplied by Sun Microsystems Inc. SunOS Version 5.0 derives additional characteristics from System V Release 4 (commonly known as Solaris Version 2.0)

> ▸ *Ultrix:* based on 4.2BSD and supplied by DEC

> ▸ *AIX:* (Advanced Interactive eXecutive) based on System V and supplied by IBM. Portions of AIX are included in OSF/1

> ▸ *NextStep:* based on the Mach operating system, is an object-oriented version of UNIX, is supplied by Next Inc. and is designed for use in client–server applications

UNIX developments

Traditional UNIX is a time-sharing, not a real-time, operating system. Real-time may be defined as the certainty that, once started, any process can finish within a pre-defined time-interval. In the latest UNIX versions, including SVR4 and Solaris, the kernel has been changed to allow real-time operation, but many existing UNIX installations do not have this facility.

From its earliest days, UNIX had good *asynchronous* communications (slow telephone-line and modem) capability. Since then, extensive high-speed networking facilities have been incorporated, allowing UNIX systems to be organised in local area networks (LANs) and wide area networks (WANs) typically using the X.25 and/or TCP/IP communications protocols.

It is now possible to internetwork UNIX systems with PC networks such as those based on Novell NetWare; with larger systems such as Digital Equipment Corporation VAX with DECnet; and with IBM systems via System Network Architecture (SNA) and System Application Architecture (SAA).

Additionally, UNIX is now the operating system of choice for high-speed workstations using RISC architectures for processor-intensive applications such as CAD/CAM.

UNIX is a character- and file- based environment and has not traditionally been good at implementing graphics which depend on bit-mapping. Several GUIs are now available for UNIX environments, including OpenLook (introduced by Sun Microsystems Inc. and AT&T) and Motif (OSF).

Most UNIX GUIs are implemented using the facilities provided by the X Windows system, both in terms of presenting a graphic interface and in controlling the underlying network in a distributed GUI system.

Partly because of the diversity of systems on which it runs, UNIX has become the basis of several recent and emerging open systems standards and application frameworks. These include:

▶ System V Interface Definition (SVID), a document produced by UNIX International (UI). This defines the standard external programming interface (API) of UNIX

▶ POSIX, the set of Portable Operating System standards developed by the Institute of Electrical and Electronic Engineers (IEEE)

▶ X/Open, a consortium specifying and promoting a common applications environment (CAE) and a portability guide (XPG)

▶ The OSF, a consortium of major computer vendors committed to implementation of standards allowing software compatibility between their various systems

UNIX, OS/2 and Windows NT compared

UNIX pre-dates DOS by ten years, OS/2 by fifteen years and Windows NT by twenty years. Many of the concepts of DOS, OS/2 and Windows NT have their origin in UNIX. It is possible that, say before the end of the century, the best aspects of these operating systems will have merged into a single, portable, environment which will be universally available and completely invisible to the application user. Comparisons of UNIX, OS/2 and NT are tabulated below.

Feature comparison of OS/2, Windows NT and UNIX

Feature	OS/2 3.0	Windows NT	UNIX
System requirements	386 or better	386 or better	286 or better
Memory requirements	4MB	12MB	4MB
Storage requirements	30–50MB	100MB	20MB
Memory management	Flat	Flat	Flat
Data exchange	DDE	OLE	Low-level only
Bundled Applications	Yes	Yes	No

Feature comparison (continued) of OS/2, Windows NT and UNIX

Feature	OS/2 3.0	Windows NT	UNIX
System Help	Excellent	Adequate	Poor
Printer Support	Many	Many	Many
Multitasking	Pre-emptive	Pre-emptive	Non-Preemptive
DOS Support	Full	Partial	Partial
GUI	Object-Oriented	Menu-Driven	Menu Driven
Data Transfer	32-bit	32-bit	32-bit
Processor Support	Intel	Intel, MIPS, Alpha	All
Networking	Client–server	Client–server	Extensive
Multiuser	No	No	Yes

Open operating system standards

Background: UNIX

The UNIX operating system was the first general-purpose small-system operating system which offered a degree of portability: the operating system itself could relatively easily be moved between different systems, and application software was portable at the source-code level between systems running UNIX.

UNIX and the C language were the first operating system and language combination to offer this kind of portability and have become the basis of efforts toward formal standardisation of open operating systems and portable application software. UNIX has been an important influence on the following standards and specifications:

▶ System V Interface Definition (SVID)

▶ Portable Operating System Interface Standard (POSIX)

▸ The Distributed Computing Environment (DCE) and Application Environment Specification (AES) originated by the OSF

▸ The X/Open Portability Guide (XPG)

▸ Common Open Systems Environment (COSE)

Each of these topics is dealt with later in this section.

Conformance to POSIX and XPG are particularly important, being required by the procurement agencies of many governments. While formal standards such as POSIX are developed, *de-facto* standards, promoted by companies including Microsoft and Novell, are often adopted instead because the processes of formal standardisation are so slow.

The UNIX operating system originated in the late 1960s as the aftermath of an effort by General Electric, Massachusetts Institute of Technology (MIT) and AT&T Bell Laboratories (Bell Labs) to develop an experimental operating system called MULTICS. For reasons caused by delays in MULTICS development, Bell Labs ended its involvement in the project in 1969. The originators of UNIX designed a small operating system, with many of the characteristics which had been incorporated into MULTICS, and made it run on a DEC PDP-7 minicomputer.

In 1973, UNIX was itself rewritten in the new language, C, which was derived from B and BCPL. C's independence of any particular type of computer meant that UNIX could subsequently be quite easily ported to many computers. This fact was to influence heavily the spread of UNIX systems. Also, the UNIX kernel has never since been completely rewritten.

In 1979, the Seventh Edition of UNIX appeared. A derivative of this version was released in 1980 by Bell Labs as UNIX System III, the first commercially viable UNIX operating system.

In 1982, Microsoft Corporation unveiled XENIX, a derivative of UNIX based on the Seventh Edition and oriented towards the new PCs and business use. At the same time, the University of California at Berkeley (UCB) released Berkeley Software Distribution 4.1 (4.1BSD), a high-performance UNIX variant for which UCB had received funding from the United States Department of Defense (DoD).

In January, 1983, AT&T announced support for UNIX System V. System V was henceforth to be AT&T's main UNIX product; the company guaranteed for the first time that programs written for System V Release 1 (SVR1) would continue to work on all future releases. In 1983 also, 4.2BSD was made available with enhancements including networking, file transfer, remote login between systems and a fast file system.

Now there were three major UNIX variants, differing significantly with respect to each other, in addition to a number of other relatively minor UNIX derivatives.

In 1985, Microsoft released XENIX 3, while AT&T offered for sale System V Release 2 (SVR2). SVR2 included file and record locking, job-control facilities and enhanced system administration procedures. XENIX development was taken over in 1985 by the Santa Cruz Operation (SCO) which, in 1986, announced SCO XENIX V.

UNIX System V Release 3, incorporating improved networking facilities, was released by AT&T also in 1986. UNIX System V and XENIX converged at UNIX System V Release 3.2 in 1987, the year in which 4.3BSD also was announced.

In January 1988, AT&T acquired an interest in Sun Microsystems, a manufacturer of high-performance workstations which had also developed its own UNIX variant, known as SunOS. AT&T and Sun announced a joint effort to design future releases of UNIX. In response, in May 1988, a consortium of computer manufacturers and vendors formed the rival Open Software Foundation.

OSF's objective was to develop its own version of UNIX – based on the Carnegie-Mellon University Mach kernel and IBM's AIX operating system – for which royalties would not be due to AT&T.

AT&T and Sun Microsystems then formed UI, an organisation to define the specifications for UNIX System V, while USL, started as a subsidiary of AT&T and now owned by Novell Inc., developed and marketed System V products. In 1990, UNIX System V Release 4 (SVR4) was released and SVR4.2 is the current version. Also in 1990, IBM produced AIX 3.0. The kernel of the full OSF competitor product for SVR4, OSF/1, is now based on the customised Mach kernel and on parts of AIX 3.0.

In 1993, Novell Inc. acquired USL and now markets its UnixWare product through Univel. In 1994, ownership of the UNIX trademark was vested in the X/Open organisation and UI was disbanded. This move completed the separation of UNIX from AT&T, the company which originated it, and its subsidiaries. The following diagram summarises the facilities provided by the UNIX System V-based environments:

UNIX System V as a subset of UnixWare

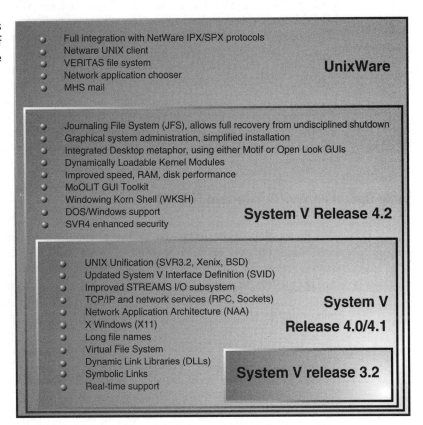

System V Interface Definition (SVID)

UNIX System V Release 4, released in November 1989, unifies four earlier UNIX variants: System V Release 3 (SVR3), XENIX, 4.3BSD and SunOS into a single package. SVR3 is a subset of SVR4, while parts of the other three systems have been incorporated into SVR4.

The parts of XENIX, BSD and SunOS not included in SVR4 have been packaged as separate *compatibility packages* which may be used with SVR4 by users wishing to retain the functionality of the earlier versions.

The SVR4 standard is codified by the System V Interface Definition (SVID). The first SVID (SVID1) was published by AT&T with SVR2 in 1985. SVID2 described the interface of UNIX System V, Release 3. With SVR4, the SVID became SVID3 and a four-volume set. The SVID defines the standard operating system interface to application programs; programs built conforming to the SVID are guaranteed to run correctly on any SVID-conforming system. Conformance of a given program in turn is verified by the System V Verification Suite (currently SVVS3).

SVR4 and OSF/1 are compliant with SVID3, as they are with POSIX and the X/Open XPG. The SVID and POSIX.1 have always been very similar and closely related. SVR4 is compatible with both SVID and POSIX.1.

Portable Operating System Interface (POSIX)

The first independent effort to define a standard operating system environment based on UNIX was begun in 1981 by '/usr/group', a United States organisation of UNIX system users who wanted to ensure the portability of application software. A public document which attempted to define formally the full UNIX system was published by '/usr/group' in 1984 – it was based on AT&T UNIX System III.

Institute of Electrical and Electronic Engineers (IEEE) Project 1003 (P1003) adopted the 1984 standard for development into the POSIX standards. '/usr/group' went on to be renamed Uniforum.

POSIX is a family of standards (as yet incomplete) which define the way application programs interact with an operating system. The POSIX standards cover issues including system calls, libraries, tools, interfaces, verification and testing, real-time features and security. POSIX has been adopted as part of the United States Federal Information Processing Standard (FIPS). This standard must be adhered to by computer systems purchased by the U.S. Federal Government. The sheer size of that Government's procurement program guarantees the importance of POSIX as a standard. POSIX compliance is also required by the Governments of the U.K. and Sweden.

Some of the POSIX standards approved, balloting and working are summarised below. Explanation of notation used by IEEE is useful at this point. The working groups dealing with the various topics covered by POSIX are called P1003.n, in the case of the operating system interface, *P1003.1*. The name of a project dealt with by a working group drops the leading 'P', so the operating system interface project is 1003.1. The approved standard based on the conclusions of P1003.1 is called *IEEE Std 1003.1-1990*. This is also called simply *1003.1* or, synonymously, *POSIX.1*.

▶ *POSIX working group P1003.0. guide to the POSIX Open Systems environment.* The document produced by this working group is a roadmap defining a complete plan for open systems; it is an overview of all the other POSIX and related standards covering, among other things, language services, system services, communication services, database services and character and Graphical User Interfaces.

▶ *POSIX working group P1003.1. system interface* The   main POSIX standard, adopted by IEEE in September 1988, is IEEE Std 1003.1-1988 (POSIX.1). In 1990, it became ISO standard 9945-1:1990. It defines the interface between portable application programs and the operating system, based on several UNIX versions including System V and BSD. In particular, it defines how application programs written in C interface to the operating system's system calls. Application programs written to meet this standard are system-independent: they can be ported at the source code level between systems running a POSIX-conforming operating system.

POSIX.1 was defined in terms of *Classic C*, the original version of the C language as codified by Kernighan and Ritchie in 1978. This was because the ANSI C standard was not approved until December, 1989. IEEE Std 1003.1-1988 has been replaced by IEEE Std 1003.1-1990, which refers to the ANSI C language.

In principle, POSIX is language independent: programs accessing the operating system interface should not have to know about C. To achieve language independence, IEEE Std 1003.1-LIS (*language independent standard*) is in draft as a replacement for POSIX.1.

▸ *POSIX working group P1003.2. Shell and tools* Specifies a shell command language based on the UNIX System V shell with some additions taken from the newer *Korn Shell*. It specifies a standard interface between application programs and shell services and defines approximately 70 utilities (tools) which may be called from shell or application programs. The standard does not specify a user interface. 1003.2 was ratified as an IEEE standard (IEEE Std 1003.2-1992) in 1992 and as ISO Standard 9945-2:1993.

▸ **POSIX working group P1003.3. Testing and verification** Defines a standard procedure for testing conformance of operating systems and environments to POSIX standards. Its document was adopted in 1991 as IEEE Std 1003.3-1991 – Test Methods for Measuring Conformance to POSIX.

▸ *POSIX real-time extensions and profiles* This working group was originally called P1003.4. It defines the minimum changes necessary to POSIX.1 to allow portability of real-time applications. The POSIX.4 definition of real-time is that the operating system must have the ability to provide a required level of service within a predictable, bounded, response time.

▸ *POSIX working group P1003.5. Ada language binding* Defines the language interface to POSIX.1 for Ada, the language sponsored by the DoD. Its document was adopted in 1992 as IEEE Std 1003.5-1992 – POSIX Ada Language Interfaces.

▸ *POSIX security extensions for 1003.1* The POSIX working group originally called P1003.6 specifies functional requirements and system interface standards for control of access to a POSIX-conforming system, auditing and access privileges.

▸ *POSIX system administration* The POSIX working group originally called P1003.7 specifies a common set of utilities and system interfaces for system administrators to use to install, configure /maintain computer operating system environments.

▸ *POSIX transparent file access* The working group originally called P1003.8 specifies a set of standards defining the characteristics of distributed file systems and network protocols as well as an Application Program Interface (API) for access to them.

▸ **POSIX FORTRAN-77 language bindings** The POSIX working group originally called P1003.9 defines the language interface to POSIX.1 for the FORTRAN-77 language.

Other POSIX working groups

▸ POSIX Supercomputing (P1003.10)

▸ POSIX Transaction processing (P1003.11)

▸ POSIX Protocol-Independent Interfaces (P1003.12)

▸ POSIX Multi-Processing Systems Profile (P1003.14)

▸ POSIX Batch Queueing Extensions. (P1003.15, now assigned to Working Group P1003.10)

▸ POSIX C Binding to System API (P1003.16)

▸ POSIX Platform Profile (P1003.18, now assigned to P1003.14 Working Group)

▸ Fortran-90 thin language-independent binding to 1003.1-LIS (1003.19, assigned to P1003.9)

▸ Ada thin language-independent binding to 1003.1-LIS (1003.20, assigned to P1003.5)

▸ POSIX Real-time Distributed Systems Communications (P1003.21)

The IEEE is a United States standards body, which refers its agreed standards to the American National Standards Institute (ANSI) for ratification. ANSI in turn proposes its standards to the International Standards Organisation (ISO) for international adoption. POSIX standards approved as of mid-1994 include the following:

▸ IEEE Std 1003.1-1990, System Interface. Also standardised as ISO 9945-1:1990

▸ IEEE Std 1003.2-1992, Shell and Tools. Also standardised as ISO 9945-2:1992

▸ IEEE Std 1003.3-1991, Test Methods for Measuring Conformance to POSIX

▸ IEEE Std 1003.5-1992, Ada Binding to 1003.1-1990

▸ IEEE Std 1003.9-1992, FORTRAN-77 Binding to 1003.1-1990

A number of other POSIX standards have been approved; these mainly specify interfaces to communications and messaging system based on the OSI (Open Systems Interconnection) model. A number of consortiums have appeared since the mid-1980s to promote open systems standards based on UNIX. These consortiums include the Open Software Foundation (OSF), X/Open and the COSE. These groupings have come about because of the market-driven need for interim open systems standards pending the final POSIX definitions. They have also influenced the direction of POSIX. The standards promoted by OSF, X/Open and COSE have much in common and all claim adherence to POSIX.

Open Software Foundation (OSF)

OSF's first UNIX implementation, OSF/1, is based on POSIX and the X/Open specification. OSF/1 also includes core technology from IBM AIX 3.0 and Carnegie-Mellon University's Mach kernel. OSF/1 is characterised by the following components:

- The OSF specification: a complete description of the OSF/1 operating environment including languages, user interface, graphics libraries, network services, database management and supported file systems

- The Application Environment Specification (AES), an operating system interface compatible with POSIX.1, SVID and the X/Open Portability Guide

- Parts of AIX 3.0 including program management facilities, logical volumes for management of file systems, the System Management Interface Tool (SMIT), a database search and retrieval system called InfoExplorer

- The Distributed Computing Environment (DCE), a platform for creating and using distributed applications in a multivendor environment. DCE includes Remote Procedure Call (RPC) for networking, the Andrew File System facility, which is compatible with NFS, and Kerberos security

- OSF/Motif Graphical User Interface, based on X Windows

- Distributed Management Environment (DME), an object-oriented approach to the systems management of heterogeneous computing networks

▸ The Mach kernel, allows multiprocessing – programs executing simultaneously in parallel – and improves on traditional UNIX security

▸ BSD Virtual File System (VFS); BSD Fast File System; BSD NFS-compatible distributed file system

▸ Support for the C and *Bourne Shell* command interpreters and support for the ISO C, Fortran, Pascal, BASIC, COBOL, LISP and Ada languages

X/Open Portability Guide (XPG)

The X/Open group was inaugurated in 1984 by a consortium of European computer manufacturers and vendors and now also includes many major North American system and software vendors.

X/Open specifies a Common Applications Environment (CAE) based on the SVID and the ISO C language. X/Open also contains all the POSIX standards and additionally specifies rules for implementation of the programming languages, file handling, database systems and communications interfaces.

X/Open aims to develop a free and open market for all its members through the supply of computer systems compliant with the international standards. X/Open members are committed to selling computer systems conforming with the CAE, ensuring source code portability of software between such systems.

The CAE is defined by the X/Open Portability Guide (XPG). XPG4 is the latest version of the portability guide. Its predecessor, XPG3, concentrated on issues of portability and UNIX SVR4 and OSF/1 conform to it. XPG4 additionally makes specifications in the area of interoperability. XPG4 contains the following components:

Base Computing Platform

▸ System Calls and Libraries
▸ Commands and utilities
▸ C Language (conforms to ISO-C)

Programming Languages

- COBOL
- Pascal
- Fortran

User Interface

- X Windows System Display
- X Windows System API
- Terminal Interfaces

Mainframe Interworking

- Common Programming Interface-Communications (CPI-C)

General Interworking

- Byte-stream data transfer
- X.400 Gateway
- X.400 Message Access
- Directory Access (X.500)
- Network File System
- Transport Interface (XTI)

Data Interchange (Media)

- Magnetic media formats

PC Interworking

- (PC) NFS Server
- LMX Server

XPG4 specifies five *profiles*:

- Base Profile
- OSI Communications Gateway Profile
- Base Server Profile
- Workstation Profile
- Database Platform Profile

System vendors who wish to achieve X/Open *profile branding* for their products must demonstrate that such products conform to, integrate with and have available all the components of the profiles.

In 1993, X/Open expanded its role in open systems by assuming responsibility for two important branding programs:

▸ Publishing specifications for, and branding implementations of, the Common Desktop Environment and Common OS API of the COSE industry agreements

▸ Owning the registered trademark UNIX and branding systems wishing to use it

Common Open Software Environment (COSE)

COSE was announced in March 1993. It is a product, not a consortium, and was announced jointly by IBM, Hewlett-Packard, Santa Cruz Operation, Sun Microsystems, Univel and UNIX System Laboratories. Digital Equipment Corporation later committed to COSE also. COSE is a profile defining standard approaches to implementing the following environments:

▸ *Common Desktop Environment:* The CDE uses existing technologies of the COSE sponsors to define the characteristics of the desktop environment across a range of client–server systems. The environment supports electronic mail, window management, GUI and security

▸ *Networking:* COSE provides tools needed by developers to build distributed application software, based on OSF DCE, Sun Microsystems' Open Network Computing and Novell NetWare

▸ *Graphics:* COSE separates graphics application software from particular graphics hardware, using common APIs supporting the X Windows imaging and graphics facilities

▸ *Multimedia:* COSE will develop a standards specification to provide users with consistent access to multimedia tools

▸ *Object Technology:* COSE is working to deliver an object-based technology allowing development of complex applications and re-use of previously developed software objects

▸ *System Management*

One of the principal aims of COSE is to act as a catalyst, basing its products on the earlier open systems work of OSF, POSIX, UI and X/Open and accelerating the implementation and acceptance of standards. Considering the market weight of the COSE sponsors, it is not surprising that the framework is gaining widespread market acceptance.

Internationalization

The market for traditional United States-produced software applications is limited to North America and the rest of the English-speaking world. Even in the English-speaking world, cultural conventions cause differences in currency representation, date and time representation, collating sequences and numeric formats.

The European languages, including Cyrillic and Icelandic, require more than 800 different characters to be fully represented. The traditional ASCII character set, with a maximum of 256 encodings, is insufficient. Non-European languages, especially the Far Eastern ones, require thousands more. Nations can have more than one set of conventions as examples such as Switzerland show. Traditional UNIX, originating in the United States, used the ASCII character set. ASCII represents 128 characters using all the combinations of seven data bits. Many early application programs developed for UNIX used seven bits of a byte to accommodate ASCII characters and the other for special purposes. This practice further reduced the international portability of UNIX and its applications.

The efforts at rendering operating systems and applications capable of handling extended character sets and conforming with locale conventions (see below) is referred to as internationalisation or I18N. Internationalisation must take account of:

- ▸ Human languages, with their different character sets, collating (sorting) sequences and informational messages

- ▸ Various code sets, both for Western and Asian languages. While ASCII (128 character combinations) can accommodate English only, EBCDIC (256) can be used to implement most European languages as well. A large number of codesets are defined by ISO for particular languages and cultures. Standards, including the Japanese Industry Standards (JIS) and Unicode, have been defined which use 16 bits to accommodate the ideographic Asian characters, where each character is a word

▸ Cultural conventions, including numeric, monetary and date formats

To implement internationalisation, computer systems implement a number of combinations of languages, coded character sets and cultural conventions as *locales*. The process of rendering software to conform with the requirements of a locale is called *localisation*. On a particular system, the required locale can be selected using shell environment variables. Modern GUIs usually provide facilities which allow the user to do this indirectly.

The POSIX standards 1003.1 and 1003.2 provide for environment variables specifying locales and conventions. OS/2, Microsoft Windows NT and UNIX support international character sets with expanded 16-bit encodings.

Standards efforts in the area of internationalisation are less formal than in many others. There is currently no POSIX working group dealing with internationalisation; instead, the X/Open and UniForum I18N groups make recommendations which are adopted (or not) by end-users as *de-facto* standards. Various national standards bodies also influence the definition and adoption of I18N standards.

Security

The DOS, Windows 3.1 and OS/2 environments provide no facilities for security against unauthorised access. Both UNIX and Windows NT by default implement discretionary security protection based on password schemes and file protection. In general the security facilities provided by these small-system operating systems are poor.

Increasingly, governmental, military and large corporate organisations using these systems require more secure environments than those traditionally provided. Standards in the area of security have been led by the United States National Computer Security Commission (NCSC), originally known as the DoD Security Center. In 1983, the NCSC published the DoD Trusted Computer Systems Evaluation Criteria (TCSEC), referred to colloquially as the Orange Book. The Orange Book defines four classes of *trusted system*:

- ▶ **Class D:** Insecure

- ▶ **Class C:** Discretionary Protection

- ▶ **Class B:** Mandatory Protection, restricting the freedom of users to grant access permissions

- ▶ **Class A:** Verifiable Design; the same as the most secure Class B level but formally provable

Classes C and B are sub-classified into further levels of trustworthiness in ascending order of security. The levels are (ascending from the least secure): D, C1, C2, B1, B2, B3, A1. Security at level B2 is required for systems used in sensitive applications.

Traditional UNIX systems meet security level C1. UNIX SVR4 and Microsoft Windows NT comply with level C2.

Under United States Federal Government pressure, some versions of UNIX, including SVR4, have been modified to comply with levels B1 and B2. UNIX System V/MLS (Multi-Level Secure) offers B1-level security. A high-security version of SVR4, SVR4 ES, is now available which offers B2-level security. OSF/1 offers three security options: traditional UNIX, C2 and B1. The vendor building the OSF/1 system can choose the required security level when compiling the operating-system source code.

It will take a completely rewritten version of UNIX to meet level B3. No commercial computer system yet built has realised the A1 security level.

Security extensions to the POSIX set of standards are being defined by the POSIX working group P1003.6 whose job it is to specify a POSIX interface to a trusted system using the DoD TCSEC criteria. The group is developing interfaces in five areas:

- ▶ Discretionary Access Control: support for access control lists

- ▶ Mandatory Access Control according to the TCSEC requirements

- ▶ Auditing

- ▶ Privileges, allowing users to perform security-related activities

- ▶ Information labelling

Language standards

Introduction

Many factors determine whether or not a computer program is portable between different computer systems. We have seen some of them: the architecture of the microprocessor on which the program is to run; the API presented by the operating system under control of which the program is to run; and the CLI or GUI which the program must use to interact with its users.

Of central importance to a program's portability is the programming language in which it is written and the degree to which that language has been standardised among the different systems the program is intended to run on.

A POSIX-compliant operating system (current examples are UNIX and Windows NT) presents an API (or system-call interface) to its client programs which the programs must agree with. For example, an OS/2 program starts a process using the OS/2 API call 'DosExecPgm'. Such a program will have no chance of running on a POSIX-compliant operating system, because 'DosExecPgm' is found nowhere in the standard 1003.1. To make the program run, 'DosExecPgm' must be converted to the equivalent POSIX 'fork' system call.

Assuming the client program conforms to the API presented by the operating system, it must also match the API of the GUI (if any) which it uses to converse with users. For example, a program containing a Microsoft Windows 'ShowWindow' API call will not run in an OS/2 or X Windows GUI environment.

Even if all APIs are conformed to, the language in which the program is written must be standardised, or portability of the program between systems is very unlikely. A C program conforming to the ISO C standard (as well as the necessary APIs) will transfer without change between different systems. So will programs written in other languages although none of them is as portable or standardised as C.

The first and second-generation languages (machine code and assembly) are completely non-portable, being intimately related to the hardware on which programs written in those languages run. The third-generation languages, of which C, Fortran, Ada, Pascal and PL/1 are examples are in principle machine independent. The degree of that independence is defined by how standard the language is and to what extent the standard is adhered to.

POSIX standards have been defined for *bindings* of three languages (Ada, C and Fortran) to the base services specified by 1003.1. A binding means a set of specifications by which a program written in one of the three languages – for example, Fortran – can use the base services. A *thick binding* specifies the base services as part of the binding; a *thin binding* does not specify base services other than as an interface. Because of their independence, thin language bindings are preferred.

The 1003.1 standard was originally (1988) defined in terms of C. The C language binding allowing programs to use the base services defined by 1003.1 is 1003.1-1990:C and is a thick binding. An equivalent language independent standard (LIS) for base services has since been approved as 1003.1-LIS and the C language binding removed to P1003.16. P1003.16 is a thin binding.

The language bindings themselves imply that the languages they refer to have been standardised to a large degree. Otherwise, for example, a non-standard Fortran program would not match the binding necessary to enable it to use the operating system's base services. Ada, C and Fortran have all been standardised and are further described in the sections following.

Ada

Ada is a *procedural* programming language designed under the direction of the DoD in the late 1970s, mainly for the purpose of eliminating the proliferation of programming languages then in military use. It was intended to be the primary language for DoD software development. Ada is named after Augusta Ada Byron, an associate of Charles Babbage in the early development of computing machines. The language was derived from Pascal but was designed to support additional features such as data hiding, concurrent processing, operator overloading and modules.

The major features which characterise Ada in contrast to Pascal are these:

▸ Module structures and interface specifications for large-program organisations and separate compilation

▸ Facilities for *encapsulation* of data and operations used to process the data

▸ Generic definitions to support *abstract data types*

▸ Support for parallel processing

▸ Control over low-level characteristics (for example, hardware interrupts) of the system on which an Ada program runs

The philosophy of Ada is very different from, for example, that of the C language used with UNIX. Ada is intended to be used for large-scale, long-lived, constantly changing and reliable applications. It is oriented towards military command-and-control applications in real-time and multiprocessor environments. It has process management, synchronisation and scheduling built into the language rather than depending on those implemented by an operating system. Ada tasks behave differently from processes as defined by the POSIX standard, and the Ada environment expects to be able to manage and monitor a user process in a way that is alien to UNIX and POSIX.

The IEEE 1003.5 approved standard defines a thick binding for the Ada language (standardised as ISO 8652:1987) to the portable operating system base services as defined by 1003.1. This means that programs can be written in Ada to interface to and use the services of POSIX-compliant operating systems.

IEEE P1003.20 will define a thin binding for Ada to 1003.1-LIS. This has been made possible by the removal of much of the C bias from the language-independent standard 1003.1-LIS as compared to the earlier 1003.1.

C

The C programming language has come into very wide use since its public appearance in 1978. It is the language in which UNIX is largely written. C has been implemented on all types of computer system from the smallest PCs to the largest supercomputers. The main identifying characteristic of C is that it specifies, in a manner independent of any particular computer system, how to do efficient, low-level, assembly-like operations. C retains the portability of high-level languages as a result of its independence of machine architecture, while its low level operations allow C programs to compete with assembly equivalents. Its flexibility and power, along with the inherent portability of software written in C, have ensured the durability of the language.

With the increasing popularity and use of C, many slightly incompatible definitions of the language came into being. In any case, there had never been a formal definition of the C language; the 1978 book by Kernighan and Ritchie 'The C Programming Language' was the accepted, if rather loose, definition.

In 1983, ANSI formed a technical committee, X3J11, on C language and run-time library standardisation. The ANSI C standard – formally referred to as American National Standard X3.159-1989 – was adopted by ANSI in 1989 and superseded in 1990 by the ISO 9899:1990 C standard.

ANSI C represents a significant change to the original C definition. The spirit of the C language is maintained, and some care is taken to ensure that almost all of the millions of lines of code written in earlier C versions are accepted by ANSI C. The major changes are in the tightening of the C language definition to remove undefined code constructs; strengthening of data type checking to reduce the risk of unexpected program crashes; formal definition of the run-time library contents; and a host of smaller yet important changes.

The ANSI C standard has gained remarkable acceptance and has no real competition; the entire C user community is converging on the single standard. The major UNIX versions, including SVR4 and OSF/1 embrace ISO C. The original 1003.1 standard – to which both SVR4 and OSF claim conformance – is described in terms of ISO C. POSIX compliance does not require the use of ISO C; it is language-independent. POSIX standard 1003.1-LIS and its C language thin binding P1003.16 reflect this independence.

Nonetheless, the ISO C (ISO 9899:1990) definition is of central importance to the various standardisation efforts and is, for the time being at least, the means by which nearly all software standards are described.

Fortran

Fortran (Formula Translation) is the world's first high-level (third generation) language, or *autocode*, as it was called at the time, developed in the mid-1950s by IBM and a number of user groups. Fortran is an algebraic language designed originally for numerically-intensive computation in the engineering and mathematical fields. The language has been standardised by ANSI three times, in 1966, 1977 and 1990 and has by now evolved from being a language useful mainly in specialised applications to one which has general-purpose uses. The 1977 version of the language is by convention spelt in upper-case: 'FORTRAN', while the 1990 revision is called 'Fortran-90'. In this book, where the language name is not qualified by either '77' or '90', 'Fortran' is used.

The most common version, FORTRAN-77 (ANSI Standard X3.9-1978), is supplied with UNIX in addition to the C environment. It has the following characteristics in addition to those defined in the original language:

- ► Character type
- ► 7-dimensional arrays
- ► Extended expression syntax
- ► IF...THEN...ELSE and DO constructs
- ► Subroutines with parameters and return values

Fortran 90 (ANSI Standard X3.198-1992) includes FORTRAN-77 and adds characteristics which include the following:

- ► Long identifiers
- ► Multistatement lines
- ► Nested procedures
- ► Recursive procedures
- ► Modules encapsulating data types and procedures
- ► Data hiding
- ► Bit and array operations

Two Fortran thin bindings for 1003.1 (standard describing POSIX operating-system base services) are in progress: IEEE P1003.9 to FORTRAN-77 and IEEE P1003.19 to Fortran-90.

C++ and object-orientation (OO)

The techniques of object-orientation, and their implementation using languages such as C++, Smalltalk, Eiffel and others, are not directly connected with the specification of open systems. However, two factors make OO and C++ in particular increasingly important to implementation of open systems and client–server solutions:

▸ OO promotes re-use of code and is useful in controlling the complexity of increasingly large application software suites

▸ C++ is the successor to and is completely compatible with C, the most popular system-programming language and the language which is at the heart of most open systems standards

It is now not possible to buy a C compiler alone for PCs: the major suppliers now integrate a C compiler with a C++ environment. A standard for C++ has not yet been approved, but the ANSI X3J16 committee is currently working on it and the C++ standard is expected to be approved in 1995. Because of the importance of C++, it is advisable to be aware of it and of the rudiments of object-oriented programming (OOP).

Object-oriented programming and design

OOP is a way of writing and packaging software so that it closely models objects and processes found in the real world. OOP is characterised by four concepts:

▸ Classes
▸ Objects
▸ Inheritance
▸ Polymorphism

OOP allows a high level of abstraction in the definition of objects. It is possible to defer design issues which might cause error if settled too early, later adding classes derived from those initially defined. Using OOP, objects encapsulate their data and the operations possible on that data. Inheritance allows common object data and functions to be shared and reused. Polymorphism allows the programmer to manipulate objects without having to take account of their types; the language system looks after type considerations and reduces the amount of code to be written.

Why OOP is necessary

To manage complexity:

- ► Software objects closely model the real world

- ► OOP systems allow a higher than conventional level of abstraction: one can think of 'window' or 'dialog' as an understandable concept rather than being concerned with their low-level implementation

- ► The programmer interface to objects is reduced by encapsulation to a number of possible function calls; the programmer does not have to know how the class is internally implemented

- ► Provided this interface is unchanged, underlying code can be maintained and modified without affecting outside code

To improve reliability:

- ► Encapsulation leads to safer data storage, and data hiding prevents undisciplined use of class members

- ► Only the function interface is publicly accessible, so outside programmers are restricted in what they can do with a class

- ► Because objects present a common interface, using them is not error-prone

To promote software reuse:

- ► Class inheritance and polymorphism save development time and reduce code amounts

- ► Classes are reusable in the same or slightly modified form

- ► Modification may reduce existing functionality; traditional systems can only add to existing code

- ► Software reuse is possible without access to source code

To improve programming flexibility:

- ► Modular classes allow rapid prototyping

- ► Classes limit the scope and effect of code changes

- ► Polymorphism allows addition of classes with the same interface as existing ones, without change to existing code

C++

The C++ language is a hybrid language based on, and almost completely compatible with, its predecessor, C. C++ was named in 1983 after being devised by Dr. Bjarne Stroustrup at AT&T. In the same year, the ANSI C standardisation effort began and C and C++ were to trade ideas from then until approval of the ANSI C standard in 1989.

It is possible to write programs in C++ which are purely procedural and have no object-oriented characteristics. Every program in the Kernighan and Ritchie 2nd Edition definition of the C language is a valid C++ program. C++ additionally supports the OOP approach with the following language features:

▸ Classes

▸ Object initialisation and destruction, using constructors and destructors

▸ Class inheritance using base and derived classes

▸ Function and operator overloading

▸ Polymorphism using virtual functions

C++ is becoming increasingly important for development of complex applications, for implementation of object-oriented database managers (OODBMSs) and for doing message-handling programming for GUIs. Its compatibility with C makes it likely that C will soon no longer be considered as a language in its own right but as a subset of the language capabilities provided by C++.

Standards for object-orientation

Two of the most common applications for object-oriented software, whether written in C++ or not, are GUIs and databases. Both lend themselves well to the OO *paradigm* (programming and design model). A GUI maintains many objects in the used display; if these objects interact with each other, it is said that they send *messages*. An object-oriented database system must have an API that it presents to programs which will use the database.

There are thus two main areas in which effort is being concentrated on the definition of standards for OO:

▸ Mechanisms for messaging between objects

▸ Object-oriented database API

The main body concerned with establishment of OO standards is the *Object Management Group* (OMG), a non-profit consortium of information system companies. Rather than addressing the issues of messaging and database in isolation, OMG decided to develop a more-general *Object Management Architecture*. OMG took submissions from a number of major system vendors and, on the basis of these, published in 1990 its *Object Management Architecture Guide* (OMAG).

In an open system environment, where software from different vendors must interact, it is necessary that there be some standard model for messaging between objects – otherwise objects created by the software of one supplier will not be able to talk to the objects created by the software of another. The OMG's recommendation in this area is the *Object Request Broker* (ORB), a mechanism for messaging between objects. ORB specifies, among other things: object naming and location; invocation of object *methods* (to pass a message to an object is to call one of its methods); and encoding of parameters accepted by those methods.

The first OO standard proposed by OMG is the *Common Object Request Broker Architecture* (CORBA), a specification which defines ORB implementations, services and interfaces. CORBA has been endorsed by X/Open and OSF. In the area of object-oriented databases, no proposal for an API standard has yet been made. The OODBMS is an emerging technology and it is still unclear whether it will exist in its own right or will be integrated into the existing relational model.

Structured Query language (SQL)

SQL (Structured Query language) is a database *sublanguage* used for querying, updating and managing relational databases. It is not a procedural language in the same sense as COBOL or C, nor is it object-oriented in the manner of C++. Instead, SQL is used in formulating interactive queries to be applied to a database, and for embedding in application programs (written in other languages) as instructions for handling data.

There are several database models, of which the most important are *hierarchical, network, relational* and *object-oriented*. Hierarchical and network databases were the earliest solutions to maintaining databases of large numbers of records with many relationships between those records. Object-oriented databases are an emerging technology.

The most widely accepted database organisation is the relational model, devised in 1970 by Dr. E.F. Codd as part of an IBM research project (System R) which created the Structured English Query Language (SEQUEL). The relational model is the only one with a theoretical basis in mathematical set theory. For a database to be fully relational it must conform to 12 rules outlined by Dr. Codd in a 1985 paper.

Under the relational model, data is presented to application programs using it in the form of tables made up of *rows*, where each row represents a record. Rows in turn contain *attributes*. Relationships between records are defined by their attributes. The relational model is described in more detail in the *Applications* section, starting on page 119.

Transactions written in SQL are used to retrieve data from relational databases according to specially formulated queries such as the following:

```
select CUSTOMER from LIST where BALANCE > 1000;
```

SQL also contains components for defining, altering, controlling and securing data in a relational database. Relational databases maintain their integrity (self-consistency) by allowing access only to requests of SQL form. Standardisation efforts for SQL began in 1983 and resulted in the adoption by ANSI of standard X3.135, informally known as ANSI SQL86, in 1986. The same standard was ratified by ISO in 1987 as ISO 9075:1987.

Critics of the initial SQL specification maintain that the language is too loosely defined, that it contains a great deal of redundancy (many different ways of doing the same operation) and that it fails to adhere to the theoretical foundations, as enunciated by Dr. Codd, on which relational databases are built. As a result of these criticisms, further, tighter, SQL standards have been adopted by ANSI: SQL89 and SQL92.

A major characteristic of relational databases is that an application program accessing the database does so only through the SQL interface;

it need know nothing of the internal representation of the database. This separation of function has become increasingly important in the implementation of client–server database systems. The client–server model is described further in the *Applications* section (page 119) and *The client–server models* section (page 245).

A shortcoming of the SQL standards is that they are *minimal standards*. This is in contrast with the example of ISO C, which is a *maximal standard*. With a minimal standard such as SQL, many characteristics of the language are not covered by the standard and are instead left to be implemented by individual vendors as they see fit. This has resulted in the situation where the version of SQL supported by every database vendor differs from all others, while still conforming to the core SQL standard. Where database software from different suppliers must be used together, for example across a network, software must be supplied to translate the different SQL versions in use.

SQL is implemented by almost all relational database management systems (*RDBMSs*) and for some non-relational systems. Examples of RDBMSs which use SQL are:

- IBM OS/2 Extended Edition Database Manager
- IBM AS/400 Database Manager
- IBM DB/2 under the MVS operating system
- IBM SQL/DS under the VM operating system
- Oracle
- Ingres
- SQL Server (Microsoft)
- SQLBase (Sybase)

Programming tools and utilities

A system interface such as that defined by POSIX.1 is useful only if there are programs which can take advantage of the facilities offered. POSIX.1 is a narrow standard in that it specifies the interface (API, or system-call interface) presented to application programs by a portable operating system. POSIX.1 is not much use on its own, in the same way that it can be said that an operating system in isolation does nothing: it is only useful when it has programs to run.

Programs written in standard languages such as C and Fortran can, through their language bindings (POSIX.16 for C; POSIX.9 and POSIX.19 for Fortran) use the system interface specified by POSIX.1. Other facilities are needed, however: the first being a shell command language with utilities; and the second *Computer Aided Software Engineering* (CASE) tools to assist in the generation of software which can use the operating system interface specified by POSIX.1.

Command shell and utilities

Before the advent in the late 1980s of GUIs as the preferred means of user interaction with a computer system, the primary interface was a text-based command-line interface (CLI). In the early days of computing, the CLI was in the form of a teletype device; this was superseded by the character-mode terminal, use of which is still extremely widespread, especially on UNIX systems.

The commands issued by the user on the CLI are interpreted by a program which is either part of the operating system controlling the computer system connected to the terminal or is a shell program supplied as an adjunct to the operating system. In the case of MS-DOS, the shell program is 'COMMAND.COM' and the CLI prompt is (typically) C:\>. The OS/2 shell program is 'CMD.EXE' and the typical shell prompt [C:\]. UNIX, being UNIX, supplies a number of standard shell programs and even allows users to write and install their own.

Even in a GUI environment, many of the actions initiated by a user using the GUI will be implemented at a lower level using shell commands and utilities. System administrators and other technical users will continue to use the more powerful and flexible CLI, even though the GUI is available, often to write *shell scripts* to automate complex and routine tasks.

Many MS-DOS and OS/2 commands are derived from the UNIX originals, as are their hierarchical filesystems and file naming conventions. The UNIX shell commands and many of the standard UNIX utilities are therefore used as the basis of IEEE Standard 1003.2-1992: Shell and Utilities, also called POSIX.2. POSIX.2 concentrates on the shell command language and tools familiar to users of UNIX, and on making the tools and programs written in the shell language portable between operating system environments conforming to POSIX.1. Shell scripts are mainly used for batch and background work, and not primarily for user interaction. POSIX.2 also defines a large number of interactive tools and commands to be used in conjunction with the shell.

The question of a graphical interface for POSIX environments was effectively deferred by POSIX.2, which confines itself to the CLI. This fact reflects the character- and text-based nature of UNIX and the relatively late appearance of GUIs (examples are Motif and OpenLook, based on X Windows) in the UNIX world. GUIs are dealt with in the *User interface* section (page 126).

POSIX.2 specifies a shell command language based on the standard UNIX System V shell (derived from and very similar to the Bourne Shell), while including some of the newer features of the Korn Shell. It describes the facilities required for shell scripts to be portable, but excludes interactive features.

POSIX.2a is a related standard, contained in the same document as POSIX.2 and also called the *User Portability Extensions* (UPE). It specifies a large number of interactive commands, closely related to the UNIX originals, for file manipulation, electronic mail, job-control, system management and other purposes. Functions are provided which allow application programs written in high-level languages to use services provided by the shell. Software development utilities, including *make*, *lex* and *yacc* are also specified.

By providing a standardised shell interface as well as many commands and utilities, POSIX.2 makes the POSIX.1 system interface more useful across many different types of computer system. A major weakness of POSIX.1, however, is that it fails to deal with GUIs and bit-mapped terminals, confining itself to character-based input and output on simple character terminals. This failure tends to reduce the relevance of the POSIX.2 standard in a world dominated by graphical interfaces.

CASE tools

The purpose of Computer Aided Software Engineering is to provide software engineers with tools which help them specify functional requirements and designs for software development projects. These tools include methodologies as well as computer programs for design and for automatic generation of code. CASE separates the design of a suite of application software from its coded implementation and automates the generation of software based on the design built with CASE tools.

Structured methodologies for software engineering cover the analysis, design, programming, review and testing phases of development. The reason structured methodologies exist is to impose some discipline on the software development process, which traditionally had been haphazard, late and poorly documented, producing software which was difficult to maintain and which relied excessively on a few guru programmers. Currently, CASE tools mainly address themselves to structured analysis and design, also generating structured code as an output of the design.

CASE is an attempt to support modern software engineering methodologies through computer-based tools. These tools provide good user interfaces to existing methodologies, such as a graphical interface for design of software modules and for keeping track of changes in the design. They may also keep track of relationships between variables in the software, as well as implementation, testing, debugging and maintenance activities. CASE represents a higher-level form of programming in which software tools are used to design and implement well-organised and easily-understood applications.

Given the breadth of the remit of CASE, it is unsurprising that few standards have been defined in the area. However, the growing number of CASE tool and vendors which are available means that, increasingly, information must be exchanged between different products. Standards under development include the following:

▶   *CASE Data Interchange Format* (CDIF), being developed by a committee of the *Electronic Industries' Association* (EIA). CDIF is a set of standards which specifies formats for exchange of data between diverse CASE tools. These formats include entity descriptions, process logic and dataflow diagrams

▶   *Information Resource Dictionary System* (IRDS), an entity-relationship model defining the contents of a CASE object *repository*, the way information is stored in the repository and how CASE tools should access this information

▶   *Portable Common Tools Environment* (PCTE), an initiative of the *European Computer Manufacturers' Association* (ECMA) to provide a reference model for software engineering environments, into which various CASE development tools can be plugged. PCTE is being considered for adoption as an ISO standard. It specifies methods of data integration, data modelling and data sharing across different CASE tools

CASE itself is a quite new technology; standards in the area are therefore in the early stages of development.

Applications

Introduction: APIs and portability

The term 'application' in the context of computers means one or more computer programs which carry out a task useful to a user in the real world. Examples include word-processors, spreadsheets, databases, *computer aided design* (CAD), manufacturing systems, airline reservation systems and accounting systems. Operating systems, communications programs and compilers are usually termed *system programs* because they do nothing of direct interest to the end user: they make the system usable by applications. Whether an application program will or will not run on a computer system or network of computers is determined by at least two factors:

▸   Whether or not the executable form of the application will run on the processor architecture of the system required

▸   Whether or not the Application Program Interfaces (APIs) – of operating system, communications, GUI and other applications – required by the application are supported by the computer on which it is to run

The various API dependencies are illustrated in the diagram below.

The application program (labelled 'Application' in the centre) runs on a computer which also supports a GUI, one or more communications device drivers and an operating system, each of which presents an API to the application. The application can present – and in the case of, for example, database programs, usually does – its own API for use by other application software.

Important
Application
Program
Interfaces

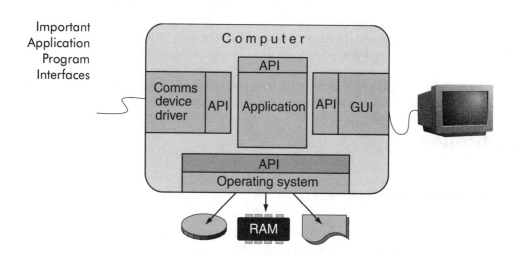

If our application contains API calls which are not matched in the operating system, GUI or device driver, then it will not run on the computer. Its API calls must be adapted to match those supported; this process is part of what is involved in porting software.

We are concerned here with open systems, so application programs which are inherently non-portable are not of interest. This includes the host of applications written for the MS-DOS and Microsoft Windows environments. Of interest in the open systems context are applications which are relatively easily portable between different (heterogeneous) computer systems and can be used by a collection of such systems in a networked environment.

There are many such applications but the one on which open, distributed, client–server systems are most often based is the database. Many, if not most, computer users, large and small, use their systems mainly for storage and retrieval of data. Examples of large users falling into this category include banks, airlines and manufacturing enterprises of all kinds. Traditionally, such organisations have implemented computerised databases as centralised systems: one large database stored on a central mainframe computer and accessed by many connected users by means of *dumb* terminals. These terminals are called dumb because all the intelligence is concentrated on the side of the central computer, which completely controls the actions of the user.

The next section deals with the various database models. Usage of database systems in distributed client–server environments is covered in Part 3, after the main technologies governing LANs and WANs are explained. For the time being, we assume that the computers and other devices linked in a networked database arrangement are connected by 'hosepipes' down which information is reliably transmitted to the intended location. Both front-end (user) and back-end (centralised or distributed database) products are therefore listed.

Database systems

Database models

A database system is usually of two parts: a DBMS and a database application program to access and update information stored by the DBMS. The defining characteristics of a DBMS are:

- It defines and stores data organised logically into records and fields

- It allows application programs to change, update, delete and sort the records

- It may provide facilities for display of retrieved and updated data

- It ensures integrity of the data it stores

The DBMS model

A DBMS is implemented according to a model which describes how data is presented to the user and the application programmer for access.

With the exception of the simple File Management System the manner in which the various models represent their data to an application bears no relation to how data is physically stored on disk.

The main DBMS models are these:

- File Management System (FMS)

- Hierarchical Database System (HDS)

- Network Database System (NDS)

- Relational Database Management System (RDBMS)

- (recently) the Object-Oriented Database Management System (OODBMS)

The file management system

With the simple FMS organisation of data, each field or data item is stored sequentially in one large file. A data item can only be retrieved by a (slow) sequential search. It is possible to maintain a pointer to the last item retrieved, so it is not always necessary to start searching from the beginning of the file. The FMS does not introduce any abstraction: it is unique in actually describing how data is stored.

A good example of application of FMS is that of a word-processor. Each line is a record. When a document is retrieved, some or all of the lines are retrieved and placed in a list in memory, where they are accessed sequentially.

It is possible to associate an index with an FMS but the price is complexity and likelihood of the index being corrupted with respect to the data. The main problem with the FMS is that it does not express the relationships between data items other than specifying the order in which they are stored. Except for simple applications, the FMS is not favoured.

The File Management System (Simplified)

FMS Database Fields

	Index	
Mary had a little lamb	1	2260
whose feet were black as soot	2	3164
and into Mary's bread and jam	3	4440
his sooty foot he put	4	1544

The hierarchical database model

Under the hierarchical database model, data is presented to the user and programmer logically as a tree structure which bears no relation to how the data is physically stored in the database. In many naturally-occurring situations, the relationships between data items can be represented as a tree, or a parent-child relationship, and the HDS takes advantage of this fact. A company organisation chart is a good example as shown in the diagram on page 123.

Searching a hierarchical database is much faster than a sequential search; the links are followed until the required piece of data is found. The network's data is usually presented to the programmer as a linked list of fields the organisation of which is independent of how the data is actually stored on disk. Because of the linked organisation, it is easy to add fields to the database.

The hierarchical
database model
(simplified)

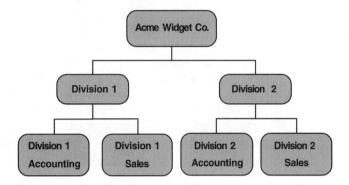

The disadvantages of the HDS are these:

▶ The structure of the database is arbitrary; it must be defined as the *schema* at the outset

▶ To change the structure, and the order in which the data is stored, it is necessary either to change the whole schema or add more fields to records. The former is a lot of trouble; the latter is inefficient and causes data duplication

▶ It is not possible to represent many-to-many relationships, for example, the case where two Divisions share an Accounting department

▶ Links between records must be physically stored along with the data. This gives rise to the possibility that these links may be corrupted and become inconsistent with the data

The network database model

The NDS evolved as a result of the deficiencies of the hierarchical model. Its main addition to the hierarchical model is its ability to express many-to-many relationships between data records, as well as the simpler parent–child relationship.

Network databases have nothing to with networking expressed in the context of communications. Network databases are referred to as CODASYL databases; they form the majority of databases in use on mainframe systems. The relationships between data items are defined as *sets*. Here is the organization chart adapted to the network model:

The network
database model
(simplified)

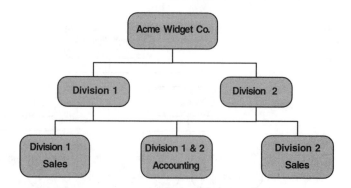

In a network database, sets are expressed using a data-description language which is part of the DBMS. The disadvantages of the network model are these:

▸ Network databases are very flexible, allow fast retrieval of data and do not have much data duplication, but the price is complexity of the database structure itself

▸ The necessity to store complex systems of pointers separately from the data threatens the integrity of the database

▸ Otherwise, the network model shares the disadvantages of the HDS

The relational database model

With the relational model, no parent–child relationships need be recorded or pointers stored. The data is organised in tabular sets where each record is represented as a row in the table. Relationships between data are expressed by means of data values in the records, not by systems of pointers. Records are fixed-length and fixed-format. Each record has a primary key to identify it uniquely.

Records are *flat*: they cannot contain arrays or repeating data. Flat records can always be achieved (at the expense of extra storage) by a process called *normalisation*.

In an RDBMS, one-to-one relationships are expressed by linking the primary and secondary keys of records:

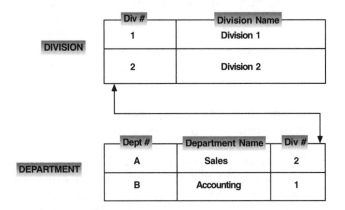

Many-to-many data relationships are expressed in the relational model using connector tables:

The relational
database model
(simplified)

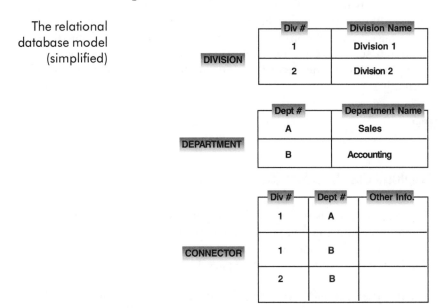

The relational DBMS preserves the integrity of the data by preventing access to the data by any means other than queries handled by the DBMS itself. Programs accessing the database do not have to know about links between records, or how or where the data is stored.

Most modern database software products are built according to the relational model. The standard means of access to a relational database is using SQL directives usually embedded in a program written in a high-level language such as COBOL or C. Using such directives, the application programmer need know nothing about the internal structure of the database. This safeguards the integrity of the data stored in the database and means that relational databases are particularly suitable for use in client–server environments.

The object-oriented database model

Object-orientation does not change the underlying DBMS, it only changes the methods by which it is accessed. Object-orientation binds the behaviour of the record to the data values which represent it. For example, the record would not simply store data but also access requests which can be made for the record. This storage of data and access methods together is called encapsulation. Object-orientation is characterised by encapsulation, inheritance and polymorphism.

One of the benefits of OODBMSs is that the normal RDBMS queries are shortened further, reducing network traffic. OODBMSs also encourage storage of non-text data, such as graphics and multimedia, in the database. The retrieving application will then use the polymorphic characteristics of the records to ensure that each one is retrieved correctly.

User interface

Origins of the Graphical User Interface (GUI)

The user interface is that part of a computer system through which the human user and the computer communicate. It is also the means by which the user interacts with applications – such as those described in the *Applications* section starting on page 119.

The first user interfaces were plugboards, or banks of switches and lights on the front of a computer; a user with the rare gift of being able fluently to read hexadecimal character representations or bit streams in binary could determine what was going on in the computer and how to make it do something useful.

Later, batch (non-interactive) mainframe systems provided *job-control languages* (JCL), which allowed users to describe to the system the requirements of their tasks. JCL allows users to identify themselves to the system's security mechanism; request resources for use by their programs; specify I/O devices and files; and define error-handling procedures for situations where their programs finish abnormally. As anyone knows who has used JCL for IBM mainframes, writing JCL is not simple, requiring as it does significant expertise and knowledge on the part of the writer.

The development of the user interface has been characterised by progressive reduction in the levels of expertise required of the user.

In the first move away from batch job-control languages such as JCL, interactive computer systems, including those running UNIX and MS-DOS, renamed their job-control languages as command languages. These, unlike JCL, can be used interactively as a stream of English-like commands submitted and interpreted one line at a time. Each time a command is entered, the user must make a judgement on the basis of the results as to what the next command should be. With batch JCL programs, it is necessary for the user to anticipate all eventualities at the time of writing; interactive command languages have the advantage of allowing users to respond to evolving situations. Additionally, the computer can be programmed to prompt the user through the command-line interface (CLI).

Command languages have become very sophisticated and powerful. Examples are the various shell command languages available with UNIX and the REXX language supplied with OS/2. They may carry out the functions of file management, screen editing, user and security control and management of electronic mail.

The main disadvantage of CLIs is that they use an artificial, imperative medium to allow the user to control the system. At all times, the system is a slave awaiting orders; no attempt is made to help or guide the user. The command languages provided by UNIX and MS-DOS are good examples of this. Also, they do not take advantage of any facilities which may be provided by the terminal display unit for controlling the cursor and the screen position of output. The screen is effectively treated as a long roll of paper, with all entry of commands taking place at the bottom left of the screen and eventually scrolling irretrievably off the top.

'Power users' of UNIX, OS/2 and MS-DOS like the CLI and the terse commands offered by it. In expert use, the CLI commands provide mode power, efficiency and speed than a GUI. However, the required level of expertise is again the problem. Most users simply do not have it and, restricted to CLIs, the potential user population is limited.

Two developments which led the move in the late 1980s away from the CLI are:

▸ Availability of cursor-addressable display screens

▸ The advent of bit-mapped graphical display screens

Cursor-addressability allowed development of business-form-style spatial layouts, with data entry taking place at many points on the screen, and allowing users control over the order in which data is entered. The introduction of screen objects such as menus, buttons and dialog boxes helped guide the user and reduce or eliminate the possibility of syntax errors when commands are entered.

Bit-mapped displays allow screen objects to be represented as icons (pictures) instead of textually; text to be displayed in multiple typographic-style fonts; pictorial artwork and the characteristic 'what you see is what you get' (WYSIWYG). A word-processing program operating in character (not bit-mapped) mode will probably not be able to display directly on screen a line of text in (say) 14.5-point Century Schoolbook font. It can print it correctly, if the printer has that font loaded, but what appears in print is not what is displayed. Bit-mapped displays allow the word-processor to display the text exactly as it is printed. Most users very much prefer this.

The iconic bit-mapped display is the basis of the modern GUI. Additionally, multiple windows in the screen display allow users easily to switch between tasks and contexts. The advent of multimedia in conjunction with the GUI – colour, motion, audio and TV-quality images – gives more realism and more sensory cues in the user's interaction with the computer. As an example use of multimedia with a GUI, consider the example of discarding a file. First, the file is dragged, with the mouse, towards the wastebasket. An attendant dragging sound is generated, to be followed by a clang or thud when the file lands in the wastebasket. This level of realism attracts users and makes the interaction more pleasant and satisfying to the senses.

Undoubtedly, the most common GUI in current use is that presented by the Microsoft Windows environment. Its lineage, and its influence on later GUI designs, are illustrated below.

Development of the Graphical User Interface

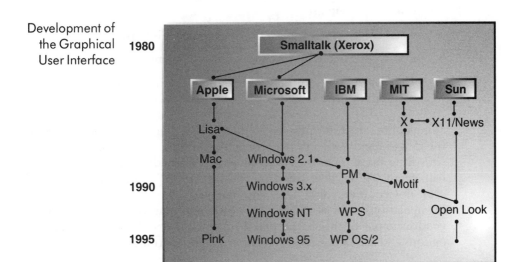

Principles of GUI design

With the great increase in interactive PCs, terminals and workstations, the importance of the ease of use (usability) of the interfaces (increasingly GUI) which they present is growing.

GUIs and application programs which have good usability encourage exploration, and increase the size of the user population, because they are attractive. Usability has its price: there is a great increase in the difficulty of programming a GUI in comparison to interacting with a CLI. GUIs consume a large part of the software construction and maintenance effort, by various estimates, anywhere between one-third and two-thirds.

With GUIs, verbs (commands) are reduced in importance as compared to nouns (objects). Objects are represented as icons, not textual entities, and are directly manipulated with a pointing device such as a mouse. The language syntax and symbolic references prevalent in the CLI environment are replaced by object manipulation.

The GUI *metaphor* is the mapping of the interface structure on some aspect of the real world. Examples include:

▸ The Desktop, representing the totality of icons, windows and other objects in use

▸ The Folder, representing a file or a physical disk drive

▸ The Wastebasket, an icon providing the means of discarding data

▸ The Calculator, an icon providing a familiar interface for performing arithmetic

A metaphor which is intuitive, familiar to the user and appropriate to the task in hand results in a system and applications which can be used with little prior training. The confusion ('What do I do next?') and bafflement ('What does this error message mean?') which so discourages novice users of a CLI are removed by *only* allowing valid manipulations of objects. Errors of syntax are removed altogether. A good example of this is the pull-down menu: it only presents valid options and it is impossible for the user to do something invalid.

Application programs which user familiar metaphors in a predictable way are said to have a consistent look and feel: even when using the application for the first time, a user can make intelligent guesses based on experience of similar programs. Training and learning time are reduced.

Because of the advantages of the GUI outlined above, users perceive tasks as being easier than the CLI equivalent, even though that equivalent may involve fewer steps. The GUI provides predominantly visual information which, especially in colour, communicates more powerfully than the equivalent textual information. Isolated objects in the GUI provide better communication than a cluttered display. A graphical element in a GUI and its function are interrelated; the element should work the way its appearance suggests.

The design of visual interfaces is based mainly on the following properties:

▸ Object 'feel'
▸ Contrast
▸ Colour
▸ Font

Feel

Any three-dimensional object can be pressed or acted on. Selection of a three-dimensional object is confirmed to the user by its appearance of having been pressed. Inactive objects (those whose selection is inappropriate for the context) are greyed out. In the example below, the illusion of buttons having been pressed makes it intuitively clear to the user that text-entry will be left-justified and that the leftmost tab button is active.

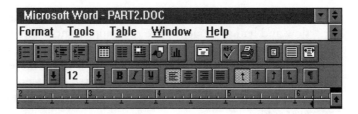

Contrast

Use of black outlines for objects, along with use of contrasting white and grey, allows crisp display of objects and the illusion of three-dimensionality.

Colour

All colours are combinations of the primary Red, Green, Blue (RGB) colours. In good interface design, groups of objects are separated by having different colours, especially if the colours, like red and green, are naturally opposing.

It is bad design, and leads to confusion, to have too many colours, especially non-opposing ones, in a graphical display. In general, the colour blue should not be used to display text, because the human eye cannot focus on blue as well as the other primary colours. This very fact in turn means that blue is a good colour for a background display. In a good design, colour should be used to emphasise grouping, opponent colours should not be used in close proximity and use of colours should, in general, be to achieve a subtle and calming effect.

Fonts

Text typeface can be used in a hierarchy of size and weight to intuitively organise information. In general, smaller, lighter, fonts are used to communicate information which is less important than that represented by large, heavy, typefaces.

Microsoft Windows

The first commercial adaptation of the GUI was the Apple Lisa in 1983. The machine was slow, because the processor technology of the time could not adequately cope with the demanding processing requirements of the GUI. The Lisa did not sell well, but its concepts survived in the popular Macintosh system introduced in 1984.

In 1985, Microsoft introduced its first Windows product. This was also slow and had an unattractive tiled appearance. The first viable version of the product was Windows 3.0. It was introduced in May, 1990 and was an immediate runaway success. To date, more than 40 million copies of Windows and its successors have been sold. This makes Windows the second most popular software program, after MS-DOS, ever sold.

Microsoft Windows NT uses the same style of GUI as the earlier Windows products. This style conforms to the IBM Common User Access 89 (CUA 89, see the next section on OS/2 and IBM usability standards) specifications and is thus application-oriented, not object-oriented like the more modern GUIs. Programs written for the Windows interface are completely non-portable, but the huge installed base of Windows means that this is not a handicap.

GUI programming: the event-driven model

Allowing for a possible over-simplification, there are two types of computer program: those which are procedural, and the rest which are event-driven.

Most of the programs ever written have been procedural. A procedural program is one which is started by whoever is operating the computer and which runs under the control of the operating system in a manner dictated completely by the sequence of instructions which make up the program. An event-driven program is one which consists of a number of largely unrelated parts. The sequence in which these parts are executed is dictated by outside events, including instructions from the operator, which occur while the program is in execution.

An example of a typical procedural program is the kind of software installation routine we were used to before the advent of Microsoft

Windows and other GUIs. This sort of installation program might be written with the C programming language or, more likely, as an MS-DOS batch file or a UNIX shell script. At the computer's command prompt (DOS is assumed) it is started like this:

```
C:\> a:\install
```

The install program immediately starts running under the control of the operating system and begins reading files off the floppy disk in order to write them to the computer's hard disk. First, however, it does this:

```
Enter the path name of the installation directory:
```

Now the operator must enter a directory pathname. If this is done, there is no problem; the files are copied and the installation completes successfully. If for any reason, however, the operator does *not* want to enter the pathname – suddenly realising there is not enough space on the disk for the installation and would prefer to stop the installation procedure – there is no graceful way out. The installation program requires entry of the pathname and offers no alternative. The best that the operator can do is probably to abort the program by entering an interrupt such as Ctrl-C. The point is that the install program is procedural: it controls completely what happens and the operator must helplessly respond. In the modern era of event-driven programs, this install program would be considered anti-social, at best. The event-driven alternative is the kind of program popularised by Windows:

All Windows programs are event-driven. Such a program at all times presents the user with a 'Cancel' option which guarantees as far as possible that the status will remain unchanged. In this case, the installation will exit without copying any files.

Not all programs before GUIs were procedural. Good examples of non-GUI event-driven programs are operating systems themselves and communications programs. Consider what happens when a communications program is running and a message arrives from the outside world. The stream of characters incoming might look like this:

SYN SYN SOH STX M E S S A G E ETX SYN SYN SYN

The message 'MESSAGE' is surrounded by a number of control characters: synchronise; start of header; start of text; and end of text. When the first SYN character appears, the communications program has no way of knowing what kind of character will appear next; it must respond to whichever one it is by quickly switching to an appropriate piece of code to handle it.

In the same way, when the message box above is on the screen, the GUI cannot know in advance which option the user will take and what the resulting event will be. It must select appropriate code to respond to the event.

In GUI environments and Microsoft Windows in particular this 'switching', or 'selection', is done using messages. When Windows is running, it, not the operating system (DOS), controls the passing of messages within and between programs. Every Windows program has two parts: a message loop and an event procedure:

The two parts of
a GUI program

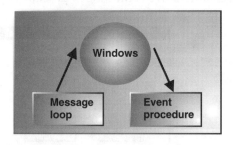

The parts are unrelated and are made to interact by Windows, which passes messages between them. Suppose an event occurs: for example, the user clicks on a screen object such as the Cancel button with the mouse. Windows gives the message to that part of the program which is the message loop. There, the message is processed and returned to Windows so that it may be passed on to the event procedure. The event procedure is the code which actually performs the response to the message. In this case, it causes the Installation message box to disappear and control to be returned to another part of the same program or to the Windows desktop. Usually, an event-driven Windows program will contain a large number of event procedures, often one for each object in a window being managed by the Windows program. Each of these event procedures will be capable of responding to any of a number of messages relating to outside events. The event procedure attached to the message box above must be able to respond to four messages relating to possible events:

- ► Click on 'OK'
- ► Click on 'Cancel'
- ► Display the message box
- ► Move the message box

In general, a window displayed on the desktop by a Windows program will contain a number of objects. For each of the objects, there is an attached event procedure. The event procedure is an independent program fragment (usually a C function) which contains logic enabling it to respond to any possible event which can happen to its attached object.

The messaging mechanism used by GUI environments imposes a significant processing overhead: Windows and other GUIs spend as much as 70% of their time passing messages and doing internal processing, which the remainder devoted to running the application. This overhead has meant that PC-based GUIs only became truly viable with the advent of fast 80386 processors succeeded by 80486 and pentium-based systems.

OS/2: System Application Architecture (SAA), Common User Access (CUA) and the Workplace Shell (WPS)

CUA is an important set of specifications which is part of the System Application Architecture defined by IBM. To describe CUA, it is necessary first to have an understanding of SAA. SAA is also interesting in its own right in that it represents IBM's approach to open systems.

CUA specifies the characteristics of a uniform, consistent GUI usable across all IBM systems. Applications written to this specification are consistent in look-and-feel and have a minimal requirement for user training.

The objective of SAA is to tie together IBM's multiple system architectures (the PC, AS/400 and 390-series mainframes are all incompatible) in a manner which ensures consistent operation of application programs across them all. SAA is a set of software interfaces, conventions and communication protocols which provides a framework for developing integrated applications for all the architectures. In principle, a program which complies with the specifications of SAA is independent of the underlying IBM hardware and operating system: it will run unchanged on any IBM SAA system.

SAA is effectively IBM's internal (for its own systems only) implementation of open systems. The benefits yielded by SAA are similar to those of open systems:

- Portability of software across IBM's disparate systems

- Connectivity, by defining how applications can be distributed among heterogeneous networked IBM computers

- Consistency of appearance and usage of application software across all systems

SAA consists of a *base foundation* and an *interface framework* which describes how the base is accessed by application programs. The base foundation is a layer of abstraction which hides the different system dependencies from applications. It consists of:

- *System Control Programs* (operating systems including VM, MVS, OS/400 and OS/2)

- *Application Enablers* (tools useful to software developers including compilers, debuggers and database management systems)

- *Communications* (communications protocols for interconnecting SAA systems with each other and with non-SAA systems running the OSI and TCP/IP protocols)

The SAA interface framework, the components of which request services from the base foundation abstraction layer, comprises of:

- CUA
- Common Programming Interface (CPI)
- Common Communications Support (CCS)

The CPI specifies standard programming languages, including ANSI C and COBOL-85, to be used on SAA systems. CCS specifies the supported communications protocols. A diagram of the full SAA structure follows:

Structure of IBM
SAA

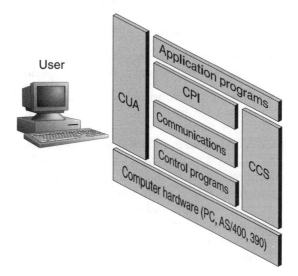

IBM's approach to achieving internal openness of its systems differs from that of the more general open systems movement based on UNIX and POSIX standards: SAA includes a number of very different operating systems, hiding them from applications with a layer of abstraction. Open systems standards, by contrast, require a single standardised operating system based on UNIX. Each approach, however, provides sufficient overlap with the other to ensure that software can be portable between SAA and open systems and that they can be networked.

CUA includes these main component requirements:

▸ *Common Presentation:* the appearance of all screen objects is consistent across all applications running under a given operating system, for example OS/2

▸ *Common Process Sequence:* a GUI object is always selected *before* the required action on it is specified. For example: a file to be deleted is first selected and only then, as a separate action, is it dragged to the shredder for deletion

▸ *Common Actions:* objects with similar appearance always behave similarly. For example, a button with an 'OK' caption is always used to signify confirmation of an action

CUA-compliant software should be easy, efficient and pleasant to use and will have the following characteristics:

▸ The user, not the computer, is in control of the interaction

▸ Users need not memorise all or most aspects of how an application works; they are prompted by menus and other cues

▸ Because of consistent look and feel, CUA applications will be easy to learn

CUA originated in 1987 and has been the subject of two revisions, CUA 89 (CUA2) and CUA 91 (CUA3). CUA2, to which Microsoft Windows conforms, is application-oriented. As an example of what this means, to delete a file, a pull-down menu must be selected from the 'File' menu option, and then the 'Delete' option selected. This is quite a simple process but, to do it, the user has to know details of how the Windows application works, that is that there exists a menu with a 'Delete' option.

Early versions of OS/2, up to version 1.3 used the Presentation Manager (PM) graphical user interface (GUI). This conformed to CUA2 and was very similar in appearance and behaviour to the Microsoft Windows 3.x GUI. PM and Windows are in many of their functions procedure-oriented GUIs.

OS/2 2.x introduces the WPS, a completely new object-oriented GUI which conforms to CUA3 and eliminates many of the procedural characteristics of earlier GUIs such as Windows and PM. For example, to delete a file, the user points at the file object, drags it to the shredder (another object on the desktop) and drops it. This has the effect of deleting the file without it being necessary to issue formal commands of the 'Delete' type. The procedure is visual and is based on the objects: the file and the shredder.

Under the WPS, the various Managers familiar to users of Windows and PM are gone. There is no File Manager, Program Manager or Print Manager. All WPS functions are carried out by means of operations on objects (programs, data files, devices and folders) which are accessible from the Desktop.

These objects hide the complexity which underlies them. It is not necessary, in order to execute a program object, to know what the OS/2 (or DOS) directory pathname is where the program file can be found. It is not necessary to change the program or its configuration files to change its behaviour; this is done via *settings notebooks*, which can be made to appear from the desktop object. If objects communicate with each other, the communication takes place at a lower level: the user may see the result, but the mechanism by which it is done is transparent.

X Windows

X Windows is a client–server communication and display protocol for implementation of networked graphics.

X began as a research project in 1980 at the Palo Alto Research Center (PARC) of Xerox Corp. The research was into methods of replacing the then-current character-based system interface with one based on the WIMP (window, icon, mouse and pointer) model. The technology was first commercially used in the Apple Lisa and the Apple Macintosh.

Project Athena, started at Massachusetts Institute of Technology (MIT) in 1983, used elements of the Xerox research to define a graphics protocol which could work on heterogeneous environments across any network. The project became known as 'X' or 'X Windows'.

X Windows comprises two major elements:

- ▶ The X *Protocol* for inter-system communication
- ▶ *Xlib* (also called the X Library), a library of C-code functions used in developing GUIs and GUI-based applications

X Windows is not itself a GUI; it merely provides the facilities for building GUIs. Xlib in functionality is very broadly equivalent to the Microsoft Windows API, which is used to build applications to run under Microsoft Windows.

X Windows is not limited to UNIX systems or any particular type of network protocol. In practice, however it is mainly supplied with UNIX and the underlying network protocol is usually TCP/IP.

In the context of X Windows, the usual meaning of client and server is reversed: the server provides the graphic display for the application program running on the client system. If the application program and the graphic display are both running on one system, then the server and client are that system. More generally, the application runs on a client which is remote from the user and connected to the user's X *Terminal* server by a network.

X Windows is still independently developed at MIT. It is not the property of any computer system supplier, which may account for its popularity: it is used as the basis for almost all GUIs developed to run on UNIX systems.

The UNIX GUIs

Motif

Motif is a GUI implementation based on X Windows and IBM's CUA specification. Motif was one of the products of MIT's Project Athena. In look and feel, Motif is similar to Microsoft Windows. The original design of Motif is due to Hewlett-Packard, which used Windows and the OS/2 Presentation Manager as the model for its development. Motif has been adopted by OSF and COSE as the standard UNIX GUI and it has gained very wide market acceptance, even among customers of the rival UNIX International camp.

Motif provides:

▸   A *style guide* and a single API, allowing development of portable Motif application programs for all systems which support Motif

▸   A high-level software development environment based on the low-level X Windows *intrinsics*

▸   A User Interface Language which describes the visual aspects of a user interface

▸   A window manager which allows users to manipulate windows

▸   Multiple-language support through compliance with the XPG4 standards for National Language Support (NLS)

Motif has the widest support of all UNIX GUIs. Its main competition is Open Look, promoted by Sun Microsystems.

Open Look

Open Look is a GUI specification developed by AT&T and Sun Microsystems. It is based on Sun's earlier SunView GUI and, because it has a clean design and a consistent style guide, products based on Open Look are held to be technically superior to Motif. But Open Look is relatively proprietary: it is a Sun product and it does not have the industry acceptance which Motif enjoys.

The Open Look specification comprises:

- A Style Guide

- The NeWS windowing-system software development environment

- Sun's XView, for building GUIs based on the X Windows X Library

- The Xt+ development toolkit based on the X Windows intrinsics

Motif and Open Look compete on a fairly even basis. However, Motif has the market edge: even Sun Microsystems supplies it in order to be able to compete for United States Government tenders.

Part 3

Standards for Interconnection and Interoperability

Introduction

Standards for portability, dealt with in Part 2, are important for implementing open systems. Standards governing connection of computer systems and related devices in networks are perhaps even more important, especially given that computer systems nowadays rarely stand alone. In client–server applications such as distributed database and on-line transaction processing, getting the network to work is all-important.

This Part deals with all main aspects of data communications, connectivity and interoperability from the hardware upwards. Part 2 starts with transistors and microprocessors; continues by dealing with operating systems and programming languages; and ends by covering application software and graphical interfaces. In much the same way, Part 3 opens with the electrical characteristics of data communications media, usually some form of cable, continues with explanation of the characteristics of the major network communication protocols and products, and finishes with coverage of distributed networks running applications including order-entry and banking systems.

The maze and alphabet-soup of standards for data communications and networking are daunting. This is partly because of the diversity of computer systems and devices which must be networked; many of them came into existence in an era where their interconnection was not a prime consideration. But even in networking similar systems, the terminology is arcane.

The goal of the sections following is to guide the intelligent but non-specialist reader from Alpha to Omega, as it were, trying not to leave out any of the Deltas or Epsilons on the way. Many textbooks on communications start promisingly but then seem, without warning, to break the continuous thread by dropping a term like 'transport layer interface service provider' on the hapless reader. The text tries to explain the components and operation of the most important protocols, all the time returning to the common thread of the OSI Reference Model. All the proprietary and *de facto* standard protocol suites described are related back to the model and may be compared for equivalence with the formal OSI standards which populate that model.

A compromise is sought between describing the protocols and technologies in great detail, thereby stranding the non-specialist, and only glossing over them, in which case the utility of the result is questionable.

Basics of data communications

Electrical interface

The first systems for communications using an electrical medium were the simple telegraph systems devised by Samuel Morse and others in the 1830s. The Morse transmission system, for example, was binary, using the presence of an electrical current to signify a dot or a dash; absence of current meant no transmission was taking place. A further binary variable, duration of current, indicated a dot or dash.

Although incomparably faster and more efficient, today's data communication systems also ultimately rely on binary transmission of ones and zeros: transmitting a positive voltage level represents binary 1 while a different, usually negative, voltage level represents binary zero. Groups of bits (binary digits) transmitted represent text and other characters. In certain types of transmission, bytes representing text and other data may be grouped in *blocks* or *frames*.

At the advent of computerised data communications in the early 1960s, the main existing electrical communication medium was the *public switched telephone network* (PSTN). The telephone network is switched to avoid the necessity of providing direct lines between every subscriber on the network and every other subscriber. An operator, nowadays often automatic, acts as a switching centre, or node, to carry out the processes of control and routing and of establishing transmission links for connecting external machines to the network. These machines can be telephones or computer equipment, the latter more generally referred to in the communications context as *data terminal equipment* (DTE).

Morse's system was digital: absence and presence of current on the transmission medium meant 1 and zero respectively. The telephone system is analogue: it relies on a frequency range or *bandwidth* within which voice conversation can be conducted. For binary data communication to take place over a telephone link, binary data being transmitted must first be converted to analogue, a process called *modulation*. When the data is received, the reverse process of conversion from analogue to binary takes place and is called *demodulation*. A device commonly called the *modem* carries out the modulation/demodulation function and allows a DTE connected to the PSTN to transmit binary data to another DTE also connected to the PSTN.

The PSTN in a recognisable form has existed for most of the 20th century. Relatively recently, most public PSTN carriers have provided a public switched data network, the PSDN, designed specifically for the transmission of data as opposed to voice.

Electrical transmission of data requires a physical medium. Available media include simple wires, more complex co-axial cables, optical fibre, radio and satellite links. When viewed from the perspective of users and application programs on separate computers sharing data stored in files, it is not very important which of the underlying physical media is used. For them, the network acts as a 'hosepipe', reliably exchanging data between appropriate connected devices. This natural layering of the services provided by computer networks is described by the ISO Reference Model for Open Systems Interconnection (OSI) in *Network architectures* (on page 166).

The different characteristics of physical transmission media have implications for the kind of devices which can be connected, the volume of data that can transferred between them and the distance by which the devices can be separated. The remainder of this section looks at a number of types of transmission media and the practical limitations they impose.

Two-wire lines

The simplest media for data communication are pairs of insulated metallic wires, either open – parallel, separate and insulated from each other – or twisted. The two-wire open line is the simpler of the two arrangements. It allows connection of DTEs up to about 50 metres apart, using slow bit-transmission rates of 9,600 bits per second (bps) or perhaps 19,200 bps. The voltage indicating one- or zero-status is carried on one of the two wires (the signal wire), while the other wire carries a reference voltage, for relative comparison of the one/zero voltage values.

The distance limitation arises from *attenuation* (reduction) and *distortion* (mis-shaping) of electrical signals transmitted over the wire. After sufficient attenuation and distortion have occurred, the receiving device becomes unable to distinguish between the signals representing one and zero and transmission errors increase sharply. All transmission media are subject in some degree to these problems, but media more sophisticated than the two-wire open line are capable of carrying data for greater distances.

Two-wire open lines can be used to connect computers (DTEs) but are more usually employed in connecting a DTE to local *data circuit terminating equipment* (DCE), of which a modem is an example. An extension of the arrangement is to place a number, often eight or 16, of open wires in a flat ribbon cable for connection of proximate devices.

The open line medium is susceptible to cross-coupling of electrical signals between neighbouring wires on the same cable, resulting in *crosstalk*. The fact that the wires are open leads to reception on the wires of external electromagnetic signals. This results in interference on the line. Both crosstalk and interference can cause erroneous reception of data. Their incidence is also a limiting factor on the distance by which the connected devices can be separated.

Arrangement of the wires in a twisted pair is a significant improvement, giving much better immunity to outside interference. The closeness of the twisted wires means that any outside interference received is induced in both the signal and reference wires simultaneously and is of equal strength. The effect on the difference signal existing between the two wires is therefore reduced.

The twisted pair medium can be used to carry relatively high bit volumes, up to 1 Mbps, over distances up to 100 metres. At lower bit rates, twisted pair cable can connect devices up to 5 kilometres apart; the extreme range for the medium is about 15km. Twisted pair is widely used in the PSDN and is also to be found in local area networks where the cable length is short, such as within one building. Although more capable than the open line, twisted pair is still quite limited in the distance over which it can reliably carry data. When digital data is being transmitted, a *repeater* is needed about every two kilometres to boost and clarify the signal. The twisted pair arrangement so far described is not in any way protected from outside interference except in the insulation on each of the wires. This is an *unshielded* twisted pair (UTP) and can be improved on by using a layer of shielding surrounding the twisted pair of wires. The result is *shielded* twisted pair (STP), which further reduces the effects of interference.

Co-axial cable

The co-axial cable provides much better performance than pairs of wires, twisted or not. The co-axial cable for transmission of data is similar in appearance to the cable (the one that carries the signal) plugged into the back of an ordinary television set. The cable consists of a hollow outer cylindrical conductor, itself covered with insulation from the outside world, within which runs a single inner wire conductor.

The inner wire is the signal wire; the cylindrical conductor acts as the voltage reference. The two should be separated by air but an inner insulating material is usually in practice used. As compared to twisted pair, both interference and crosstalk are greatly reduced. This is because the electromagnetic fields are almost completely confined within the outer insulation and because the outer conductor is earthed. Using the co-axial medium, very high transmission rates, of up to 150 Mbps, can be carried over short distances. More typically 10 or 20 Mbps are carried over distances of several hundred metres. This makes co-axial cable the ideal transmission medium for local-area networks spanning one or more buildings.

For LANs, two types of co-axial cable are in general use. First there is a cable of 50 ohm resistance that is quite bulky, about one half inch in diameter, and when used in Ethernet LANs is often referred to as *thick Ethernet*. More commonly a 75 ohm cable, of quarter-inch diameter, is used; in the context of Ethernet LANs, it is called *thin Ethernet* or *Cheapernet*. 75 ohm co-axial cable is the same as that used in cable television projects. Both the cable itself and terminators used with it are standardised and widely used, so its cost may be only 20% that of the heavier cable. Additionally, it is easier to cable buildings for LANs using the thinner cable.

There are two possible transmission modes over co-axial cable, *baseband* and *broadband*. With baseband, the full bandwidth of the cable is used for signals representing a single message. If there are multiple messages, they are arranged to follow each other sequentially using a technique known as *time-division multiplexing*. In broadband mode, several messages can be transmitted simultaneously, each at a frequency lower than the baseband bandwidth capacity of, typically, 10Mbps. The messages are arranged in several side-by-side channels governed by the technique of *frequency-division multiplexing*.

Baseband transmission uses both thin wire and thick wire co-axial cable. With both cable types, the bandwidth is the same, 10Mbps, but greater attenuation on the thin wire type means that its transmission range is limited to about 200 metres, at which point a repeater must be used to perpetuate the signal. Thick wire co-axial cable has a transmission range of 500 metres at 10Mbps. Thin wire, baseband and 200 metres together give rise to the term *10 Base 2*; the alternative is *10 Base 5*. Both these terms are used as a shorthand for describing the co-axial cabling arrangements used in LANs.

Unshielded twisted pair cable can also be used for 10Mbps transmission in LANs. Such use is designated by the term *10 Base T*. Typically co-axial cable is used in LANs organised in a bus *topology* – a length of cable with devices attached at intervals on a multi-drop basis – while UTP is used in LANs of a star topology.

Optical fibre cable

Optical fibre cable differs from the metallic media so far described in carrying its binary data in the form of a fluctuating beam of light in a glass fibre rather than as an electrical signal on a wire. Very high transmission rates, running into hundreds of megabits per second, are possible with optical fibre cables because of the higher bandwidth of light waves as compared electrical waves.

An optical fibre cable consists of a glass fibre for every signal to be transmitted, surrounded by a protective cladding which protects the fibre from external light sources. The light signal is generated at the transmitting end by an optical transmitter which converts the electrical signals used by the DTE to binary optical equivalents. This is done with a light-emitting diode (LED) or injector laser diode (ILD). At the receiving end of the transmission, the signal is extracted by a photodiode and converted to the required electrical signal. Advantages of optical fibre cabling include:

▸ High bandwidth and consequent very high data transmission rates

▸ Immunity from electrical interference and crosstalk; this is especially useful when transmitting in an electrically noisy environment

▸ Smaller and lighter cables

▸ Lower attenuation over distance compared to co-axial cables

▸ Electrical isolation and consequent high security when optical fibre is used in a network; it is difficult to intercept a signal carried by an optical fibre cable

Optical fibre cables of very high bandwidth – 565Mbps is a typical value – can carry very high volumes of data. With this bandwidth, more than 3,000 simultaneous telephone conversations can be multiplexed on the cable, replacing the twisted pair telephone cable and resulting in enormous space saving. Optical fibre cable, because of its high performance, has application in new high-speed LANs which operate at a bandwidth of 100Mbps and upwards.

Non-physical transmission media

Under circumstances where connection of locations and devices by physical media – twisted pair, co-axial or fibre optic cable – is difficult or impractical, wireless media may be used. The two principal wireless media in general use are radio and (higher-frequency) microwave links. Wireless links may be chosen where the source and destination of transmission are widely geographically separated or where they are separated by an obstacle (eg a road) which makes laying of physical cables difficult.

Data communication by radio with a fixed computer network is achieved using one or more radio transmitters, called base-stations, connected to the fixed network. The power output of a base-station determines the extent of its coverage. Within that area of coverage, computers and terminals can perform wireless communication with the base-station within a particular frequency band. Depending on the total area and number of devices to be covered, further base-stations may be needed. Other base-stations in the network are also connected to the fixed network but operate on different frequencies, unless they are far enough away to duplicate the frequency without interference. Transmission rates achieved using wireless radio links are quite low, usually less than 100Kbps. Radio links may be an acceptable alternative to twisted pair media but probably not for an application requiring the 10Mbps bandwidth provided by co-axial cable. If a new computer is installed or moved, no rewiring need be done but, in the case of a new system, a radio unit must be provided to convert digital data to and from the form of radio signals.

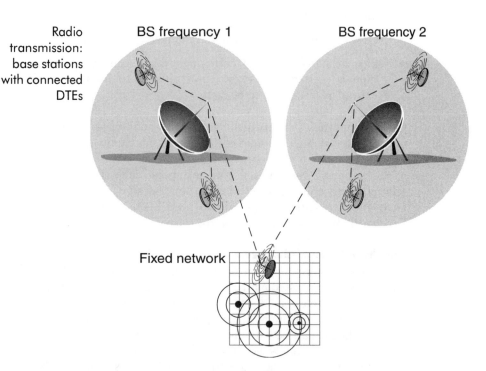

Radio transmission: base stations with connected DTEs

BS frequency 1

BS frequency 2

Fixed network

Where low-frequency radio links are inadequate in bandwidth or coverage, microwave links may be used. These fall into two categories: terrestrial microwave and satellite microwave links.

For data communication using a satellite link, a geostationary satellite is used which is in line of sight of both the transmitting and receiving stations. A microwave beam, carrying modulated data, is transmitted from the ground along an *uplink* frequency band. The beam is received and retransmitted to its destination ground station by the satellite using an antenna and a *transponder* covering a different (*downlink*) frequency band. Depending on how finely focused the microwave beam retransmitted by the satellite is, different kinds of ground stations are used. For finely focused beams, it is possible to use small-diameter receivers called *very small aperture terminals* (VSATs) or, in the vernacular, just 'dishes'.

Extremely high bandwidth of up to 2,000 Mhz can be provided by modern satellite microwave links; in practice, many high-bit-rate transmissions are multiplexed on to the bandwidth.

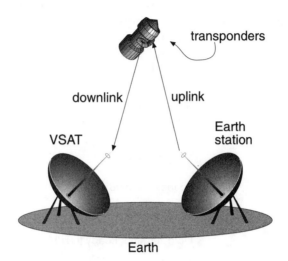

Satellite microwave transmission (simplified)

transponders

downlink   uplink

Earth station

VSAT

Earth

The main disadvantage with satellite transmission is caused by the very large distances which must be covered. A geostationary satellite operates nearly 23,000 miles from the earth's surface and the round trip time for the transmission is significant even in the context of the speed of light. The transmission delay is in the order of a quarter of a second. This delay is noticeable in some ordinary telephone conversations and can cause problems of flow-control and high error-incidence in digital data transmission.

Line of sight microwave transmission on earth (terrestrial microwave) is also possible over distances measured in hundreds of kilometres although the transmission can be disturbed by buildings and bad weather conditions.

Interface standards

Binary data is transmitted between DTEs (computers, terminals, printers and other devices) along physical media including those described above. DTEs are not directly connected; the transmission medium is connected to an interface which uses a set of electrical signals to control the order and timing of data transfer between them.

This set of signals constitute the physical level protocol, or level 1 of the OSI seven-layer reference model and is described in the *Network architectures* section, starting on page 166. The most common interface standard is RS-232C. It is very widely used to control interconnection of DTE and DCE (modem) equipment over short (typically less than 100 metres) distances. RS-232C defines a set of signals numbered from 101 to 125. These signals include:

Signal name	No.
Transmit Data (TD)	103
Receive Data (RD)	104
Request To Send (RTS)	105
Clear To Send (CTS)	106
Data Terminal Ready (DTR)	108

and are used to control orderly flow of data between DTEs or between DTE and DCE. Originally, RS-232C standard was defined for connection of DTE and DCE only; connection of DTEs is made possible using an RS-232C signal configuration called a *null modem* which causes one of the DTEs to emulate a modem device.

Simplified view of RS-232C transmission

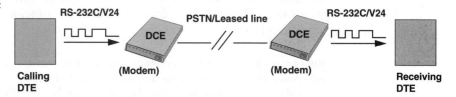

Signal numbering in the RS-232C standard is reflected in the typical 25-pin adapter used with a serial (low-speed, bits transmitted in sequence over a single wire) data *port*. Serial ports are used on many types of computer especially for the connection of dumb terminal and printer equipment. Not all of the signals defined are needed to control communication: a nine-pin adapter is often used as a simpler alternative.

The RS-232C interface allows serial data transmission at low speeds such as 9,600 bps and 19,200 bps. The RS-449 interface, which includes the RS-422a and RS-423c sets of electrical signals, is used to control higher-speed transmission of about 2Mbps over twisted-pair media for distances up to 60 metres. Interfaces such as the *de facto* Centronics standard control parallel (higher speed, bits transmitted in parallel over several wires) data transmission. For access to the high-speed transmission media used in LANs such as Ethernet and Token Ring, *network adapter cards*, also called *network interface cards* (NICs) are used.

Standards bodies

The RS-232C standard defines the signals used by the serial interface. RS-232C originated with the United States Electronic Industries' Association (EIA). V.24 and V.28 are, taken together, the equivalent recommendations made by the International Telegraph and Telephone Consultative Committee (CCITT) in Europe. A large number of standards have been defined by ISO as part of the OSI Reference Model described in *Network architectures* (on page 166). A number of national and international bodies, have defined standards for communications for which corresponding standards are found in the OSI model. These bodies include:

▸ EIA, ANSI, IEEE (all U.S.A.)

▸ The Government of the U.S.A., in the Federal Information Processing Standard (FIPS)

▸ CCITT

Data transmission

Data link

The purpose of data transmission is to exchange encoded binary data reliably between DTEs connected by a data link. The term 'data link' is a generic one which covers all types of transmission media, including those described above.

There are several ways in which binary data can be encoded. Two of the most common are *return to zero* (RZ) and *biphase* (Manchester) coding. The details of the encoding methods are not important here: whichever scheme is used, different electrical voltages are used to represent bits of data sent over a data link. The distance by which DTEs are separated and the speed and throughput of transmission required will influence the kind of data link and transmission methods used. For example, if character data is to be transmitted from a computer and displayed in screenfuls on a VDU then asynchronous, serial transmission may be suitable. On the other hand, if a bitmapped graphic image is to be displayed on a high-resolution terminal on the other side of a network, a high-speed data link using *synchronous* transmission will be needed.

To regulate the data communications conversation across any kind of data link, a set of rules is needed. The DTEs must exchange control data, in addition to ordinary data, as part of all transmissions. The rules agreed by both DTEs are applied to the control data and used to govern the sequence of transmission and reception. A set of such rules, along with the control data, is referred to as a communications protocol. In general, communications protocols perform the following functions:

▶ Framing the bits or characters within a transmission which constitute actual data as opposed to control codes surrounding that data

▶ Error control: detection of errors and retransmission

▶ Sequence control: defines the method of numbering messages to detect lost or duplicated messages and to identify messages retransmitted following detection of error

▶ Flow control (in network communication): selection of a route to the destination of transmission which avoids congesting the network

▶ Initiation, maintenance and termination of connection for transmission

▶ Recovery from line, equipment or software failure

There is a very large number of protocols – increasingly standardised – which govern data communications over all kinds of data links, from the slowest short-distance connection to high-speed networks spanning continents. When considered at the lowest level, all these protocols govern transmission and reception of streams of bits organised in bytes or, to use a more general term, *octets*. The remainder of this section briefly considers the main techniques and protocols used to transfer octets across a data link.

Character representation

Characters are represented by digital computers as sequences of bits organised in octets. Bit patterns within octets are interpreted to mean printable or non-printable characters according to coding systems defined by a number of internationally-accepted character codes. The two major codes in use are ASCII and EBCDIC. These are briefly described in *Background to open systems* (on page 15). Any ASCII or EBCDIC pattern can be accommodated in one octet. If the data being transmitted is treated as character data, an octet may be interpreted according to its ASCII or EBCDIC encoding. For non-text data, such as a file containing a bitmapped graphic display, each octet represents merely an arbitrary eight-bit grouping; any character interpretation is incidental.

Communications protocols can broadly be classified into character and bit protocols: the first where the individual octets are interpreted as encoded characters; the second where the octets collectively represent a stream of bits having a greater meaning. A typical character protocol is the Binary Synchronous specification. In Bisync, non-printable characters including STX (Start of Text), ETX (End Of Text) and ACK (Acknowledge) are used as control characters. These characters are members of both the ASCII and EBCDIC encodings. A standard bit protocol is the Higher Level Data Link Control protocol (HDLC). Both Bisync and HDLC are described later in this section.

Transmission modes

We have seen that bits being transmitted are logically grouped in octets, even if the character representation associated with an octet has no character meaning. Two fundamental modes of data transmission, serial and parallel, are differentiated by the manner in which an octet or group of octets is transmitted in those modes. In parallel mode, the bits within an octet or group of octets are sent in parallel along many wires with a single reference wire as shown:

Parallel
transmission of
ASCII 'a'

Transmitting unit

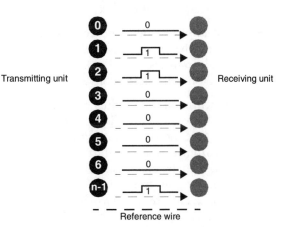

Receiving unit

Reference wire

In serial mode, the bits within an octet or group of octets are sent in sequence along two wires: a signal wire and a reference wire:

Serial
transmission of
ASCII 'a'

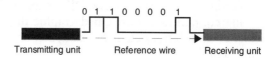

Parallel transmission is useful where transmission distances are very short, no more than about 5 metres, and typically between subunits contained within a single piece of equipment. The most common form of parallel transmission between a computer and an external device is that to a parallel printer, a short distance away and connected by a parallel cable using a Centronics-type interface.

For longer-distance communication, of up to about 100 metres, between DTEs serial transmission is used. Serial cable is less expensive than parallel and its performance is often sufficient for slow peripheral devices connected directly or by modem over the PSTN to a computer. Serial transmission may be:

▸ *Simplex:* in one direction only at a time. Simplex transmission is useful for applications such as unidirectional file transfer at low line cost

▸ *Full duplex:* fully bidirectional, where required transmission performance demands it and the extra cost of PSTN or leased lines is justified. Most modern bit-oriented communications protocols are full-duplex

▸ *Half duplex:* where the connected devices can operate in send and receive mode and do so alternately, giving alternate bidirectional transmission. Traditional character-based protocols are based on half-duplex conversations

▸ *Asynchronous:* individual characters that are part of the transmission between two DTEs are preceded by a *start bit* and appended with one or more *stop bits*. The clock in the receiving DTE synchronises on the start and stop bits added by the sending DTE. Each character is therefore clocked in individually. Asynchronous transmission is slow and suitable to use with serial mode. The terms asynchronous and serial are often used interchangeably, if inaccurately, 'asynchronous terminal' being taken to mean the same as 'serial terminal'

▸ *Synchronous:* characters are not clocked individually, instead they are grouped in a *block* or *frame* and the receiving DTE attempts to stay synchronised with the sending DTE for the entire extent of the frame. The frame contains a part constituting the actual data being transmitted; this may be a pattern of characters or a sequence of bits with no character meaning. Surrounding the data part are control characters or bit sequences which are used to ensure orderly transmission and reception. Synchronous transmission is more efficient than asynchronous and is used where higher-speed communications are necessary. The factors involved in transmission of blocks of characters as opposed to bit sequences are explained next

Data link control protocols

Introduction

Data link control protocols exist to effect accurate data transfer over serial data links. These protocols occupy the data link layer (Layer 2) of the ISO Reference Model. They can be used to transfer data over any of the kinds of physical media described in the earlier part of this section, over simple point-to-point connections or by an addressing mechanism through a switched network. Transmission controlled by data link protocols can be synchronous or asynchronous, character-oriented or bit-oriented.

To summarise, all modern data communications and networking relies on the operation of an underlying data link protocol, usually invisible (transparent) to the network programmer never mind the end-user of a networked application program. There are two broad classifications of data link control protocol:

▸   Character-oriented
▸   Bit-oriented

All modern network protocols are based on bit-oriented data link protocols. These are either implementations of HDLC (High-level Data Link Control) or derivatives of it; HDLC is briefly described below. Character-oriented data link protocols are still, however, in wide use; the archetype is IBM's Binary Synchronous Communication protocol (Bisync or BSC). It relies on encapsulating the data to be transmitted in sequences of non-printable character codes the interpretation of which governs the half-duplex transmission and reply.

Character-oriented data link control protocols

Character protocols are characterised by their use of predefined transmission control characters to surround the data being transmitted and to provide the required control functions. Many software products exist that are based on simplex character protocols; these are mainly used for unidirectional file transfer. Examples common in the PC environment are Kermit and Laplink.

The basic message format of Bisync is this:

Binary synchronous message format

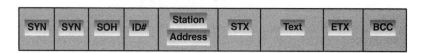

The transmission consists of two or more SYN characters to synchronise the receiver and transmitter followed by a start-of-header (SOH) character to mark the optional header information following; a start-of-text (STX) and end-of-text (ETX) characters to frame the actual data being transmitted; and a block check character, generated based on the data preceding it, for error control. In a multi-block message, the ETX character is ETB (End Text Block) for all but the last block.

Bisync uses a well-defined set of rules for establishing, maintaining and terminating transmission, including use of the synchronise character seen above and a set of special control characters: acknowledge message (ACK), negative acknowledge (NACK), enquiry (ENQ), wait and end-of-transmission characters.

A variation on the character protocol, the byte-count protocol, has been implemented to cater for situations where actual data in the text contains control characters or the generated BCC character coincidentally has a control-character meaning.

Bit-oriented data link control protocols

Bit-oriented data link protocols use predefined bit patterns, rather than transmission control characters, to delineate the start and end of the frame of data being transmitted. A unique flag character such as 01111110 delineates individual frames. The general format of a HDLC frame is shown below.

Standard
HDLC frame
format

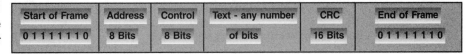

Start of Frame	Address	Control	Text - any number	CRC	End of Frame
0 1 1 1 1 1 1 0	8 Bits	8 Bits	of bits	16 Bits	0 1 1 1 1 1 1 0

The address bits identify the destination of the frame. The control bits specify the type of the message: whether it is an information frame carrying data, or a supervisory frame for controlling the data link. HDLC guarantees that there will never be transmission of six consecutive one-bits except in the start-of-frame and end-of-frame octets. This guarantee provides better transparency – protection against interpretation of data as control characters – than is possible in character protocols. Transparency is achieved by the transmitter inserting a binary zero after every five consecutive one-bits. The receiver in turn removes every zero that follows five consecutive 1s.

The method of error checking is called *cyclic redundancy checking* and the process of inserting binary zeros to preserve transparency is referred to as *bit stuffing*. Cyclic redundancy checking is a more powerful error-checking mechanism than the systems of *parity checking* which preceded it. On transmission, all the bits in the frame, including control and address bits, are treated as a serial string of bits representing a binary number. This number is then divided modulo 2 by a predetermined binary number and the remainder stored in the frame as the CRC. On reception, the same procedure is carried out. If the CRCs agree, transmission is assumed to have been error-free, otherwise the receiver will request a retransmission.

HDLC is a widely-accepted technology and many of the data-link control protocols used in current LAN and WAN (wide-area network) arrangements are derived from it. The main advantages of HDLC, as a bit-oriented protocol, over the character-oriented alternatives include the following:

▸ Better data transparency, as noted above

▸ Better efficiency for transmission of binary data

▸ Character set independence: character-oriented protocols depend on a character set being in use which contains the required control characters even though the actual data being transmitted may be binary

- ▶ Frames may freely contain either character (printable and non-printable) or binary data

Network protocols: summary introduction

HDLC is an accepted international standard for link control and acts as a basis for all modern network data link protocols. It does not, however, provide sufficient facilities for packet switching or for networks making use of higher-level protocols for connection of end computers. Further protocols are therefore needed to satisfy these requirements.

X.25 is a standard protocol set used for interfacing a DTE to a DCE across a packet-switched network.

There are three main communications switching techniques: packet switching, circuit switching and message switching.

- ▶ *Circuit switching* is analogous to a telephone call: the line over which the transmission takes place is dedicated to that transmission only until the conversation is completed. A major disadvantage of circuit switching is the difficulty of re-establishing calls if the circuit is broken

- ▶ *Message switching* operates on a store-and-forward basis: the whole message is sent through the network from node (switch) to node. This method is not good for real-time interaction over the network or for time-critical applications

- ▶ *Packet switching* is a technique for delivery of transmitted messages in which small units of information (packets) are relayed through stations in a computer network along the best route available between the source and the destination. A packet switching network breaks long messages into multiple packets before transmission. Packets constituting a message may travel by different routes across the network and arrive out of sequence; it is up to the receiving system to reassemble them. The process of breaking messages into packets and then reassembling them is called *Packet Assembly/Disassembly* (PAD)

Packet switching systems are very reliable because of built-in redundancy: if one route to the destination is not available, another is tried. The disadvantages are the overhead of the packaging and routing information which must be sent across the network with the actual data and the need for powerful computer systems to act as packet switches.

The X.25 packet switching protocol consists of three levels:

- Physical
- Data Link
- Network

The physical level is defined by the X.21 recommendation for linking synchronous devices. X.21 provides full-duplex serial transmission between DTE and DCE across a *Circuit Switched Public Data Network* (CSPDN). X.21bis is an alternative interim recommendation for the same purpose; its operation is similar to RS-232C. At the data-link level, frames are transmitted between DTE and DCE using the Link Access Protocol-Balanced (LAP-B), a subset of HDLC. The network level manages connection across the network between a pair of DTEs.

Many DTEs, such as dumb asynchronous terminals, are unable to support X.25 directly. Instead, they use a PAD protocol converter which allows such devices to access the X.25 packet-switching service. Three further protocols, X.28, X.29 and X.3 (*Triple-X*) govern the DTE and the network. X.28 operates between the terminal and the PAD, breaking up the message into packets for transmission through the network. X.29 carries out the reverse operation at the receiving end to form the original unbroken message. X.3 contains parameters which govern the operation of the other two protocols.

Higher-level network protocols, such as TCP/IP and protocols from the OSI suite can use the lower-level network and data link connection services of X.25. X.25 is a particularly suitable protocol for use with WANs and is widely implemented in public networks. It is less so for LANs, although there are LAN implementations which use it, because it does not have broadcast facilities and its underlying addressing scheme may not be able to handle the large number of addresses which are often present in a LAN environment. The most important LAN protocols are developed under IEEE Project 802 and are compatible with the OSI Reference Model. They are confined to the two lower layers of the Model (Physical and Data Link) and they adhere as closely as possible to HDLC. They are:

- IEEE 802.3 CSMA/CD Bus Network
- IEEE 802.4 Token Passing Bus Network
- IEEE 802.5 Token Passing Ring Network
- IEEE 802.6 Metropolitan Area Network (MAN)

CSMA/CD stands for *Carrier Sense Multiple Access/Collision Detect* and is the basis of operation of the Ethernet network. The characteristics of this and the other standards are described in the *Network architectures* section starting on page 166.

Public network services

As we have seen, X.25 usually runs over public networks. A range of public network services is available; in North America and Europe, they include the following:

- Dial-up telephone service (PSTN)
- VSATs
- Packet-switched data
- Narrowband Integrated Services Digital Network (ISDN)
- T1 and E1 digital channels
- Frame Relay
- Switched Multimegabit Data Service (SMDS)
- Asynchronous Transfer Mode (ATM)
- Broadband ISDN (B-ISDN)

Wide-area network requirements needing relatively low transmission speeds – approximately in the range 10Kbps to 100Kbps – are generally met using the PSTN, VSATs and public packet switched networks.

ISDN is a worldwide digital communications network and is an outgrowth of existing telephone services. Its goal is to replace current telephone lines, which require digital to analogue conversion, with digital switching and transmission facilities capable of supporting a variety of digital services including transmission of voice, data, music and video. The ISDN uses two channels, the B channel and the D channel. The latter carries control information; the B channel carries data at a rate of 64Kbps. Many B channels can be multiplexed onto higher-capacity trunk lines.

Telecommunication service providers in North America and Europe provide leased, point-to-point fixed-bandwidth services operating at the T1 (1.544Mbps) and E1 (2.048Mbps) rates. Each carries a number of 64Kbps B channels: 24 in the case of T1 and 32 for E1. Using the ISDN standard, the available T1 and E1 capacities are 23 and 29 B channels respectively.

X.25 packet
switched network

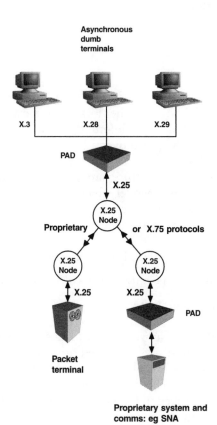

Asynchronous
dumb
terminals

X.3   X.28   X.29

PAD

X.25

X.25
Node

Proprietary   or X.75 protocols

X.25
Node   X.25
Node

X.25   X.25

Packet
terminal

PAD

Proprietary system and
comms: eg SNA

T1 and E1 dedicated WAN links provide higher bandwidth than the
PSTN and other low-speed services but may be insufficient for high-
volume data transfer, such as that involved in LAN-to-LAN communi-
cation, or for full integration of data, voice, audio and video services.
For these, higher-speed alternatives are Frame Relay, SMDS, ATM and
B-ISDN, all of which are described in the *Network architectures*, below.

Network architectures

Introduction

There are two main classes of network architecture, the wide-area network (WAN) and the local-area network (LAN). Distributed computing systems, which form the basis of client–server implementations, are usually spread over a large geographical area and connected by switched media such as the PSDN. The suites of protocols used by existing WAN architectures are to a greater or lesser extent reflected in the OSI Reference Model which is described in 'The OSI Reference Model' below. Later sections in Part 3 describe the predominant architectures. These are:

- ► The Open Systems Interconnection (OSI) protocols
- ► Transmission Control Protocol/Internet Protocol (TCP/IP)
- ► IBM Systems Network Architecture (SNA)

The Local Area Network constitutes a group of computers and other devices dispersed over a limited area, all connected by a high-speed communications link which allows any device to interact with any other on the network. The physical medium of the link is typically co-axial cable, (as described in *Basics of data communications*, page 146), providing bandwidth in the range 4 to 16Mbps. More recently, LANs have been implemented using optical fibre media of higher (over 100Mbps) bandwidth; these are described in *LAN Protocols and Standards*, below.

In the section *Basics of data communications* (page 146) physical media and low-level transmission protocols are described. The protocol layering mechanism of the OSI Reference Model is referred to as an aid to understanding but is not fully described. In the introduction to Part 2, the layered Reference Model is outlined and then used as part of an analogy in which system software and hardware are considered as a series of layers, from the microprocessor and operating system up to high-level end-user application programs. Before describing LAN concepts, protocols and implementations, as well as the linking of LANs by WANs, we need first to understand the need for layered protocols and how the layering is implemented by the Reference Model.

Layered protocols

Programmers and to a lesser extent end-users of computer systems are familiar with the ways in which software subsystems are layered in a modular fashion, with the lower layers providing services to the higher layers. Consider what happens when a command-line user of an operating system such as UNIX or DOS displays the contents of a text file using the system utility provided for that purpose. These are the steps for accessing the file, from highest to lowest:

Layered
procedures

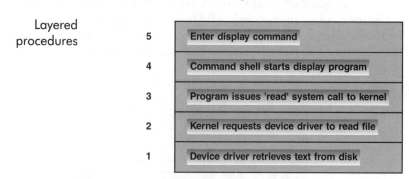

Consider layers 1, 2 and 3. The program treats the kernel as a *service provider*; the program issues a system call on the kernel and accepts the data returned without caring how the kernel retrieved it. In this context the kernel regards the program as a *service user*. The kernel itself is a service user with respect to the device driver. The function of each of the layers is quite separate, with each service user making minimal requests on the service provider immediately below and accepting the reply returned.

The same principle is used for the process of communicating between a data sender and receiver. The functions which provide the communication service are similarly partitioned into a number of vertical layers. All but the top and bottom layers act as both a service provider to the layer above and as a service user of the output of the layer below. In general, a layer does not know or care how the layer below it provides a service or how the layer above it uses the service provided. In an actual product implementation of the communications system described by the layers, each layer, apart from the one describing the physical and electrical characteristics of the transmission medium, corresponds to a software module.

Each additional layer builds on the functionality provided by the supporting lower layers. An increasing level of functionality is provided the higher up the stack we go. As a simple illustration of the need for layering, consider the case of system A on a network wanting to send a message to system B elsewhere on the network. If the highest layer on our communications stack were the data link layer (level 2), we might try firing unsequenced HDLC frames across the network and hope that they would be received correctly by system B. If the application program on B has its own sequencing and error-recovery mechanisms, this may work. More generally, and to avoid duplication of this functionality in applications using the network, a higher layer on the protocol stack will be used. Layer 2 will supply its frames to layer 3 for reliable network transmission. The three layers can be depicted like this:

Protocol layering

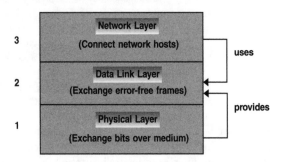

Systems A and B on the network will in practice both have software implementing these layered protocols. The communication is two-sided: the protocol at a given level on A (sending) will converse with the equivalent level on B (receiving). The two-sided stack diagram looks like this:

Communication using layered protocols

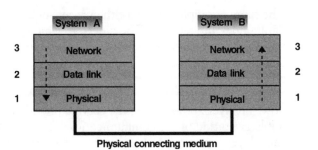

Physical connecting medium

When the message is initiated by A, it is passed by A down through the levels from Network to Physical and then actually transmitted over the physical link to B. On B, a reverse process takes place in which the message is passed up the layers for eventual processing by an application program.

On transmission, each time the message is passed down between layers, the service provider (for example, Data Link with respect to Network) adds a protocol header to the message. The message eventually sent out on the physical medium is encapsulated in protocol headers corresponding to each of the layers through which it has been passed. A protocol header from, say, layer 2 on A contains information which makes the message (containing a further protocol header for layer 3) it encapsulates recognisable to layer 2 on B. On reception, each time a message is passed up between layers, the service provider removes the protocol header for that layer and passes on the encapsulated message. Eventually, when all the layers have been traversed, the message as it was originally sent can be read free of all protocol headers. The process is now depicted graphically:

Layered protocols and protocol headers

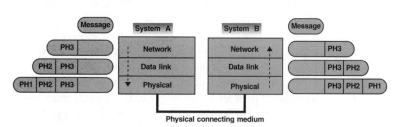

Appending protocols in this way is elegant and symmetrical; the main disadvantage is one of degraded performance caused by the sending and receiving systems appending and removing the protocol headers, as well as the increased line traffic caused by those headers. The advantages of the layered-protocol approach are, however, significant and considered sufficient to outweigh performance considerations. The advantages include:

▸ The layered architecture makes for robust communications implementations: new functionality can be added by way of new layers and applications without regard for how the underlying layers are implemented

▸ The services provided by a given layer are well-defined and consistently made available to the layer next above. This modular approach means that protocol stacks for particular purposes can be constructed on a building-block approach with all the

> advantages to the software development process of modularity and encapsulation of function

▸ A given layer presents a black box interface to the layers immediately above and below. Provided that interface is unchanged, the protocol(s) implemented at that layer can be replaced or changed without affecting the rest of the system

The OSI Reference Model

The Reference Model for Open Systems Interconnection, standardised as ISO 7498 and CCITT X.200, was devised by the International Standards Organisation in 1977. Also known as the seven-layer model, it is a formal, abstract description of a protocol stack architecture. It acts as a framework for development of protocol suites for communication between open systems. The Reference Model consists of seven layers, extending from, at the high level, the application program using a communication system down to the actual physical medium over which the communication takes place.

Since the late 1970s OSI protocols corresponding to each of the seven layers have been devised and, in many cases, adopted as standards. The motivation behind definition of the OSI Reference Model and the associated protocols was to provide a formal framework for communications protocols and to define a single set of standard protocols drawing on the best features of existing practice. Widespread implementation in software of the ISO protocols would then make possible communication between any two computer systems, regardless of their origin, using the ISO protocols.

As is the case with many excellent ideas, practice has not matched the theory. It has taken many years since introduction of the Reference Model for a coherent body of actual protocols to be standardised. In the meantime, there was a pressing need to be able to connect systems and LANs in internetworked WANs. One of the *de facto* protocol standards for this purpose is TCP/IP, originated by the United States Department of Defense (DoD). IBM introduced its own SNA, APPC and APPN products for similar purposes. TCP/IP and the SNA family are described below, respectively in sections: *Transmission Control Protocol/Internet Protocol (TCP/IP)* (on page 201) and *Systems Network Architecture (SNA)* (on page 222).

Whether products based on the ISO protocols will ever supersede systems such as TCP/IP is uncertain. The Reference Model, on the other hand, has achieved international acceptance and is the abstract model against which major protocol suites, including TCP/IP, are measured. It is described in the remainder of this section and repeatedly referred to for the rest of Part 3.

OSI Reference
Model

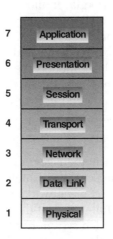

7	Application
6	Presentation
5	Session
4	Transport
3	Network
2	Data Link
1	Physical

The Reference Model reduces the complexity of software systems written to implement it by making each of the seven layers responsible for one particular aspect of the communication problem. Seven layers (as opposed to more or fewer) were defined because they resulted in minimal information flow across layer boundaries; were not too numerous and yet not individually too large; and were extensible without affecting the existing services. The model is very widely used to describe network architectures in general even though not all those architectures implement all its layers.

The highest layer is the Application layer, which performs the functions that are the reason for the communication i.e. those required by an end-user application program needing to communicate across a network. The lowest layer is the Physical layer and is concerned with access to the physical medium over which the communication takes place. Looking at the Reference Model from an end-user viewpoint, we describe the seven layers from the top down.

Application layer
Provides services, in the form of operating-system commands and function calls, which may be used by application programs to access the

facilities of the network. The application layer includes application programs such as electronic mail, file transfer, airline reservation systems and remote database access. It is the main provider of services for open, distributed systems.

Presentation layer

The presentation layer allows the application layers of two networked systems to communicate without knowing or caring how data is represented on those systems. Thus, details of system architectures such as word size, byte ordering and character sets are hidden. To do this, the presentation layer models the types of data and operations used by the application and then maps the data representations and operations required by each end user to this common model so that exchange of data may be effected.

Session layer

The session layer manages orderly exchange of data between connected systems. It supports the establishment, control and termination of the dialogue between networked applications, including whether that dialogue is full- or half-duplex. If the dialogue is half-duplex, it determines which system has the right to send at any given time. The session layer also reports to the application process errors arising at lower layers.

Transport layer

The transport layer acts as the interface between the application-oriented layers (5 to 7) and the network-dependent protocol layers (1 to 3). It provides an ordered, end-to-end, error-free message transfer service to the session layer, independent of the type of network over which the transfer is carried out. The transport layer provides the session layer with a set of message transfer facilities and thereby hides from the session layer the operation of the underlying network. To cater for the quality of service provided by different network types, the transport layer provides five different classes of service, ranging from zero (basic connection and data transfer) to 4 (full error- and flow-control procedures).

Network layer

The network layer establishes and clears a network-wide connection between two systems needing to communicate over the network. It controls routing, flow-control and sequencing. If there is no direct connection, data packets are transmitted on a store-and-forward basis between systems and networks.

Data link layer

The data link layer defines protocols for transferring messages between adjacent systems either directly connected by means of a point to point serial data link or by a shared-bandwidth medium. It performs error detection and correction, thereby turning the simple but unreliable connection provided by the physical layer into an error-free connection between the two systems. HDLC is a prime example of a data link layer protocol.

Physical layer

The physical layer drives the electrical interface between the sender and receiver, transmitting across the medium a series of electrical impulses representing data bits. It specifies the physical and electrical characteristics of the medium for signal exchange, as well as the procedures for establishment of transmission. The most common layer 1 standard is RS-232C. An example of a real application used over WANs for file transfer is the 'ftp' (File Transfer Protocol) utility supplied with the TCP/IP, or Internet, protocol suite. A user on a networked system can issue an 'ftp' command like this:

```
ftp lab.research.widgetco
```

thereby requesting setup of an 'ftp' conversation. The remote system is specified using the Domain Name Service (DNS) addressing scheme. With the subsidiary 'user' command of 'ftp' the identity of the other party to the conversation is specified. After the link is established, the sender can issue specific commands for transferring file data to and from the remote system – which might be 5 or 5,000 miles away.

The 'ftp' application operates at Layer 7 of the Reference Model. In a manner transparent to the user it packages data in a series of protocol headers which ensure correct routing and error-free transmission of the data to the intended recipient. On the receiving system, the protocol header information is stripped off by each successive level of the TCP/IP communication software until the actual data is accessed. As we shall see in the section *Transmission Control Protocol/Internet Protocol (TCP/IP)* (on page 201), the organisation of the TCP/IP protocol stack does not exactly match that of the OSI Reference Model. This is because the TCP/IP protocols were designed some years before adoption of the OSI Model. Nevertheless, there is enough similarity between the OSI Model and TCP/IP (as well as other non-OSI systems) for the Reference Model to be used as a yardstick for describing and evaluating them all.

LAN definition and characteristics

The first computer networks were developed during the late 1960s and early 70s. A good example is the DoD ARPANET – see *Background to open systems* (on page 15). These networks were based on packet switching over the telephone system and could therefore interconnect computers nationally and internationally. Transmission speeds were low, ranging from 1,200 bps up to 64Kbps, and error rates high, about 1 error in 100,000 bits transmitted. The LAN, introduced in the 1970s, is characterised by a number of attributes which differentiate it from such wide-area networking schemes:

▸ It restricts transmission distances to no more than a few kilometres

▸ It uses high-quality transmission media which allow high data transfer rates (somewhere in the range 100Kbps to 100Mbps) and very low incidence of error (perhaps a million times less than the WAN error-rate)

▸ All devices are directly connected to the high-speed transmission medium used by the LAN, in contrast to the PAD arrangement used in X.25 networks

▸ All devices on the LAN must use the same physical and data link protocols at the lower layers, in order to access the LAN medium. Applications needing to communicate across the LAN must use the same protocols at the higher layers

▸ Transmission is on a broadcast basis: each packet transmitted by any station, or node, on the LAN is seen by all others; the potentially receiving stations examine the destination address on the packet to determine if they should in fact receive it

▸ Because transmission is broadcast, a LAN does not have to perform routing of messages as does a WAN

▸ Because of their limited geographical extent, LANs are often owned by a single organisation. There is less need than with WANs to accommodate equipment of diverse suppliers on the same network. Complex multi-layer protocols for interconnection of such devices is usually not necessary, with the result that LANs are generally less cumbersome

> ▸ LANs used to interconnect other LANs restricted to a building or department are called backbones. Similar LANs are linked by bridges acting as transfer points between LANs; dissimilar LANs are connected by routers and gateways which both transfer data and do any necessary protocol conversions.

A common use of LANs is in a small area to allow a number of PCs to share peripheral devices such as disks and printers.

Typical LAN
environment

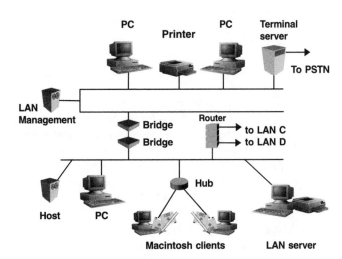

The LAN can be used to allow several PCs to connect to a remote host (mainframe or minicomputer) through a single channel. LANs can be used to support a range of engineering, professional and administrative workstations requiring shared access to information and processing power as well as interchange of graphic and other documents.

LAN architectures and access methods

The purpose of LANs is to implement orderly transmission of data frames between nodes over a high-speed medium. LANs can be organised in different arrangements, or topologies, but in all cases, the frame format will be similar to the following:

General format of
LAN frame

| Preamble | Destination | Source | Data | Error-check |

The two fundamental LAN topologies are linear (either bus or tree) and ring. The best known example of a bus LAN is Ethernet and of a ring LAN, Token Ring. The topologies are illustrated by diagrams:

Network topologies

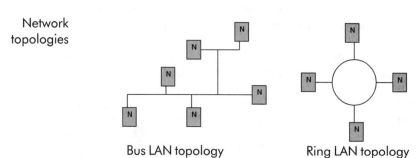

Bus LAN topology   Ring LAN topology

In a linear LAN system such as the bus topology, the network connecting a number of nodes accepts any information presented to it for bidirectional transmission along the physical medium to all the nodes. The nodes must contend for use of the network. Bus LANs run *contention protocols* which try to avoid the situation of simultaneous use of the network by multiple nodes. The best-known contention protocol is the CSMA/CD protocol used by Ethernet.

LANs using the ring topology avoid the contention problem by ensuring that only one node on the LAN can transmit at any given time. This is ensured by two main methods. Using the first method a token is passed (in one direction only) around the ring and only the node in possession of it can transmit, to the next node; with the second, a *slotted ring* system is used, in which a few empty frames (slots) circulate on the network, and any station receiving an empty slot can fill it with data and thereby transmit. The token method is prevalent and is exemplified by IBM's Token Ring LAN protocol.

Bus LANs using contention protocols are broadcast systems: any node can transmit whenever it wants. Ring LANs using tokens are likened to *polling* systems, whereby nodes wait until they are signalled to transmit.

Protocols controlling ring LANs are complicated by the need for data termination procedures. These are to counter the tendency of messages to circulate endlessly around the LAN. The advantage conferred by LANs such as Token Ring is predictable response time: the length of time that any node may possess the token is limited. By contrast, with contention protocols, heavy LAN traffic (with attendant high incidence of frame collisions) can cause serious and sudden delays in network response time.

Both the linear and ring topologies represent compromises. The ring system guarantees availability of bandwidth on the LAN for a node to transmit, but at the expense of a predictable delay. The contention protocol used on a bus LAN allows immediate transmission but does not guarantee bandwidth. With low network traffic, very high performance is achieved but, as the rate of collisions increases, LAN performance is degraded by unpredictable delays in transmission.

Ethernet

Ethernet is by far the predominant type of bus LAN and was designed at the Xerox Corp. PARC facility (see the section *User interface* on page 126) in 1976. It was intended to provide communication between PCs and to allow sharing of facilities in an office environment. Ethernet was designed to be inexpensive in terms of both transmission media and equipment needed for a node to access the transmission medium – nowadays usually a *network interface card*. Ethernet is intended specifically for burst transmission, where traffic is usually very light but is punctuated by concentrated bursts equating to situations such as that arising when a file is written back in full from a node to the network server.

Usually in LANs using Ethernet, co-axial cable is used as the physical medium. Either 50 ohm or 75 ohm coax can be used. The latter (thin wire, or Cheapernet) is favoured because it is easier to handle and is less expensive, but it has a shorter transmission range (about 200 metres as opposed to 500 metres for thick-wire) before a repeater is needed to amplify the signals transmitted. The bandwidth provided is usually 10Mbps. The cable is terminated at the ends to prevent signal reflection and stations are attached to the cable using passive *taps*. These are connectors which are coupled to a cable without blocking the passage of signals through the cable.

A node needing to transmit a frame first checks to see if another node is transmitting. If not, it begins its own transmission. There is a delay before all the other nodes become aware that a transmission is in progress. During this delay, called *acquisition time*, another node may transmit and a collision results. The originating node listens to its own transmission and, if it detects a collision, aborts the transmission, which is scheduled for retry after a randomly-generated time interval. Usually, there is no collision the second time. If there is, a third transmission is attempted and the procedure is repeated to a limit of 16 transmission attempts.

The complex collision avoidance protocol, CSMA/CD, required by Ethernet LANs is the major drawback of the system. Because the protocol relies on collisions, 100% use of the network bandwidth cannot be achieved. On the other hand, the transmission delay inherent in ring systems is avoided. At up to 30% bandwidth usage, Ethernet performance is excellent; thereafter, depending on the number of nodes on the network and how busy they are, performance degrades exponentially as the number of collisions multiplies. In extreme cases, Ethernet nodes simply hang up, waiting for access to the network which may never become available. The performance characteristics of Ethernet networks are summarised by a diagram:

Ethernet LAN
performance

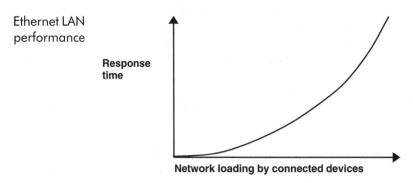

Token Ring

Probably because of its IBM origin, Token Ring is the predominant type of ring LAN. While providing many of the same capabilities as Ethernet networks, Token Ring is more expensive in terms of both transmission media and equipment needed for a node to access the transmission medium. Although the network is organised in a ring topology, individual nodes are connected to the ring not directly but via a Multistation Access Unit (MAU). Up to eight stations can be connected to the MAU in a star topology. The MAU contains circuits which cause the physical star to be treated as a logical ring. Individual stations can be up to 150 feet distant from their MAU, by which they are in turn connected to the ring network.

Token Ring networks can use standard telephone wiring or shielded twisted-pair cable as the physical medium. The bandwidth provided in the original Token Ring specification (IEEE 802.5, see 'High-Speed LANs' below) was 4Mbps but Token Ring with a 16Mbps signalling rate was introduced by IBM in 1989. The following is a simplified diagram of a Token Ring network:

Token Ring
network topology

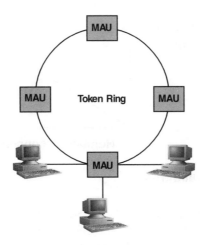

A node needing to transmit a frame waits until it receives a free token. The token is itself a frame of data which circulates in one direction only through the network stations when they are idle. When the transmitting station receives the token, it changes the free token to a busy token and transmits a frame of data immediately after the busy token. The frame contains all or part of the message the station has to send. When the station transmits the frame, there is no free token on the network, so the other nodes must wait. The receiving station copies the data from the frame and the frame continues around the ring back to the transmitting station. The transmitting station inserts a new free token on the ring.

The drawbacks of the Token Ring system are its complexity and the expense of its controlling hardware, as well as the predictable delay on all transmissions. Much of the complexity is associated with ensuring successful data termination and that the token is not lost, duplicated or corrupted. Failure of one station adapter in a Token Ring network can cause the whole network to fail because every node in the ring must be available to pass every token and message. Its great advantage over

Ethernet is that it is not a collision-based system using a protocol such as CSMA/CD. All the bandwidth can be used and, as the number of networked nodes increases, performance degrades slowly in a predictable, linear, fashion:

Token Ring LAN
performance

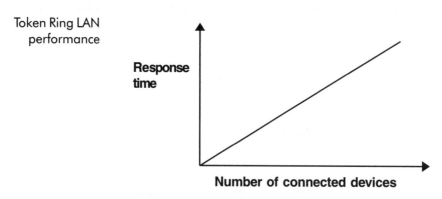

LAN protocols and standards

Standardisation of LAN protocols has been conducted by the IEEE committee 802 and has resulted in a series of standards covering bus LANs such as Ethernet; ring LANs including Token Ring; a linear variant of Token Ring called Token Bus; and most recently, the Metropolitan Area Network (MAN). The operation of LANs at the link and physical layers of the Reference Model varies widely. At the physical level, for example, Ethernet LANs can exist on a straight (coaxial) cable with nodes connected (tapped) into the cable. A Token Ring network, on the other hand, must form a circle which closes on itself, using MAUs to treat stations organised in a star topology as being part of that circle.

The mechanisms of transmission over the physical layer are diverse. Ethernet uses baseband signalling with Manchester encoding; the main protocol complication is concerned with detection of collisions and their avoidance on retransmission. Rings can use several types of physical media, the commonest being STP and fibre-optic cable. Signalling is baseband with Manchester encoding; the protocol must avoid frames endlessly looping around the ring. As a result of these differences, Layer 2 of the Reference Model has been subdivided (for LANs only) in two parts: the *media access control* (MAC) sublayer and the *logical link control* (LLC) sublayer. The MAC encapsulates the principles on which the different LAN types operate, including CSMA/CD for

Ethernet and token-passing for Token Ring. The upper sublayer, LLC, provides a level of abstraction to the network protocol, hiding the underlying protocol details. At the end of the section *Basics of data communications* (on page 146), the IEEE 802 series of LAN protocols is introduced. The following diagram shows how they form part of the MAC sublayer and how the MAC and LLC relate to the Reference Model.

LAN standards and the Reference Model

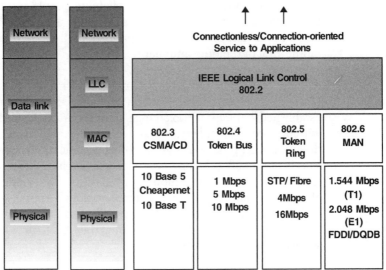

The LLC is common to all of the underlying LAN transmission standards. The LLC provides two principal modes of service to those applications:

▸ Connectionless (datagram) service
▸ Connection-oriented (virtual circuit) service

Using a connectionless service is analogous to the action of posting a letter, while using a connection-oriented service is like making a telephone call. When a letter is posted, the sender operates on the 'fire and forget' principle: no special measures are taken to ensure safe passage of the letter and no explicit check is made to verify its safe delivery. In the rare case in which a letter does not arrive at its destination, a copy is sent.

With a telephone call, on the other hand, before conversation begins, a virtual circuit, or end-to-end connection is established. The conversation then takes place and, when complete, the link is shut down.

In the context of data networks, a connectionless service supports the exchange of single data packets (datagrams) without prior establishment of a data link connection. No flow-control, error-recovery or acknowledgement mechanisms are used. Because of the absence of the checking mechanisms, such transmission is fast and efficient but is referred to as unreliable. This unreliability should not be overstated: connectionless transmission is suitable and reasonably reliable for small amounts of non-critical data. Applications include data-capture and monitoring of remote equipment.

A connection-oriented service supports transmission of larger messages containing several packets. A data link connection, or virtual circuit, is established before data exchange. Frames are delivered in sequence, with flow-control and error recovery. At the end of data exchange, link disconnection procedures are invoked. Connection-oriented transmission is often called reliable. Applications include those which involve transfer of significant amounts of data, such as file transfer and electronic mail, as well as continual remote terminal access (remote login). The LLC provides both connectionless and connection-oriented services; it is up to the application using the LLC to decide which type of service is suitable for its purposes.

IEEE LAN standards

IEEE Project 802 restricts its standardisation activities to the Data Link and Physical layers of the OSI Reference Model. Major guiding principles during the specification of the standards were that their mechanisms for frame transfer should be as similar as possible to the widely-accepted HDLC standard, and that the underlying link medium, transmission rate and network topology should be transparent as far as the higher-level protocols such as 802.2 are concerned.

The LLC standard IEEE 802.2 defines the function and operation of the logical link control sublayer. Because it is common to the various medium access control (MAC) methods, it provides a uniform interface between user equipment and application software and the different underlying media technologies and link protocols. When a message arrives from an application to the LLC, the LLC encloses that message in protocol header information specifying source and destination

Service Access Points (SAPs) equivalent to network nodes. The underlying MAC protocol – say 802.3, Ethernet – adds a further protocol header containing access-control and destination address fields. Finally, the physical layer adds start-of-frame and end-of-frame delimiters. The last of the IEEE 802 standards – 802.6 – specifies the protocols which implement Metropolitan Area Networks (MANs). The MAN is essentially a halfway house between the traditional LAN and WAN architectures and exhibits the following characteristics:

► Geographical extent of between 1 and 100 kilometres

► High-quality link medium, usually Fibre Distributed Data Interface (FDDI, see the next section)

► Some routing capability

► With FDDI, 100Mbps throughput

► Low error-rate in the region of one in 10 billion

The need for MANs (and high-speed LANs, described in the next section) has arisen from the fact that the bandwidth provided by conventional LANs such as Ethernet and Token Ring is insufficient for some applications, particularly backbones linking LANs, and multi-media transmission. Digitised speech and video are transferred in small fixed-size cells of 53 bytes, including control information. These are switched through the network by hardware switching devices. Because of the hardware switching and the fact that cells are fixed-length, performance is very high. By contrast, most LAN and WAN protocols use large, variable-length messages switched by software. Almost any type of information can be transported by breaking it down into a sequence of these cells.

The standard protocol for MANs, approved by the IEEE 802.6 committee, is Distributed Queue Dual Bus (DQDB) which specifies two parallel fibre-optic cables connecting network nodes. The parallel cables offer redundancy and good reliability, while the realistic throughput is 80Mbps, a rate sufficient for a backbone connecting LANs, or almost any other application. DQDB offers connection-oriented, connectionless and *isochronous* (transmission of equal time segments). The last is particularly for voice and video applications that require consistent and continuous timing between source and destination in order to function correctly.

Based on IEEE 802.6 and DQDB, the Switched Multimegabit Data Service (SMDS) is offered in a number of cities in the U.S.A. by the Bell companies. SMDS is suitable for transmission of traffic in concentrated bursts of the type common with many LAN architectures, including Ethernet. Consequently, SMDS is useful for linking conventional LANs within a metropolitan area.

High-speed LANs

The bandwidth limitations of conventional LANs – 10Mbps and 16Mbps for Ethernet and Token Ring respectively – are sufficient for most LAN applications to run with acceptable performance. For a few LAN applications, however, much higher bandwidth is desirable. These include supercomputing applications, CAD/CAM (Computer Aided Design and Manufacturing), LANs acting as LAN-to-LAN backbones and Metropolitan Area Networks. Several technologies exist and are emerging which deliver LAN performance in excess of 16Mbps bandwidth. Those which are briefly described in this section are:

> ► 100Mbps Ethernet
> ► FDDI
> ► Asynchronous Transfer Mode (ATM)

100Mbps Ethernet

One of the practical consequences of replacing traditional LAN media with fibre-optic cable is the cost of recabling, and retooling for connection of nodes to the new medium. In an effort to avoid this cost and to extend the life of the Ethernet architecture, the IEEE 802.3 (Ethernet) standards committee is specifying a faster Ethernet which will operate at bandwidth comparable to that of FDDI (100Mbps).

Ordinary unshielded twisted pair telephone cable is not reliable enough for such performance; instead, a superior ('category 5') twisted pair cable will probably become standard. Category 5 suffers less from crosstalk and interference than the earlier UTP, 10 Base-T and should cost no more than twice as much.

Fast Ethernet relies on use of a packet-switched hub which can provide either a normal (10Mbps) or high-priority (100Mbps) service. When a transmitting node signals the hub that it has information to send, it requests one of the two services. The hub then switches the request to an appropriate transmitting port.

Fibre-Distributed Data Interface (FDDI)

FDDI is a standard specified by ANSI for high-speed fibre-optic LANs. It provides specifications for transfer rates of 100Mbps over Token Ring-based networks. The network is arranged in a ring topology. This avoids cable tapping which, with optical media, tends to increase the error rate. A dual cable ring is specified which operates at 100Mbps for each ring, giving a total bandwidth of 200Mbps. The total cable distance (that is, the circumference of the ring) is limited to 100km and up to 500 nodes can be attached. A distance of no more than about 2 kilometres is allowed between adjacent nodes.

The ring operates in a manner similar to Token Ring LANs. A node in possession of the token can begin transmitting packets. When the last packet is sent, the node issues a new token. Under Token Ring, a new token cannot be issued until the message has reached its destination. In addition to the inherent speed of the medium, FDDI yields better performance than Token Ring, eliminating the waiting time on the part of the transmitting node.

An extension of the FDDI standard, FDDI II, contains additional specifications for the real-time transmission of analogue data, including voice and video, in digital form. The total bandwidth is allocated (*multiplexed*) into 16 channels each of bandwidth 6.144Mbps and one of 1.696Mbps which carries control and timing information. Graphic images can be carried on a 6.144Mbps channel, while a single one of those channels can carry 96 64Kbps voice or data channels.

SONET (Synchronous Optical Network) is an alternative to FDDI for implementation of fibre-optic LANs. It was adopted by ANSI in 1990. SONET allows transmission products from different vendors to be connected on the same link. It provides extremely high bandwidths, in the range 51.84Mbps to 2,488.32Mbps, but there are currently few actual products which implement the standard.

Asynchronous Transfer Mode (ATM)

ATM is a high-speed packet-switching LAN architecture and is one of the central technologies on which B-ISDN is based. It offers such high performance, in the range 100Mbps, that its natural use is as a switch between conventional LANs:

LANs interconnected
with ATM

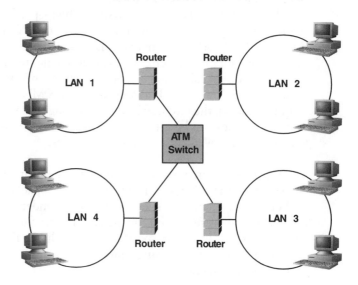

ATM is based on fixed length frames, called cells, each of 53 bytes, including five bytes for header and address (*virtual path*) information. The cells are fixed in size to reduce the complexity of switches in the network; a variable-length packet such as that used by X.25 is more efficient in terms of data storage but slower through a switch. The cells are small, as well as fixed length, in order to be quickly transmitted and to meet requirements for short delays when transferring audio or video data.

The designers of X.25 in the mid-1970s had to assume that the quality of the media over which transmission would take place would be poor and error-prone. Consequently, X.25 has sophisticated error-checking and correction procedures which degrade network throughput but are necessary in the context of older link media. Development of high-speed media, such as those outlined in the section *Basics of data communications* (on page 146), have made it possible for ATM to dispense with any error-checking and retransmission facilities and further increase efficiency. It is assumed that such checking will be done at higher levels in the protocol stack.

ATM is a basic data transport mechanism within broadband ISDN. It uses small fixed length cells into which packets from other protocols are decomposed and from which they are later reassembled. ATM can, at the Network layer of the OSI Reference Model, support a large number of higher-level protocols, acting as a common carrier transparently to applications using those protocols. When B-ISDN becomes available, it will be easier to convert to its services users who have already implemented ATM.

Interconnection of LANs and WANs

Soon after the appearance of the PC in 1981, users began to connect them in LANs, first for the purpose of sharing expensive devices such as printers and plotters, later for running shared and client–server application programs. As LANs grew haphazardly, it seemed reasonable that LANs separated by wide distances should themselves be internetworked. Often, the LAN grew as a somewhat unofficial alternative to the corporate IBM mainframe system. Having attained a degree of maturity, the LAN was now required to be integrated with more established long-haul wide area networks. The subject of LAN/WAN internetworking occupies the attentions of many large books. To treat it fully is beyond the scope of this section, which will confine itself to introducing some of the main technologies involved and giving a few pointers for the future.

Devices for linking networks

To internetwork a LAN and a WAN, or a LAN with a LAN, they must be physically connected. A number of types of device exist which do this connection, with varying degrees of sophistication. The devices are broadly classified as the repeater, *bridge, router, gateway* and *hub*. The function carried out by each has a parallel in the OSI Reference Model.

Repeaters: Repeaters operate at the physical layer of the Reference Model. Repeaters which link two LAN segments blindly pass on all data they encounter, in both directions, between those segments. A repeater essentially acts as a signal booster. Recall from *Basics of data communications* (on page 146) that every electrical signal transmitted along a medium is subject to attenuation: it loses its definition and becomes blurred in proportion to the distance it has travelled and depending on the physical transmission medium being used. In a network, a repeater deals with frames containing data. The repeater does not have the intelligence to discriminate between the bits with a frame; it can only detect where the frame starts and ends. It then resynchronises and retransmits the frame.

The practical effect of using repeaters is to extend the network cable beyond its usual limits. For example, the normal 500 metre extent of a thick Ethernet cable might be extended using repeaters to 2 kilometres or more. A repeater provides no insulation between LAN segments: whatever it receives, it retransmits to the other segment. Neither does it perform any functions of routing or addressing between nodes on adjoining LANs. Finally, a repeater is a completely transparent device and can only be used to connect networks of identical type.

Bridges: Repeaters always link segments of local area networks; bridges can be used to link both LANs and long-distance cable systems.

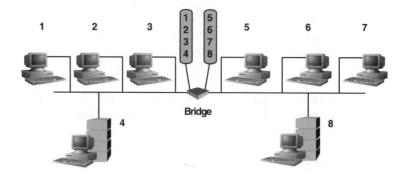

By contrast with a repeater, which passes on whatever it receives to an adjoining LAN segment, bridges discriminate among frames, blocking packets destined for nodes on the local LAN and transferring only those that are addressed to external devices.

Bridges operate at the MAC sublayer within Layer 2 of the Reference Model and are sometimes referred to as *MAC-layer bridges*. The physical media connected by a bridge can be different, for example coaxial Ethernet cable could be connected to twisted pair. But the same MAC level protocol, for example IEEE 802.3 (Ethernet) must be used on both sides. An Ethernet bridge can be used to connect Ethernet LANs, a Token Ring bridge to connect Token Ring LANs and so on. Such bridges can read the address of an Ethernet packet or Token Ring frame to determine the destination of the message. They cannot, however, look deeper into what is encapsulated in the MAC-layer frame and read, for example, encapsulated TCP/IP or ISO protocol addresses.

By transferring only those frames not addressed to nodes in the local network, bridges perform a useful service in partitioning traffic and increasing network throughput. Because bridges operate independently of protocols higher than the MAC layer, they can pass between networks LLC frames containing higher-level protocol formats, for example TCP/IP or DECnet. Networks using the same higher-level protocol can be connected with a bridge. A bridge also learns: it listens to frames as they pass through and records the addresses within adjacent networks for which it is acting as the relay. Additionally, the network manager can reprogram specific addresses to restrict what information is sent to external locations.

Bridges are categorised as local and remote. Local bridges link proximate LANs; only one is needed for that purpose. Remote bridges link LANs to thin long-distance cables in order to connect over the WAN to geographically distant networks. There must be two remote bridges to link distant LANs via a WAN. Put at its most general, whether local or remote bridges are concerned, the only function of a bridge is to transfer MAC-layer frames to a distant cable segment; it does not have the intelligence to inspect what is inside the frame or attempt routing of the data within.

Routers: Routers are more powerful than bridges. They operate at Layer 3 of the OSI Reference Model. A router is a packet switch with the ability to connect a LAN to multiple destination LANs or WANs or both. Unlike bridges, routers can read network layer addresses within, for example, TCP/IP, X.25, DECnet or SNA packets and, using this protocol-specific information, decide on the best routes for those packets.

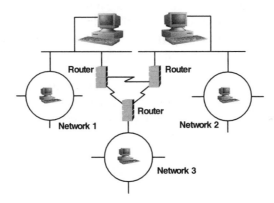

A router can connect different media, for example Ethernet and T1, but the network protocols used must be the same. Multiprotocol routers have been introduced which can route packets of several different network layer protocols, for example TCP/IP and X.25. Even so, like network layers must be connected to like.

The essential difference between a bridge and a router is this. Using a bridge, if a packet is not addressed to a node in the local LAN, the bridge 'throws it over the wall' and hopes that an adjoining LAN or cable segment will contain the destination node. In the case of a router, the packet is only forwarded if its address is known to the router as a node on a remote network.

Routers only read network packets specifically addressed to them, causing less loading on the local processor than does a bridge; they also only pass on packets known to be destined for remote addresses, so they cause less network traffic than bridges. Routers are more expensive than bridges but the differential is falling to a point where there is no reason to select a bridge in preference to a router when connecting LANs to LANs or LANs to WANs.

Gateways: Gateway is a term often used very loosely. In common use, it can mean a bridge, a router or a full-scale application-level protocol converter. Here, its meaning is taken to be the last of these.

A gateway is a protocol converter which is able to translate from one seven-layer protocol stack to another. It is used to convert all the protocols underlying an application into the protocols expected by an application running on a remote networked node. An example of actual applications connected by a gateway is that of the Internet Simple Mail Transfer Protocol (SMTP) sending mail via a gateway to the OSI X.400 mail application. The conversions needed in this case are illustrated by the diagram on page 191.

Gateways are usually implemented in software residing on a quite powerful computer system. Because of the complexity and depth of the required protocol conversions, gateways are slow and impair overall network performance.

Internet OSI mail conversion by gateway

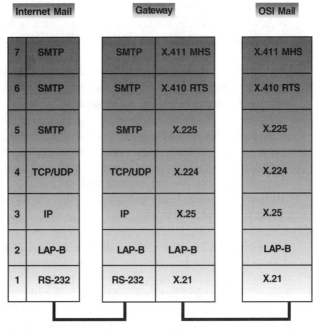

	Internet Mail	Gateway		OSI Mail
7	SMTP	SMTP	X.411 MHS	X.411 MHS
6	SMTP	SMTP	X.410 RTS	X.410 RTS
5	SMTP	SMTP	X.225	X.225
4	TCP/UDP	TCP/UDP	X.224	X.224
3	IP	IP	X.25	X.25
2	LAP-B	LAP-B	LAP-B	LAP-B
1	RS-232	RS-232	X.21	X.21

Physical Media

Intelligent hubs: The hub is the most powerful of all devices for connecting networks. It acts as a device for media connection, as a multiprotocol router and as a station for network management. The hub does the job of, and often replaces, a backbone network, connecting many network types and doing routing of packets between them.

Network interconnection with a hub

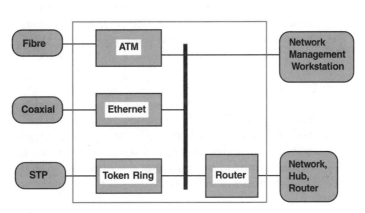

WAN protocols: X.25, Frame Relay and B-ISDN

LANs to be internetworked with other LANs may be connected to a WAN using bridges, routers or gateways. The WAN will likely be based on services provided by the PSDN such as 64Kbps, T1 or E1 media.

The conventional WAN packet-switching protocol is X.25, described briefly in the section *Basics of data communications* (on page 146). Newer alternatives include Frame Relay and B-ISDN.

X.25 protocols and products based on them are proven, reliable and stable. X.25 assumes that transmission media are unreliable and it therefore is a conservative design which numbers, acknowledges and supervises every packet transferred and requests retransmission on failure. The design leads to high reliability but needs a lot of processing power within the network.

The Frame Relay protocol is a derivative of X.25 which is simpler and does relatively little error-checking. It assumes the availability of high-quality digital and fibre-optic physical media. The protocol functions at Layer 2 of the OSI Reference Model, providing a connection-oriented service called the permanent virtual circuit (PVC). Traffic is moved from source to destination over a series of fast packet switches. Given the lack of overhead compared to X.25, the fast packet switching approach leads to high performance over T1 or E1 media and over ATM and B-ISDN networks when they become widely available.

Currently, Frame Relay is threatening the predominant position of X.25 because it is cheaper to implement and gives higher performance. X.25 implements all of the protocol functions needed to complete the three bottom layers of the OSI Reference Model, up to the Packet Layer Protocol which implements Layer 3. Frame Relay includes only the bottom and half the second layer, replacing LAP-B with LAP-D. LAP-D is the Link Access Protocol – D Channel signalling standard developed for ISDN.

Thus Frame Relay avoids much of the protocol header processing necessary for X.25. Performance achievable with Frame Relay is far higher than with X.25 given the same processing power and complexity in network nodes. Also X.25 data channels are generally limited to 64Kbps bandwidth; Frame Relay is operable up to the 2Mbps of the E1 medium and will in future be used at much higher speeds.

B-ISDN represents the 'Grand Slam' approach to integration of video, voice and data services over the public network. It is still under development and it is by no means certain that it will become the public network standard of the future. On the other hand, no current approach is so comprehensive.

The ATM cell-based protocol is the underlying transfer mechanism of B-ISDN. As has already been noted, the fixed length of ATM cells leads to very high-speed network performance. ATM switched virtual will operate at speeds of 1,000Mbps and upwards, possibly taking advantage of the higher SONET speeds. Enough bandwidth is provided, therefore, to more than meet the most demanding network applications.

Based on the common-denominator ATM cell protocol, B-ISDN will be able to support any current digital transmission protocol by decomposing packets and frames on transmission and reassembling them on delivery. Within B-ISDN, the 64Kbps B channels of narrowband ISDN might be the best medium for voice services; high bandwidth requirements can be met by T1, E1 and SONET; while Frame Relay and SMDS will also run over B-ISDN using ATM as the underlying protocol. Any LANs using ATM will also be able to access a B-ISDN network.

LAN network operating systems

Introduction

The need for stand-alone PCs to be able to share expensive peripheral devices such as printers led, in the early 1980s, to their being organised in local-area networks using technologies such as Ethernet, described in the section *Network architectures* (on page 166). It was soon also required that PCs should be able to exchange data files and share the file systems of remote computers. This led to the development of distributed file systems. A distributed file system creates the illusion that files located throughout the network are local to the user of an individual PC and its application programs. This is achieved by extension of the local operating system to a Network Operating System (NOS).

When an application program running on a stand-alone computer needs a system resource such as access to a data file, it issues a request on the operating system, in the form of a system (API) call, for retrieval of the file from the filesystem. In the case of a PC connected to a LAN, the required file may be on a remote filesystem rather than the local one. It then becomes the job of the network operating system to redirect the request for the file to the operating system of the machine where the file is resident. Filesystems distributed in the network are mapped in NOS tables local to each connected computer. A request is sent by the NOS to the server with the required mapped filesystem and the file is returned to the originator.

File retrieval by a network operating system

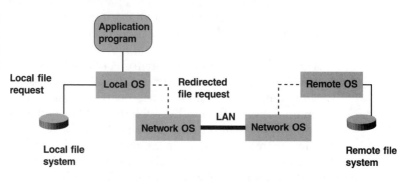

Examples of network operating systems and protocols for PC LANs include Novell NetWare, LAN Manager and NetBIOS. Distributed filesystems used with versions of the UNIX operating system are the System V Remote File Sharing (RFS) system, Sun Microsystems' Network File System (NFS), the Andrew File System (AFS) and the OSF Distributed Computing Environment (DCE). The DCE also contains many features other than the distributed filesystem capability.

The following sections briefly describe the facilities and operation of the major LAN NOSs.

Novell NetWare

NetWare, supplied by Novell Inc., is the dominant LAN NOS accounting for, by some estimates, up to 70% of the LAN market. Because of this dominance, NetWare LANs ('Novell networks') have become important components in open and client–server systems.

The NetWare NOS behaves as described in the Introduction above. Typically, the NetWare NOS and associated application programs reside on a network server connected to the LAN. This server is usually a powerful 80486- or Pentium-based PC. Also connected to the LAN can be up to 250 client systems which can be PCs running DOS or Windows; PCs running OS/2; Apple Macintoshes; workstations running UNIX; or 3270 terminals.

These clients to the NetWare server run a Novell software component, the NetWare Redirector. This intercepts requests from applications running on the client for files and other services which can only be met by the server. In a manner completely transparent to the user of the client system, the requests are redirected to and satisfied by the server. In this way, server files and application programs resident on the server are available to the client user exactly as if they were resident on that user's system.

At the physical and data-link layers, the network underlying NetWare can use Ethernet, Token Ring, T1/E1, asynchronous and other connections. The network- and transport-layer protocol software is the SPX/IPX suite, SPX ensuring reliable delivery of packets carried at the network layer by IPX. At a higher level, client users access server resources using the NetWare redirector, or requester, running under the control of the client operating system, on PCs usually DOS.

NetWare on the LAN server is organised as a System Executive and a Network Loadable Module (NLM) Bus. Network applications, which run on the server and can be used from client systems, are written as NLMs which access the server via the bus. Applications written as NLMs can be considered in two categories: application facilities provided by the NetWare environment; and popular third-party application software ported to NetWare.

Functions carried out by NLMs supplied with NetWare include the following:

- ▶ Device drivers
- ▶ Communication and mail gateways
- ▶ Network management and security
- ▶ Print server, including spooling and queueing services
- ▶ Back-end client–server database, Btrieve
- ▶ NFS shared filesystems

Netware protocols with DOS
applications

Application			
Presentation	DOS Shell	DOS Requester	
Session			
Transport	SPX (Sequenced Packet Exchange)		
Network	IPX (Internet Packet Exchange)		
Data Link	Link Support Layer Open Data Link Interface (ODI)		
	802.3	802.5	X.25
Physical	Co-axial	STP	T1/E1

NetWare communications services are available from all LAN clients. The server acts as a bridge, router or gateway to external LANs and WANs. Both the TCP/IP and OSI WAN protocol sets (see *Transmission Control Protocol/Internet Protocol (TCP/IP)* (on page 201) and *Open Systems Interconnection (OSI)* (on page 215)) are supported, the latter with Transport Protocols TP0 and TP4. At the middleware level (see *Middleware* (on page 230) and *Distributed system models* (on page 238)), the Transport Layer Interface, Remote Procedure Call and Sockets are all supported. Since its initial release in the early 1980s, there have been three major versions of NetWare, versions 2, 3 and 4. Version 4, often called 4.X, is current, but a large number of LANs still exist which run the earlier software. Characteristics of the three versions are summarised below:

NetWare 2.x

- ▸ Designed for 80286-based PC clients
- ▸ Up to 100 users
- ▸ Files up to 255MB in size
- ▸ Up to 32GB of disk storage
- ▸ Up to 1,000 files concurrently open
- ▸ NetBIOS API and emulation
- ▸ Not peer-to-peer (clients cannot share resources)
- ▸ Good security mechanisms

NetWare 3.x

- Designed for 80386-based PC clients
- Peer-to-Peer
- Up to 250 users
- Files up to 4GB in size, spread across multiple disk volumes
- Up to 100,000 concurrently open files
- Security auditing
- Encrypted backups
- Access multiple servers directly, and transparently to the client, using NetWare Naming Service

NetWare 4.x

- NetWare Directory Services, using X.500 naming conventions
- Improved memory protection for applications on server
- Larger IPX packets, resulting in higher network throughput
- Improved network administration facilities
- Extended security auditing
- Memory allocation for applications running on servers no longer in fixed segments

UnixWare

UnixWare is an enhanced version of the UNIX System V (SVR4.2) operating system and environment, marketed by Univel. UnixWare incorporates both the Motif and Open Look GUIs as standard. It additionally provides the MoOLIT (*Motif Open Look Intrinsics Toolkit*), a set of software functions based on the X Windows 'intrinsic' facilities, which makes it possible to run application software through either of the GUIs.

UnixWare integrates UNIX and its TCP/IP-based communications with LANs running Novell Netware and the IPX/SPX protocols. This improves the already strong networking capability of UNIX systems and facilitates their use as components in client–server configurations. Because both the TCP/IP and IPX/SPX protocol suites run concurrently, a NetWare client can log in to a UnixWare host, while a UnixWare user has full access to a NetWare server. UnixWare supports the following integration with Novell NetWare LANs:

> ▸ DOS command-line and Windows support
> ▸ Access to NetWare printers
> ▸ The ability to run DOS applications resident on the LAN
> ▸ Transparent file access to NetWare servers
> ▸ File transfer to and from NetWare servers

The integration is achieved using two built-in software suites: NetWare NFS and NetWare FLeX/IP. NetWare NFS is a suite of NLMs. It makes NetWare file volumes available as filesystems for NFS mounting by UnixWare clients. Thus NFS clients running under UnixWare gain transparent access to LAN-resident NetWare files. In addition to acting as an NFS server, NetWare NFS includes these services:

> ▸ File Transfer Protocol (FTP) server
> ▸ UNIX to NetWare print service
> ▸ NetWare to UNIX print gateway
> ▸ Lock Manager daemon (monitor program)
> ▸ Status daemon
> ▸ Remote X Windows console

FLeX/IP is used where the main requirement is bidirectional printing between UnixWare and NetWare environments. It does not contain the NFS shared-filesystem portion of NetWare NFS; otherwise it is the same.

Other LAN network operating systems

Most NetWare installations up to Version 3.X were of small LANs, linking relatively few PCs in office environments. Two viable alternative NOSs are LAN Manager, supplied in different forms by Microsoft, IBM and a number of other companies, and Banyan Systems' VINES (VIrtual NEtworking System). Both LAN Manager and VINES maintain their file servers on computers running multitasking operating systems: OS/2 in the case of LAN Manager and a special version of UNIX for VINES. This provides advantages in performance and in connectivity with disparate external networks and computer systems.

The diagram following shows the approximate parallel which can be drawn between the Reference Model and the LAN Manager and VINES NOSs.

NetWare protocols with DOS applications

OSI		LAN Manager	VINES
Application		Services: File, Print, Comms... OS/2 named pipes	Services: File, Print, Comms... NETBIOS
Presentation		LAN Manager Core Protocols	VINES Matchmaker Data Type
Session		NETBIOS Interface	Matchmaker RPC
Transport		NETBIOS Extended User Interface (NetBEUI)	IPC/SPP
Network			VINES IP Protocols
Data Link		Network Driver Interface Specification (NDIS) Driver or PC/TCP Packet Driver	
Physical		Network Interface Card for Ethernet, Token Ring...	

LAN Manager

LAN Manager was jointly developed in the late 1980s by Microsoft and 3Com as a potential competitor to NetWare. Many other companies, including Digital Equipment Corporation, IBM, HP and AT&T back the product and supply their own version.

LAN Manager was first introduced by 3Com in 1988 and was called 3+Open LAN Manager 1.0. Its performance fell short of that yielded by NetWare 2.X and it was only when version 2.1 of the product was released in 1992 that real competition between LAN Manager and NetWare began.

IBM's version of LAN Manager is called LAN Server and that of Digital Equipment Corporation is named Pathworks. At the time of original LAN Manager development, IBM and Microsoft were still collaborating on development of early versions of OS/2; perhaps because of this, the file server in a LAN Manager system must run OS/2 while the clients connected to the LAN can be PCs running either OS/2 or the more common DOS/Windows combination.

Because of OS/2, the file server must be powerful; anything less than an 80486-based PC is impractical. On the other hand, the multitasking characteristics of OS/2 and its High-Performance File System (HPFS) give good performance. The file server can run both network functions and OS/2 applications concurrently. A LAN Manager network can have multiple servers, any of which can be used as gateways to NetWare, TCP/IP or SNA networks.

VINES

Banyan VINES uses as an underlying operating system on its file servers a modified version of UNIX – SVR3.2.1 – which performs symmetrical multiprocessing (SMP, see *Operating systems* on page 72). A file server, perhaps an 80486-based PC can have up to eight processors, and the load of network processing is evenly spread out among them. This contrasts with less-powerful asymmetric multiprocessing (ASMP), where each processor is assigned, and can only handle, specific types of work. While eight processors in a symmetric arrangement never yield an eightfold increase in performance, thry do improve it significantly.

SMP requires that UNIX, which is fundamentally a uniprocessor system, must have its kernel modified so that it can keep track of simultaneous activities on each of the processors. Having a special version of UNIX requires that Banyan keep it up to date in other respects and continue to port it to the systems of many suppliers.

On VINES networks, the underlying UNIX is not visible to end-users or usable directly by application software. The UNIX foundation provides both powerful multitasking on servers and good connectivity over WANs to many other types of network and protocol.

Many servers can be configured in a VINES network and a scheme called Global Naming Services, similar to Domain Name Services (see *Network architectures* (on page 166) and *Transmission Control Protocol / Internet Protocol (TCP/IP)*, below), is used to access resources on widely-separated servers. This directory service is transparent to client systems: to them, all the resources needed appear to be on the local file server.

VINES file servers were among the first to provide relational databases using SQL access. They can be internetworked with almost all other network types over X.25, TCP/IP and Token Ring/SNA connections. VINES servers can also reach the IBM mainframe environments using 3174 terminal concentrators and 3725/3745 front-end processors.

Transmission Control Protocol/Internet Protocol (TCP/IP)

Introduction

TCP/IP, collectively also referred to as the *Internet protocols*, is a standard suite of open protocols which allow communication between different types of computers in a multinode network. Applications for which TCP/IP is used include file transfer, electronic mail, remote login from a local system to a distant one and network management. Unlike the protocols underlying the network operating systems described in the last section, TCP/IP can be used either as a LAN protocol or as a WAN protocol to internetwork LANs. The TCP/IP protocols predate the 1977 OSI Reference Model and are in more widespread use than the equivalent OSI protocols, which are dealt with in *Open Systems Interconnection (OSI)* (on page 215).

The TCP/IP suite is supplied as standard with all major versions of the UNIX operating system. Many PC-based TCP/IP products are available for the DOS/Windows environments. The protocol grew up in a research and university setting and is the basis of the Internet, the world's largest public network. These factors together have helped ensure very wide acceptance of TCP/IP, to the point where it is the *lingua franca* of today's LAN/WAN backbone protocols.

In this section, 'Internet' with upper-case first letter denotes the public network referred to above; 'internet' can mean any arrangement of connected networks.

The OSI Reference Model was defined before protocols to realise the various layers of the model existed. With TCP/IP, the opposite is the case; the protocol suite came into being in the mid-1970s as a result of a DoD project to implement a decentralised WAN protocol which would allow the network to be theoretically survivable in the event of a local nuclear war. The Defense Advanced Research Projects Agency (DARPA) originated the ARPANET in the early 1970s as the first wide area packet switching network. TCP/IP was not, at the beginning, used in the ARPANET but the early ARPANET protocols began to be replaced by TCP/IP in 1980 and, in January 1983, DARPA specified that all computers attached to the ARPANET had to use TCP/IP. Around the same time, DARPA funded integration of TCP/IP with the version of UNIX developed by the University of California at Berkeley. The resulting UNIX version was BSD 4.2. DARPA also commissioned several large computer system vendors, including IBM and Sperry (now Unisys), to provide TCP/IP with mainframe systems purchased by the United States Government. TCP/IP made the ARPANET viable on a nationwide basis in the U.S.A.; the network became the backbone of the Internet which succeeded it.

The ARPANET was finally dissolved in 1990, having served for many years as the test vehicle on which TCP/IP was refined and improved. One of the strengths of TCP/IP is in linking very different types of computers. It had to have this ability to cater for the diverse systems connected to the ARPANET. DARPA also entertained suggestions from many quarters for the development of TCP/IP; this democratic approach has also contributed to the success of the protocol.

In 1984, the DoD adopted TCP/IP as its official networking standard. In doing so, as the world's largest user of computers, the DoD made TCP/IP an international *de facto* standard and created a large market for software products implementing the protocol. Currently, TCP/IP ranks second in worldwide use behind SNA (see *Systems Network Architecture (SNA)* on page 222) as a long-haul communications protocol but, not being mainframe-based, is in use on a far wider variety of systems. The official OSI protocols, by comparison, lag badly, only enjoying any widespread use in Europe. Organisations often adopt TCP/IP for some or all of the following reasons:

- ▸ To connect LANs and WANs
- ▸ To connect a computer or network to the Internet
- ▸ To link heterogeneous computer systems
- ▸ To connect remote host computers
- ▸ To use the application services provided with TCP/IP including File Transfer Protocol (FTP); the TELNET remote login facility; electronic mail and directory services

Other reasons for the adoption of TCP/IP are that implementations are available inexpensively, often bundled with standard operating systems; and that specifications for the TCP/IP protocols are in the public domain.

Transport and network protocols

The Transmission Control Protocol (TCP) part of TCP/IP provides connection-oriented (reliable) network services to TCP/IP applications such as FTP. It operates approximately at Layer 4 of the OSI Reference Model, ensuring orderly, end-to-end, error-free transfer of packets (*datagrams*) defined by Layer 3. TCP software runs on networked systems, establishes connections between them, manages the flow of data and replaces any missing data blocks. TCP is called a 'reliable stream' service. TCP presents to applications above it a number of well-defined APIs. These are used by applications to access the network without regard for what happens at the lower protocol layers.

Also occupying approximately Layer 4 is the User Datagram Protocol (UDP), a more rudimentary protocol than TCP, which provides connectionless (unreliable) transport services typically used by applications which send isolated messages to each other, such as those making sporadic database queries. The underlying datagrams are transferred without the extensive checking and error-correction facilities provided by TCP. UDP software running on a networked system specifies the address of an application to which a datagram is delivered when it reaches the network address used by the Internet Protocol.

The Internet Protocol (IP) underlies both TCP and UDP and is the protocol which governs connectionless transfer of packets between systems and subnetworks within the TCP/IP network. These packets, or datagrams, use an internet address (see 'IP Addresses' below) uniquely to identify the destination system. The IP layer describes connectivity over the network, while TCP ensures that the data being transferred is correct. UDP, the opposite of TCP in terms of reliability, is above IP but provides few extra services.

The IP layer, implemented in software, routes datagrams through the network. The datagrams contain the addresses of the source and destination nodes. Routers, containing the IP software (called variously gateways, *internet routers* and *TCP/IP routers*), choose from many available paths when directing a datagram across the network. The path for an indirect transmission begins with the first router, which decides the destination for the next hop. The router at that destination repeats the process and so on until the datagram is delivered. The format of the addresses contained in the datagram allows a router to find the address of the adjoining network segment (subnetwork). Address tables on a router are simplified by only having to store the addresses of other subnets and the routers on those subnets and not the address of every end node on the greater network.

Client–server networks

Diverse types of computer, connected with appropriate LAN adapter cards, can communicate over Ethernet and Token Ring LANs using TCP/IP. To connect a LAN running TCP/IP to a WAN using a long-distance transmission scheme such as X.25 packet-switching, an X.25 gateway is provided from the LAN to the WAN. On the LAN, the TCP/IP transmission is carried by Ethernet or Token Ring protocols while it rides over X.25 on the WAN.

Once implemented, a TCP/IP-based LAN/WAN architecture allows client systems (often PCs) to access the resources of remote servers (for example mainframes and powerful workstations running UNIX). The same services are available to all systems on the network. They include:

- Remote login
- File transfer
- Electronic mail
- Use of shared remote file systems
- Execution of tasks on remote systems

Internet governing bodies

DARPA was the original organising body that funded TCP/IP and Internet development. The Internet Society (ISOC), formed in 1992, is an international administrative body for the Internet which defines and publishes technical, procedural and operational standards and policies. The Internet Activities Board (IAB), appointed by ISOC, is responsible for setting the technical direction and defining the standards to be used on the Internet. The IAB was originally set up by DARPA to encourage exchange of information between those involved in Internet research but in 1992 was placed under the aegis of ISOC. It oversees the Internet Engineering Task Force (IETF) and the Internet Research Task Force (IRTF). The IETF is concerned with resolving engineering problems associated with the implementation of Internet protocols while the IRTF carries out longer-term research work in information science and networking technology.

Internet protocols and standards start life as requests for comments (RFCs) which are submitted to the IAB, the IETF and the Internet community for examination and approval. Not all RFCs are accepted by the IAB. Those that are have become known as the Internet protocols. Although TCP/IP only explicitly refers to the transport and network layer protocols, the Internet protocol stack contains many more protocols and applications. The more important ones are listed and described later in this section.

RFCs are published by the IAB and may be obtained from the Network Information Center (NIC), which also administers and issues Internet addresses.

Integration with NetWare and UNIX

The Internet is, as we have seen, the world's largest public network. The predominant LAN operating system is Novell NetWare, running the SPX/IPX protocols. A number of ways have been defined for connecting TCP/IP and NetWare networks, including SPX/IPX tunnelling and Novell's NetWare IP, which allows NetWare users to send data over TCP/IP without using the IPX protocol.

Univel's implementation of UNIX SVR4.2 is UnixWare. UnixWare also provides full network integration of UNIX and its TCP/IP-based communications with LANs running Novell NetWare and the SPX/IPX protocols. This improves the networking capability of UNIX systems and facilitates their use as components in client–server configurations. Because both the TCP/IP and SPX/IPX protocol suites run concurrently, a NetWare client can log in to a UnixWare host, while a UnixWare user has full access to a NetWare server.

Mapping to the OSI model

The TCP/IP stack architecture devised by DARPA predates the OSI Reference Model and does not conform exactly to it. It is close enough, however, for an equivalence to be illustrated as shown in the diagram below.

There are more than 100 protocols in the TCP/IP suite; only a subset consisting of the most important ones is shown here along with the RFC numbers used when they were originated. The Application/Process layer specifies applications supplied with the TCP/IP suite which use the underlying internet and network protocols.

OSI and
Internet
protocol
mapping

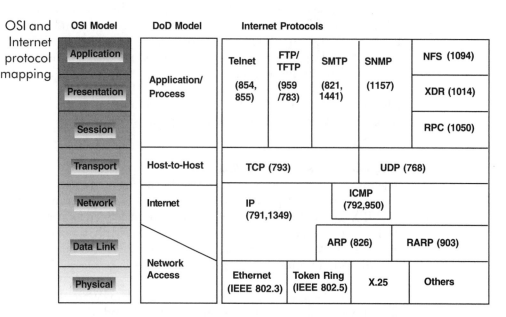

OSI Model	DoD Model	Internet Protocols				
Application	Application/ Process	Telnet (854, 855)	FTP/ TFTP (959 /783)	SMTP (821, 1441)	SNMP (1157)	NFS (1094)
Presentation						XDR (1014)
Session						RPC (1050)
Transport	Host-to-Host	TCP (793)			UDP (768)	
Network	Internet	IP (791,1349)		ICMP (792,950)		
Data Link				ARP (826)		RARP (903)
Physical	Network Access	Ethernet (IEEE 802.3)	Token Ring (IEEE 802.5)	X.25		Others

These applications are described in 'TCP/IP Applications' below. A summary of the function of each of the underlying protocols follows:

- ▶ *Transmission Control Protocol (TCP):* the transport layer protocol responsible for reliable end-to-end delivery of messages. It provides a reliable connection-oriented service and uses IP to deliver its datagrams

- ▶ *User Datagram Protocol (UDP):* routes datagrams across the network on a store-and-forward basis. Provides a relatively unreliable connectionless service using IP as the network protocol

- ▶ *Internet Control Message Protocol (ICMP):* records error and control information generated by TCP/IP software and notifies concerned parties about errors which occur in transmission. ICMP enables hosts and routers to exchange information about the state of the network so that, for example, the most efficient route can be used. ICMP data is transmitted within IP datagrams

- ▶ *Internet Protocol (IP):* provides a datagram (packet) delivery service for TCP, UDP and ICMP. IP is a connectionless protocol. TCP can alternatively use at the network layer connection-oriented protocols such as X.25 and Frame Relay

▶ *Address Resolution Protocol (ARP):* maps an internet address to an underlying hardware address such as Ethernet

▶ *Reverse Address Resolution Protocol (RARP):* the complement of ARP; maps a hardware address such as Ethernet to an internet address

The operation of the TCP, UDP and IP protocols is described in the Introduction above. The Internet Protocol, including its addressing and naming schemes, and routing protocols, is examined further here.

IP addressing

The Internet Protocol requires that a unique address be assigned to every device on the network. This includes routers, also called internet gateways. Two layers of address information make up a TCP/IP address. At the TCP (Transport) Layer, the address is a port ID identifying the application program running on the system (also variously called node, device, host or server) connected to the network. This is a 48-bit encoding, of which 16 bits identify the application process and the remaining 32 bits constitute the internet address.

IP addresses contain four bytes of routing information, consisting of a network ID and a host ID. The host ID identifies the destination system on the network, while the network ID provides routing information. IP addresses take the form of four numbers separated by three dots, for example:

194.17.10.2

The IP network address is 194.17.10 and the IP host address – the address of the destination system connect to the network – is 2. All systems on the same network must have different host addresses and the same network address. Routers also have internet addresses. All networks linked by a particular router must have different network addresses and the router's host ID must be unique for each connected network.

There are five classes of internet address: A, B, C, D and E. All these address classes have 32 bits, but use different numbers of bits from within the 32 to specify the host and network IDs. Class D is for broadcast use across the internet, while class E is for experimental and future uses by the U.S.A. National Science Foundation (NSF). Classes A, B and C are the IP address classes most often used by organisations for TCP/IP access. The characteristics of these classes are summarised in the following table:

Class	Nodes	Initial bits	Starting address
A	16,777,216	0xxx	0–127
B	65,536	10xx	128–191
C	256	110x	192–223

The form of internet addresses for all the classes is the same but the individual fields mean different things for each class.

Class A networks are indicated by the first bit of the address being '0'. The next seven bits form the network address with the remaining three fields used for the addresses of systems on the network. This form of addressing allows a small number of networks (127) with a very large number of systems: $256 \times 256 \times 256$ or 16,777,216. An example of a Class A internet address is **20.0.0.51**.

Class B internet addresses have their first two bits set to '10'. The first two fields are used for the network address; the last two for the addresses of systems on the network. 64×256 (16,384) networks and 256×256 (65,536) systems may be configured. An example of a Class B internet address is **128.10.2.1**.

Class C internet addresses have their first three bits set to '110'. The first three fields are used for the network address; the last for the addresses of systems on the network. This scheme allows a huge number of rather small (up to 256 systems) networks. The vast majority of internet addresses are of Class C. An example of a Class C internet address is **197.13.4.2**. Assuming that a Class C network is being configured, the administrator assigns each of the systems in the local network an address with the first three fields the same and the last field unique.

Although large, the number of addresses provided by the IP addressing scheme is finite. With the recent explosive growth in participation in the Internet, it has become clear that the addresses will quickly be exhausted. At the time of writing, the addressing scheme is being revised to expand the number of available addresses. For most network users, the IP address is hidden by the fully-qualified domain name defined by the Domain Name Service:

```
lab.research.widgetco
```

The DNS is the Internet's directory service and provides for mapping the symbolic names, based on network domains, to their IP address equivalents.

IP routing

When an internet router forwards an IP datagram in the network, it uses tables of routing information in deciding the next destination. Routers exchange information to keep their routing tables current. Routers must be aware of addition or deletion of networks and routers in the internet as well as failures which make part of the network inaccessible. There are no standard routing protocols but several popular ones have been implemented:

► *Routing Information Protocol (RIP):* the most popular of the internet routing protocols; it was developed at the University of California at Berkeley and is included as part of the TCP/IP protocol suite

► *Interior Gateway Routing Protocol (IGRP):* improves on RIP in supporting larger networks with better routing and faster re-routing around failed links

► *Open Shortest Path First (OSPF):* developed by the IETF as a replacement for RIP and available over the Internet

TCP/IP applications

The set of TCP/IP applications shown in the mapping of the TCP/IP suite to the OSI Reference Model are not strictly part of the TCP/IP suite of communications protocols. Rather they are utilities supplied with popular computing environments, including UNIX, which make calls on the APIs presented by the TCP and UDP transport protocols.

TCP/IP APIs

There are several popular APIs which application programs may call to access remote computers and networks using the TCP/IP protocols. Three of the most important are:

- ▸ Sockets
- ▸ Transport Layer Interface (TLI)
- ▸ Remote Procedure Call (RPC)

Sockets originated with BSD UNIX and has been implemented on many other types of system including, importantly, for the DOS/ Windows combination as Windows Sockets. A socket is an abstraction representing an endpoint of communication. Application programs request the host operating system to create a socket when they want access to the network. The system returns a number, similar to a file descriptor, which the application then uses as its handle on the network connection.

Sockets provide both TCP and UDP access. Applications select from a number of system calls including *listen* and *accept* to wait for and establish a network connection; *read* and *write* for exchanging data; and *close* to terminate the connection.

Less popular than sockets but still important because it is supplied with UNIX SVR4 is the Transport Layer Interface (TLI). TLI uses the underlying Streams mechanism which provides a bidirectional, full-duplex, connection between an application process and a device driver. TLI is a set of user-callable C-language functions which implement the *transport endpoint* and provide an interface to the *transport provider*. The endpoints are similar to sockets, while the provider is a set of software routines on the host computer which provides communications support for application processes. The application calls the TLI to access these routines and gain network access. The transport provider software need not necessarily be for TCP/IP; other network protocol suites are also supported.

The Remote Procedure Call interface is used by important applications such as the Network File System (NFS) originated by Sun Microsystems Inc. and supplied with all major UNIX versions. RPC is a Session Layer protocol, often classified as middleware, and as such is described in *Middleware* (on page 230). NFS allows a network user to mount a file system on a remote computer and access the files as if they were resident on the local system. External Data Representation (XDR) is a machine-independent standard for the description and encoding of data and is used by RPC to transfer arbitrary data between networked systems of different internal architectures. RPC can be executed over either TCP or UDP, but UDP is more common since RPC applications are usually transaction-oriented, involving transfer of relatively small (less than 4KB) volumes of data at one time.

TCP/IP applications

The set of standard applications supplied with the TCP/IP suite and identified in the Reference Model mapping is described below. In summary, they are:

- TELNET
- File Transfer Protocol (FTP)
- Trivial File Transfer Protocol (TFTP)
- Simple Mail Transfer Protocol (SMTP)
- Simple Network Management Protocol (SNMP)
- Network File System (NFS)

Software developers at the University of California at Berkeley, which was funded by DARPA to integrate the TCP/IP protocols with UNIX, also developed their own set of utilities for file transfer, remote login and other services. These are collectively known as the 'r*' (as in 'remote') commands and they all use TCP for end-to-end network connection. The commands are restricted to use with UNIX, unlike FTP and the other TCP/IP applications, which can be used with other types of system including DOS/Windows PCs. The more important 'r*' commands are listed below, with the TCP/IP application closest in functionality (if any) suffixed in parentheses:

- 'rlogin':remote login (TELNET)

- 'rcp':remote file copy (FTP)

- 'rsh':remote shell, execute commands on a remote system

- 'ruptime':manage computers in a network (SMTP)

- 'rwho':list users signed on to a network (SMTP)

The TCP/IP applications are in more widespread use than their 'r*' equivalents and they are briefly described below.

TELNET

TELNET provides access, in the form of a terminal session, to a remote computer connected to the network. TELNET accommodates equipment of different vendors so that a client user logged in to a networked system can remotely log in to any other host on the network.

TELNET uses the underlying Virtual Terminal Protocol (VTP) which transfers characters typed at the client system over the TCP/IP connection to the remote host and maps the characters to and from an intermediate format called the Network Virtual Terminal (NVT). VTP client and server software at either end of the connection shields the application running on the server from having to know the characteristics of the client terminal. Each side converts characters to and from the NVT format and the client user only sees a transparent login session to the remote host, regardless of its type. TELNET is designed for use with character-based terminals but does not preclude future development to support block-mode and graphics terminals. TELNET is preferred to 'rlogin' for use with networks of heterogeneous systems.

FTP

FTP provides a simple mechanism for transferring files between remote networked systems. To use FTP, the command 'ftp' is generally entered at the prompt provided by whatever operating system is in use on the client system. By additionally supplying identification and password information, the user establishes a connection – with an underlying virtual circuit using TCP – with the remote system.

FTP makes available to the user a number of commands which allow files to be exchanged with the remote host, as well as to be listed, renamed and deleted. Because an FTP session is established with the server, the client user can move among directories. FTP stops short of providing a full remote login service and any file or directory access allowed the client is subject to access permissions maintained at the server side. FTP has no knowledge of the type of file being transferred; the user is required to specify either ASCII or binary.

With some FTP services, notably on the Internet, it is desirable for a given host to provide restricted access to general, unidentified clients. This is achieved by means of anonymous FTP. A casual user can log in to a remote host with the user name 'anonymous' and the password 'guest'. The user than has access to public files on the server. Availability of anonymous FTP has been important in popularising use of the Internet.

TFTP

In the same way as FTP, TFTP allows exchange with remote networked systems of text and binary files. Unlike FTP, it does not perform user authentication, uses a connectionless UDP link between client and server systems and has a more restricted command set. Because it uses a connectionless underlying protocol, the client user does not establish a session on the server in the same way as with FTP. With FTP, the TCP protocol assures reliability of transmission; TFTP is itself responsible for reliability using algorithms of its own including time monitoring and file retransmission. Because of its relative lack of capability, TFTP is rarely used in preference to FTP. Its most common application is being implemented in read-only memory (ROM) and used to load server programs and fonts in X Windows terminals and bootstrap diskless workstations.

SMTP
SMTP is, eponymously, a simple protocol for transfer of interpersonal mail messages between users on a distributed TCP/IP network. Its operation is similar in some respects to that of FTP. SMTP has become popular because of its rudimentary nature. It only allows transmission of ASCII data: telex, fax, binary data and non-English character sets are excluded.

SMTP is implemented by a mailer program – on UNIX systems, the 'sendmail' program – which transfers mail messages to the next system on the route to their destination. A front-end application is also provided for composing, editing and browsing mail messages to be processed by the mailer. The addressing scheme used for the destination system is that of the Domain Name Service.

SNMP
TELNET, FTP, TFTP and SMTP are all concerned with providing services to users connected to a network. SNMP is concerned with management of all the communication protocols within each network host as well as all the items of networking equipment – routers, bridges, repeaters and so on – which help provide those services.

In distributed computing and client–server architectures, there is a need for central access to information about resources on the network. With this information, a network manager is in a position to trouble-shoot problems on the network from a central location as well as to optimise performance; configure and manage network devices and their associated names; and implement security and accounting procedures.

SNMP is a network management protocol which originated in the Internet community as a means of managing TCP/IP and Ethernet networks. The devices in a SNMP-managed network are referred to as *managed objects*. Associated with each managed object is a set of management information including variables which can be read or written, over the network, by the network manager. The protocol underlying SNMP which enables the network manager to find the status of managed objects is ICMP.

Management information associated with devices on the network is kept at the network manager station in a Management Information Base (MIB). The network manager can read the information in the MIB. If necessary, in response to a fault on the network or a perform-ance bottleneck, the network manager can specify changes, from the central location of the network manager station, to the configuration of the network.

MIB objects are named with a hierarchical naming sequence defined with a language called Abstract Syntax Notation 1 (ASN.1), which is part of the OSI Reference Model, and which also defines the formats of packets exchanged by the network management protocol.

The role of SNMP is to enable the network manager station to exchange messages with the management processes running in the managed objects. These processes are written specially to perform management and configuration functions for the devices in which they reside. SNMP is easy to use, uses less resources than its OSI equivalent, the Common Management Information Protocol (CMIP), is stable and is widely available in product form. The weaknesses of SNMP include poor security and documentation and the fact that a number of incompatible product variants have appeared.

NFS

The Network File System (NFS) was introduced in 1985 by Sun Microsystems Inc. and forms the basis of most implementations of distributed filesystems using UNIX and other system types. The essence of NFS is that a client system can 'mount' a filesystem resident on a remote host and a user on the client can access that filesystem without being aware that it is remote. The filesystem can be concurrently shared by several clients.

NFS runs on a client system and intercepts operating system requests for file services. If a request is for a file which has been mounted from a remote system, the remote system is asked for that file. Systems running

NFS can act as both client and server in peer-to-peer operation: connected systems can effectively exchange filesystems while autonomously running their own applications. NFS uses the RPC and XDR mechanisms (see *Middleware* on page 230) to provide file services. An alternative to NFS, but restricted to use among systems running UNIX, is Remote File Service (RFS) introduced by AT&T in 1986. RFS hasn't gained the same wide acceptance as NFS, which is now predominant.

Open Systems Interconnection (OSI)

Introduction

The OSI Reference Model is a framework describing the natural layering of functions within communication software systems. The Reference Model was specified before actual protocols to fill it out had been defined. Since that time, many protocols for each of the seven layers have been agreed and have become international standards.

The adoption of multiple protocols per layer is deliberate: depending on the application for which communications software is being designed, one protocol or another will be more or less suitable. A case in point which we have already seen is that connection-oriented transport and network layer protocols suit file transfer applications better than do the connectionless equivalents. The protocols selected for an application constitute an *open systems interconnection profile* (OSIP); as a consequence, both the U.S.A. and U.K. Governments have selected protocols suiting their needs which are referred to as GOSIPs.

Three major international bodies, the ISO, IEEE and CCITT, are concerned with defining standards and recommendations for data communications. Broadly, the CCITT makes recommendations for rules governing connection of equipment to public communication networks including the PSTN (the 'V' standards), PSDN (the 'X' standards) and ISDN (the 'I' standards). ISO and IEEE on the other hand set standards for use by computer manufacturers and vendors in local- and metropolitan-area networks.

The DARPA Internet protocol suite, including TCP/IP, evolved outside the context of these international bodies but development of protocols and standards continues in parallel with significant overlap in functionality. The OSI protocols tend to be comprehensive, full-featured, realisations of the Reference Model layers, while the Internet protocols are simpler but more restricted in application.

Comprehensiveness means complexity: achieving consensus in the adoption of OSI protocols is a slow process; and development of software products implementing the protocols is difficult and expensive. The complexity of the OSI protocols relative to their Internet counterparts means that many more software implementations of Internet protocols are available than is true for their OSI counterparts. This fact itself promotes the market acceptability of the Internet protocols.

One of the few OSI protocols which has proven popular and for which there are many actual implementations is the X.400 Message Handling System (MHS). Broadly, this is equivalent to the SMTP application in the Internet stack. But SMTP cannot handle international character sets or character codes other than ASCII, while X.400 can, with consequent increase in relative complexity. In practice, X.400 is tending to be adopted as a backbone technology, providing connection between other, proprietary, mail systems using protocol gateways.

The OSI protocols represent undoubtedly the most complete integrated set of specifications available, but the popularity of the Internet and mainframe (see *Systems Network Architecture (SNA)* on page 222) communications facilities has resulted in a situation where it is unlikely that OSI will ever be the victor in the market. Also, the OSI protocols are not widely being implemented in aggregate; instead, attractive OSI standards, such as X.400, are adopted by users to co-exist with other technologies. Finally, OSI has since its inception tended to be more popular in Europe than in North America, where the U.S. GOSIP specification is being resisted and the Internet protocols are preferred.

Description

In OSI data communications, peer-to-peer communications is by means of exchange of Protocol Data Units (PDUs). PDUs are equivalent in purpose to the Internet datagram. The OSI physical layer and the MAC sublayer of the data link layer are usually implemented as hardware devices such as bridges. Protocols occupying the higher layers are generally implemented in software.

As with the IP layer in the Internet stack, the OSI Network layer is concerned with routing information in PDUs between network nodes, independently of the network's topology and of the physical media used. Unlike IP, OSI Layer 3 provides protocols implementing both connection-oriented (CONS) and connectionless (CLNS) services.

Layer 4 of the OSI model ensures reliable end-to-end exchange of messages across the network. Again, both connection-oriented transport service (COTS) and connectionless transport service (CLTS) protocols are defined within ISO 8073. The COTS is further subdivided in five parts, or *transport classes*, Transport Protocol zero (TP0) to TP4. If the underlying network is inherently unreliable TP4 is used; on modern reliable network media, one of the lower classes would be suitable. TP4 provides a level of transmission checking and error-correction similar to that provided by TCP in the Internet suite. Although the two protocols have similar designs, they are not compatible.

The Session layer protocols are responsible for establishing, containing and maintaining sessions between two network nodes. Layer 6 (the Presentation layer) ensures that data is presented correctly on reception, taking account of the display conventions used at the receiving station.

Mostly, the end-user is not aware of the existence of protocols between layers 1 and 6; all that is visible is the Layer 7 application. A number of specifications for OSI applications are provided. They, along with a subset of the lower-level protocols, are listed by layer in the following diagram and the commonly-used ones are briefly described in 'OSI Applications' below.

OSI applications

The following layer 7 applications specified by OSI are described in summary in this section:

- ► X.400 Message Handling Service (MHS)
- ► X.500 Directory Service (DS)
- ► File Transfer Access Method (FTAM)
- ► Common Management Information Protocol (CMIP)

	ISO Standards		CCITT Recommendations
		Application	
7	ISO 8571 File Transfer Access Method ISO 9040/1 Virtual Terminal ISO 9579 Remote Database Access ISO 10026 Distributed Transaction Processing ISO 8831/2 Job Transfer Access & Management ISO 8649 Common Application Service Elements		Common Management Information Protocol *(CMIP; ISO 9595/6; CCITT X.710, X.711)* Inter-Personal Messaging *(IPM; ISO 10021-7; CCITT X.420)* Message Handling System *(MHS; ISO 10021-1; CCITT X.400)* MHS Message Store (CCITT X.413; ISO 10021-5) EDI Messaging System over X.400 (CCITT X.435) Directory Services (DS; ISO 9594-1; CCITT X.500)
6	Connection-Oriented Presentation Service ISO 8822/3/4/5	**Presentation**	Presentation Service for CCITT Applications X.216, X.226
5	Connection-Oriented Session Service ISO 8326, ISO 8327	**Session**	Session Service Definition for CCITT Applications X.215, X.225
4	Transport Layer Protocol Specification COTS/CLTS ISO 8073 (TP 0-4)	**Transport**	Transport Service Definition for CCITT Applications X.214, X.224
3	Connectionless-Mode Network Service (CLNS) ISO 8473 Connection-Oriented Network Service (CONS) ISO 8208	**Network**	Network Service Definition for CCITT Applications X.213 - X.25
2	Logical Link Control (LLC) ISO 8802.2 (IEEE 802.2)	**Data Link**	Data Link Service Definition for CCITT Applications X.212, X.222
1	Ethernet ┊ Token Bus ISO 8802.3 ┊ ISO 8802.4 (IEEE 802.3) ┊ (IEEE 802.4) Token Ring ┊ MAN ISO 8802.5 ┊ ISO 8802.6 (IEEE 802.5)┊ (IEEE 802.6)	**Physical**	Physical layer Interface for X.25 X.21, X.21-bis

◄─────── LAN/MAN ───────────────────────►◄──── PSDN ────►

Summary of OSI and CCITT recommendations

X.400 MHS

X.400 covers a series of CCITT recommendations defining Message Handling Systems. MOTIS (Message-Oriented Text Interchange Systems) is the ISO mail transfer system, based on X.400 and defined by the series of ISO standards starting from ISO 10021. MOTIS is often inaccurately used as a synonym of X.400, to mean an e-mail system.

Under X.400, messages are sent to a named user across a network on a store-and-forward basis. On its initial release in 1984, the only application type defined for use with X.400 was interpersonal mail. Because of this, X.400 is often used as a term to describe electronic mail. Subsequent (four-yearly) revisions of X.400 in 1988 and 1992 have added new application types, including Electronic Data Interchange (X.435) and automatic storage of messages for later retrieval (Message Store).

Under X.400, a network over which messages are to be transferred is treated as an arrangement of User Agents (UAs) and Message Transfer Agents (MTAs). A UA is usually an application program, such as mail software, under the control of a human user. The UA sends messages it composes to the Message Transfer Service (MTS) and receives messages from the MTS. The MTS comprises a series of store-and-forward MTAs. MTAs provide routing, security, alternate addressing, forwarding and other services. Only the UAs actually see the contents of the messages sent or received.

Access Units (AUs) allow access to the X.400 system for messages in non-X.400 formats, such as fax and telex. The Message Store facility provides a storage area for messages before they are retrieved by a UA. Since a UA is often represented by a PC, this allows the PC to be disconnected from the MTA (also possibly a PC or more powerful router system) and switched off, while still being able to receive messages.

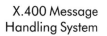

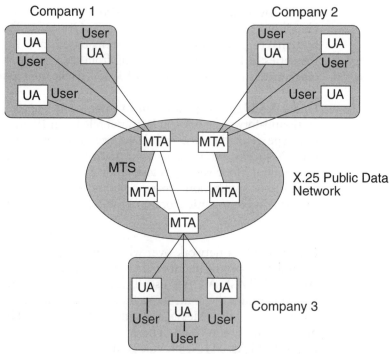

X.500 Directory Service (DS)

The X.500 Directory Service is used within an X.400 network to provide a directory of users who can be reached over the network.

Directory services such as the Internet Domain Name Service are more restricted than X.500 in that they provide only the minimum necessary mapping of names to network addresses. X.500 additionally offers the ability to store general user information (attributes) and therefore constitutes a general-purpose directory service.

The directory is a physically distributed database which appears to a Directory User Agent (DUA) to be centralised. Directory System Agents (DSAs) hold the information contained in the directory and provide a centralised view of the data by chaining the directories of multiple DSAs.

All entries in the directory, typically network users or other entities, are represented in a Directory Information Tree (DIT) as objects. Each object is uniquely identified by a Directory Distinguished Name (DDN) and is described with a hierarchical naming sequence defined with the Abstract Syntax Notation 1 (ASN.1) language.

DUAs are application software processes which interact with the end-user. The DUAs compose requests and present users with the results of those requests. Available request types include reading, listing and searching the directory, as well as addition, change and deletion of directory entries.

File Transfer Access Method (FTAM)
FTAM provides the means whereby distributed client application programs can access a remote file server, possibly with a different operating system and filesystem from those of the clients. FTAM also allows transparent transfer of files between systems differing in these characteristics.

FTAM defines a virtual file store which it uses in order to avoid dealing with the details of the filesystems maintained by the client systems. The format of files being transferred between server and client are converted to the format required by the virtual file store and then further converted to the conventions of the client.

Common Management Information Protocol (CMIP)
CMIP performs much the same network management functions as SNMP. The CMIP protocols and software products based on them manage objects stored in a Management Information Base (MIB).

Network entities are described in an object-oriented way. This allows definition of more specialised objects by using an existing object as a basis and inheriting its characteristics into a derived object. The object-oriented mechanism of polymorphism, by which actions on related but different network entities can be carried out without regard for their types, can be used to hide network complexity.

Five main areas of network management service are defined by ISO:

- Configuration Management
- Fault Management
- Performance Management
- Security Management
- Accounting Management

CMIP provides facilities to implement all these services. CMIP is preferred to SNMP for management of complex networks although, because SNMP is easier to implement and is associated with the Internet protocols, the latter is in more widespread use, particularly in North America.

Systems Network Architecture (SNA)

Introduction: traditional SNA

Originally announced by IBM in 1974, SNA was the first complete data network architecture capable of linking all the computing devices used by an enterprise and of allowing them to share and transfer data. Currently, there are more than 50,000 installed SNA sites, making SNA the world's predominant proprietary network architecture.

The original SNA was mainframe based and allowed devices of the 3270 family to be connected to networked mainframes in a hierarchical master/slave relationship. This contrasts with the peer-to-peer nature of the Internet and OSI protocols, which in turn allows applications to be distributed in a client–server arrangement.

In a standard SNA arrangement, 3278 or 3279 terminals are connected with coaxial cable to 3174 or 3274 terminal controllers. The controllers act as concentrators by gathering messages from the terminals for more efficient transmission to the mainframe. Groups of terminal controllers are connected to 3725 or 3745 front-end processors (FEPs), also called communications controllers. The FEPs serve to offload responsibility for terminal handling from the mainframe processor.

A traditional SNA network consists of nodes, of which the terminals, controllers and mainframes are examples, connected by physical links over which data is transferred in frames according to the rules of the Synchronous Data-Link Control (SDLC) protocol. SDLC is IBM's version of the HDLC protocol described in *Basics of data communications* on page 146. SDLC implements a primary/secondary mechanism in which one of two connected systems always assumes a master role. All the intelligence in the traditional SNA network is for this reason concentrated on the side of the mainframe. SNA was the first network architecture to be based on a bit-oriented data-link protocol, such as

SDLC, rather than an asynchronous or character-oriented protocol like Binary Synchronous.

The hierarchical network

Hierarchical SNA originated in an era when the predominant kind of computing was that based on the centralised mainframe. Users interacted, by means of sessions, with application programs running in the mainframe. Sessions ran on dumb terminals with no processing or networking capability of their own. The applications on the mainframe had no ability to communicate either; both the sessions and the applications needed the Systems Services Control Point (SSCP) to maintain the link.

The hierarchy is in the layering of Virtual Telecommunications Access Method (VTAM), a program running in the mainframe and supporting the SSCP; the Network Control Program (NCP); and the Physical Units (PUs) which act as concentrators for the Logical Units (terminals) at the bottom.

PUs and LUs of type 2.0 have no networking capability without the help of the SSCP. LUs of this type are called *dependent LUs*; any interaction or sharing of data between them must be routed up and down the hierarchy via the mainframe. This process, and the entities in the traditional SNA network, are depicted in a diagram:

Traditional
hierachichal SNA

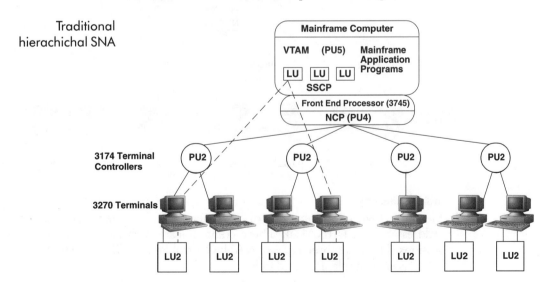

With the emergence of PCs which, in contrast to 3270 and other dumb terminals, could do their own processing, the need became clear for more direct communication between LUs running on PC workstations. This necessitated the introduction of a new type of LU, LU6.2, of which there is more below. PCs could still use the traditional SNA services by emulating 3270 terminals, acting as both PU2 and LU2 and communicating hierarchically via the SSCP.

Direct sessions between end stations

To allow direct communication between distributed SNA nodes, PU Type 2.1 and LU6.2 were introduced. Two end-node PCs, or other systems such as AS/400s, are physical units of type 2.1 and run network programs which are logical units of type 6.2. (Traditional terminals are controlled by PUs and LUs of type 2.)

Two PU2.1 running LU6.2 are capable of establishing direct sessions and of communicating independently of the SSCP and VTAM. LUs of this type are called *independent LUs*.

Direct sessions with LU6.2

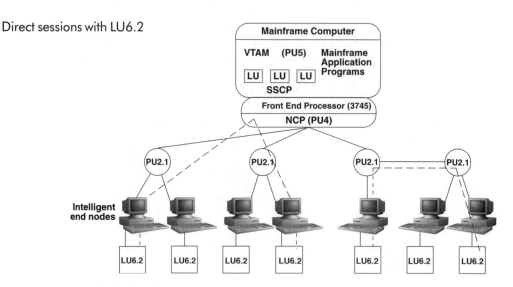

SNA terminology

Elements, logical and physical, of SNA networks are called Network Addressable Units (NAUs). These communicate with each other in sessions. There are three types of NAU: Control Points (CPs), of which SSCP is an example, PUs and LUs.

There are three traditional types of Physical Unit: types 5, 4 and 2. PU type 5 controls the network and is implemented in software by VTAM which accesses the network by means of the SSCP. PU type 4 nodes are optional. They act as communications controllers and as routers in large distributed networks. PU type 2 is the least capable, serving as a terminal concentrator supporting dumb terminals, or PCs emulating dumb terminals, which run LU2.0.

PU2.1 are intelligent, do not require SSCP to establish network sessions and can maintain peer-to-peer (LU-LU) communication with each other. They are sometimes referred to as Low Entry Networking (LEN) End Nodes and are usually implemented with PCs or other computers.

LU6.2 runs in a PU2.1 and using its own API allows programs running in distributed systems to communicate and share data directly. The LU6.2 API (called a *verb set* by IBM) is known as Advanced Program to Program Communication (APPC). In modern distributed SNA systems, functions equivalent to the Network and Transport layers of the OSI Reference Model are carried out by Advanced Peer-to-Peer Networking (APPN), a set of session and routing functions of which LU6.2 and APPC present the programmatic interface.

Peer-to-peer SNA: APPC and APPN

LU6.2, APPC and APPN have been introduced since the mid 1980s to support non-hierarchical networks and peer-to-peer communication in ways which traditional SNA could not.

LU6.2 is communications software which supports sessions between application programs running on different computers in a distributed data processing environment. APPC is the API, or verb set, presented by LU6.2 to application programmers.

APPN is a suite of network software underlying LU6.2 which is broadly equivalent to Layers 3 and 4 of the OSI Reference Model. It also has some responsibility for initiating sessions between LUs. APPN presents a common interface to network programs on IBM systems including AS/400, PCs with OS/2, 3174 terminal concentrators and 370-architecture mainframes. It handles all network routing, configuration, directory and other services and reduces the VTAM and NCP customisation needed to allow the different systems to act as network nodes.

The difference between APPC and APPN can be equated to the process of posting a letter. APPC is equivalent to the acts of writing, enveloping and posting the letter. APPN is analogous to what happens after the letter is posted: route selection, class of service and eventual delivery. The APPN environment defines several types of network nodes. The most important of these are the Network Node (NN), End Nodes (EN) and Low Entry Networking (LEN) End Node. These can be computer systems of the types referred to above and are all physical units of type 2.1.

NNs have Control Points (CPs) which communicate with the CPs of other network nodes. A CP-CP session is part of an LU-LU session. NNs maintain directory, routing and configuration databases which enable them to find and communicate with LUs anywhere on the network.

ENs are less capable than NNs but contain CPs which know about all end-node LUs which may be set in session with LUs on remote nodes. The end node relies on a network node to find remote LUs; this NN is known as the end node's network node server.

The LEN does not maintain a CP-CP session with a network node server; instead, it must maintain locally a list of all remote LUs needed for sessions with local LUs. The remote LUs are then located and sessions initiated by the connected NN.

All APPN communication is peer-to-peer. Traditional hierarchical SNA communication is still possible with devices which need SSCP and NCP support but is no longer necessary:

Nodes in APPN
network
(simplified)

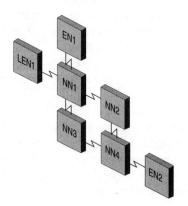

The SNA architecture does not exactly map to the Reference Model. It was, however, designed about the same time so there are parallels. The following diagram attempts to summarise the relationships between SNA, LU6.2, APPC and APPN and between them all and the layers of the Reference Model.

Relationship of
SNA to the
Reference Model

OSI Model	SNA Layers		
Application	Application/Transaction Services		
Presentation	APPC API (verb set)		
	LU6.2 Presentation Services Data Services	Function Management Transmission Control	
Session	Session Control Internetworking Network Management Directory Services	Intermediate Session Routing Topology and Routing Services Path Control Configuration Services	
Transport			
Network	APPN		
Data Link	LLC/DLC		X.25
	Ethernet (802.3) Token Ring (802.5) SDLC		
Physical	Co-axial STP FDDI		

There are two main classes of APPN services, those concerned with establishing a session between LUs running on networked nodes and those performing routing of transmissions between the nodes.

APPN sets LUs in session with each other. Network nodes located on the route between the LUs perform Intermediate Session Routing. A request for APPN session establishment services is made by an application program using an LU as a network port. In a manner transparent to the application, the other participant in the session is located using APPN Directory services and the session is initiated. Data is transferred between the communicating applications using the APPN Path Control layer. The underlying link layer (Data Link Control) carries blocks of data between the two end nodes running the applications, routed if necessary by APPN routing services.

LU6.2 provides a reliable, connection-oriented service for networked communication between application programs. In this respect, it is similar to the TCP Internet protocol but, unlike the full-duplex TCP, LU6.2 is half-duplex; transmission can only take place in one direction at a time.

The API presented to application programmers requiring an interface with the network is APPC. This consists of a number of verbs (equivalent in the TCP/IP context to the sockets function calls) including the following:

Verb	Meaning
ALLOCATE	Establish a conversation between two applications and set up an LU–LU session if necessary
DEALLOCATE	Deallocate a conversation
SEND_DATA	
RECEIVE_AND_POST	Be ready to receive data from the remote application; while waiting to receive, a local application can perform other tasks
RECEIVE_AND_WAIT	Be ready to receive data from the remote application; while waiting to receive, no other tasks are performed

Client–server SNA

The addition to SNA of facilities, in the form of APPC and APPN, which support decentralised networking has made the SNA environment capable of running distributed client–server applications

Applications divided in parts and running co-operatively using the facilities of an underlying SNA/APPN network usually communicate by one or more of three methods:

- ▶ Conversational (similar to APIs such as sockets for TCP/IP)
- ▶ Messaging Model
- ▶ Call Model (can be referred to as Remote Procedure Call)

These techniques, which make distributed applications possible can collectively be classified as middleware and are described as such in *Middleware* on page 230.

The APPC API provides verbs that allow conversation in an LU-LU session, messaging between LUs and remote execution of an application using an LU on the remote system. The conversational model depends on the LU-LU session being continuously available and is suitable for transfer of large volumes of data. The messaging model, on the other hand, provides asynchronous services. No session need be active. Messages and procedure calls are stored in queues until the required sessions and applications are running and available.

The IBM System Application Architecture (SAA) is intended to make application software portable across the VM, MVS, OS/400 and OS/2 operating systems. To address interoperability as part of SAA, IBM has introduced a strategy where multiple incompatible protocol stacks can be used transparently by means of a standard API.

To establish such an API, IBM introduced the CPI-C (Common Programming Interface for Communications as part of the Common Communications Access (CCA) component of SAA). The CPI-C command set is based on the APPC verbs and allows establishment, control and synchronisation of sessions and data transfer. CPI-C is also intended to support OSI OLTP services (see *The client–server model* on page 245).

Using CPI-C, application software can be written without regard for the underlying protocol stacks. The abstraction provided below CPI-C, RPC and the other distributed services is referred to by IBM as *common transport semantics*, meaning that the method used by applications to access the low-level network protocols, of whatever stack, is consistent. IBM's strategy, called the Open Blueprint, is shown in the diagram following. IBM software products that implement the functions in the Common Transport Semantics layer are described as Multi-Protocol Transport Networking (MPTN). These include the AnyNet series for the MVS and OS/2 operating environments.

The Distributed Computing Environment (DCE, see *Distributed system models* on page 238) is IBM's product strategy for open operating systems and networking. SAA represents IBM's open systems approach in the context of its own proprietary systems. IBM apparently intends to provide a 'bridge' between DCE and SAA, using common transport semantics to allow DCE applications access SNA/APPN and proprietary applications use the TCP/IP and OSI protocols.

IBM's Open
Blueprint

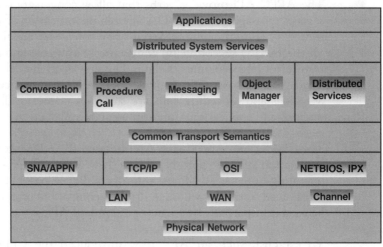

Middleware

Definition and characteristics

Middleware is a modern term which represents a logical abstraction of the middle layers of the communications software stacks used in distributed computing systems. Middleware is used to isolate application programs from the details of implementation of the underlying network. Thus, applications can be distributed – that is, operate transparently across a network – without having to be concerned whether the underlying network protocol is TCP/IP, APPN, NetBIOS or SPX/IPX.

Middleware is implemented in software as a set of services. These services are presented to developers of applications as a consistent set of APIs and help to reduce the complexity of application development. In the context of the OSI Reference Model, network software can be said to occupy layers 1 through 4, distributed applications interface to level 7, and middleware occupies levels 5–6.

The practical implementation of Reference Model levels 5–6 and the application layer 7 is less well defined and understood than that of the lower levels. Neither is it always well-defined whether or not a particular aspect of a distributed system should be thought of as middleware. For example it is disputed whether SQL and associated database APIs are middleware. However, when SQL requests are sent across a network to a remote database engine, hiding from the software developer the implementation details of the network, they accurately meet the definition of middleware given above. SQL is described in *Language standards* on page 105.

The importance of middleware is in hiding complexity and details from the application developer. Applications can be written to take advantage of a common API for network access. Middleware provides the services behind the API, reconciling the differences in the underlying network.

The three major categories of middleware shown are widely accepted. They are described in more detail later in this section. To summarise: an application program can be distributed, in that it interoperates with other computers in a network, even though it need know nothing of the details of the network over which it is communicating. Its handle on the network is a set of well-defined APIs which in turn use middleware facilities to gain access to the network.

Middleware in a
distributed system

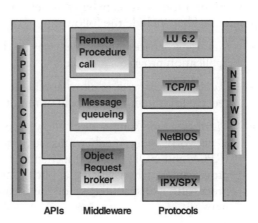

Middleware benefits

One of the major benefits conferred by middleware is in simplifying the software development process. Suppose that a distributed application were written to interact directly with the API provided by a commercial TCP/IP implementation. This API consists of a large number of functions and to use it requires significant additional knowledge on the part of the developer. When programming for the TCP/IP API has been completed, the job must be repeated for any other protocol set with which the application is to interface. The middleware approach to this problem is to implement a simple messaging service for use by the application. The messaging service would have a few simple operations and few parameters and return codes. It could then be ported to match the different protocol APIs, in much less than the time needed to rewrite the application for each of the APIs.

Application development is greatly simplified, as the middle layers of the network stack are not re-invented each time an application is written.

Access by applications to services provided by the distributed network is implemented in a consistent manner. This shortens development time and improves subsequent application portability: applications can easily be moved between systems providing the same interface to the network regardless of the underlying protocols used.

Middleware services

Middleware services are those which provide common information services or processing capability usable across multiple application programs. They include the following:

▸ *Messaging services* allow messages to be sent and received by application programs and users

▸ *Database access services* allow application programs to request and receive information from local or remotely distributed databases

▸ *Distributed processing services* allow processing to be shared across a network using mechanisms such as *Remote Procedure Call* (RPC) and SQL. These mechanisms make it unnecessary for programmers when writing applications to be aware of how the processing is distributed or of the location of any server on the network

▸ *Transaction processing services* allow co-ordination and synchronisation of operations across a distributed computing network. These services are most important in the context of database systems, where operations must be carried out consistently and fully, or not at all

▶ *Directory services* allow identification of users, applications and systems on a network using convenient names

▶ *Security services* facilitate authentication of the identity of networked users and applications, as well as access control and data confidentiality

Application Program Interface (API)

The API makes available to the application program the services provided by and over the network. APIs are stable and long-lived interfaces to these services. When APIs are standardised, the interface to network services is not proprietary, and application development is open: all application software can use the standard network interface, thereby also improving the portability of distributed software using the standard API. The X/Open consortium, which makes no standards of its own but promotes and sanctions standards proposed by others, is dominant in sanctioning standardised APIs for distributed systems. X/Open-sanctioned APIs with wide usage include the following:

▶ *X/Open Transport Interface* (XTI), which specifies a universal interface to network transport services

▶ *X/Open Directory Services* (XDS), which provides access to X.500 directory services

▶ X/Open API for access to X.400 electronic mail and transaction-processing services

▶ The X Library, providing the interface to the X GUI service

One of the most important APIs for client–server and transaction processing systems is the API accompanying each database vendor's implementation of the SQL language. Database system vendors have invariable produced extended and changed versions of SQL to suit their product and commercial needs. This diversity also reflects in the APIs offered by these vendors for access to their databases.

Middleware for database languages constitutes the pairing of SQL and the database API. If this middleware is (even slightly) proprietary to a given vendor, then database access (front-end) software which may work with other database engines will be useless. To remedy these incompatibilities, there is a need either for standardised SQL and APIs or for a body of software which will work with a large number of database front-ends and database engines. Several standards have been proposed, but Microsoft is currently attempting to impose on the industry a *de facto* standard database API system called *Open Database Connectivity* (ODBC).

Database access using ODBC

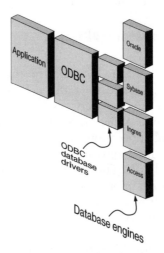

This is in turn a part of Microsoft's Windows Open Services Architecture (WOSA), which is designed to hide network details from Windows application software developers. ODBC provides drivers for a number of supported database systems. To access multiple databases, a user need only have driver software for all the databases required.

Remote Procedure Call (RPC)

RPC is a powerful mechanism for sharing across a network the processing carried out by application software. RPC takes the form of a function or procedure call from an application which causes the remote execution of that procedure or function call. The local application and user need not know that the resources of a remote system are being used. Application developers need have very little awareness that they are developing distributed software because RPC calls to a remote procedure do not differ syntactically from a call which would otherwise execute on the local system. One of the benefits of RPC is that application programs which would normally execute on a single system can, with very little change, be converted to distributed applications. Reasons for wanting to execute a procedure on a remote distributed system, using RPC, include these:

► The distribution can benefit efficient load-balancing of processing across the available resources of the network

► An application may require execution of one or more procedures concurrently on distributed systems in the network. This may anyway be possible on a single local (for example UNIX or OS/2) system but, in the case of a single-tasking (for example, DOS) system, RPC gives the ability to perform apparently local multitasking

► A remote system may be more suitable for executing a particular procedure than a local one, for example if the remote system is a database server and the required data is stored by it

The following is a pictorial representation of how RPC operates.

Remote Procedure
Call Operation

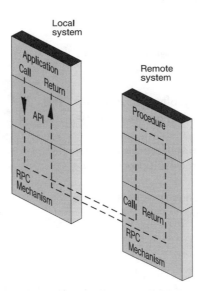

The application program on the local system calls the required procedure in the same way as it would if the procedure were to be executed locally. The call is intercepted by the local RPC mechanism which packages it and sends it over the network to be received by the RPC mechanism on the remote system, which executes the required procedure there. When the procedure on the remote system terminates, the RPC returns to the local system the name of the procedure together with any changed parameter values. The separation of function offered by the RPC model is particularly suitable for use in a client–server system. Where the client–server system implements a database, a call might be sent from the local system to execute remotely a pre-prepared SQL request and return the selected data. RPC is widely used in the OSF, UI/ATLAS and ONC+ specifications for distributed computing. These are described in *Distributed system models* on page 238.

Message queueing

Whereas RPC is based on the function call-return model of the procedural programming languages, message queueing uses the messaging paradigm more familiar to programmers of object-oriented languages and GUIs. Actual implementations of message-oriented middleware (MOM) are much less mature than RPC but some now exist, supplied by companies including IBM and Digital Equipment Corporation.

Messaging model

Step 1: The local application sends a message to the remote program.

Step 2: Message queueing software sends the message across the network to a remote queue.

Step 3: The remote queue software sends the message to an application, which processes it.

Lastly: The application sends back its response encapsulated in a message.

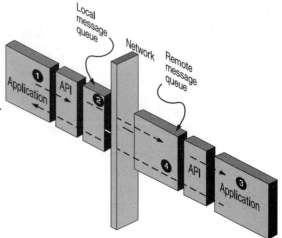

While RPC involves intercepting a call to a procedure on a local system and transferring it across a network for the procedure to be executed on a remote system, MOM presents a high-level API consisting of a few command primitives (for example: *send* and *receive*) for transmission of messages. The above diagram presents a simplified idea of how MOM operates.

Object Request Broker (ORB)

An ORB is software which manages the exchange of messages between objects across a network. Under the object-oriented paradigm, a characteristic of an object is not just that it is described by its data but that it also defines the operations which can be carried out on it. Invoking such an operation on an object is referred to as *sending a message* to the object.

An object on a local system can send a message to an object on a remote system. Currently, this is done mostly using RPC but there is no reason why MOM or other communication methods could not instead be used.

ORBs have been to a great extent standardised as part of the activities of the Object Management Group (OMG), a consortium of more than 400 system vendors. The OMG has defined an API by means of which client applications can access ORBs. The API is documented in OMG's CORBA specification. A diagram of the main interactions in the ORB model follows:

Object Request Broker Model

Step 1: Objects exchange messages across the network by means of ORBs.

Step 2: Requests from local objects are managed by the remote ORB and processed by remote objects.

Step 3: The results of remote processing are returned to the requesting objects.

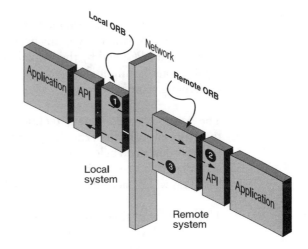

Distributed system models

Introduction

In recent years, particularly since 1988, a number of models for distributed computing have been proposed and at least partially implemented by consortia of computer systems vendors. These models incorporate the technologies and standards of open systems: they promote portability of application software among different system architectures; portability of software among different networked systems and interoperability of that software, running on different systems, across the network.

Portability is determined mainly by operating system and other APIs; by the degree of standardisation of programming languages in which application software is written; by the requirements of hardware including peripheral devices and microprocessors; and by the nature of graphic or command-line interfaces being used.

Interoperability is determined by standardised and widely-used communication and networking protocols; by standardised middleware such as the RPC; and by the availability of standardised APIs to allow applications communicate across a network independently of the underlying protocols.

The range of open-system technologies embraced by the models is therefore large. Each of the significant models for distributed computing is briefly described below. If their potential is fully realised, they promise an efficient, cost-effective world of open and interoperable computing based on widely-accepted *de jure* and *de facto* international standards.

The purpose of these models is to provide a stable common environment for development and execution of value-added application software, without the developer having to be concerned with the details and complexity of the underlying network system.

The hardware and software used to implement distributed systems can be considered as being organised in three layers, related to the OSI Reference Model:

Components of a
distributed system

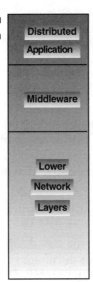

OSI Reference
Model

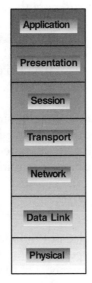

Concepts and software products categorised as middleware are summarised in *Middleware* on page 230. In this section, a number of more-or-less complete models for distributed computing are described. These incorporate operating systems, languages, database systems and GUIs – which are important to software portability – as well as specifications for networks, communications and distributed processing.

It is intended that compliance by system vendors with these models will promote the increase in portability and interoperability of application software products.

Underlying network protocols and operating systems

In describing models for distributed systems, it is very much taken for granted that the lower-level network protocols and mechanisms described in earlier sections, and the software products which implement them, exist and work. The major commercial LAN operating systems and protocols are these:

- Novell NetWare
- Microsoft LAN Manager
- NetBIOS
- Banyan VINES
- UnixWare

The predominant protocols used for communication over LANs and wide-area networks are the following:

- ▸ TCP/IP
- ▸ The OSI Protocols
- ▸ IBM LU 6.2
- ▸ SPX/IPX

In this section, these protocols and operating systems are merely acknowledged: it is assumed in the text which follows that one or a combination of these systems is in use and that, using them as a medium, distributed computing systems are implemented.

Open Software Foundation (OSF)

OSF was founded in 1988 with the stated objective of providing vendor-independent open platforms for distributed computing. A major goal of the founding members of OSF (IBM, HP, Digital Equipment Corporation, Siemens and Bull) was to eliminate dependence for UNIX source code on AT&T. UNIX was by this time effectively the open operating system, standards based on it having been approved by the IEEE (POSIX) and X/Open. But UNIX was widely viewed as being under the proprietary control of a single vendor.

OSF devised a blueprint for an operating system and computing environment which was independent of UNIX but which provided an open platform for distributed computing systems. This included a common user interface, a UNIX-like operating system not dependent on AT&T source code and licensing and a distributed computing environment. The user interface is Motif, the operating system is OSF/1, DCE is the distributed environment and DME is the technology for managing systems and networks in a distributed environment.

Distributed Computing Environment (DCE)

The OSF DCE is an integrated set of services which provides an environment for the development of distributed computing applications. The DCE is an implementation of middleware which isolates software developers from the underlying network and presents its services as a convenient set of APIs.

DCE is designed primarily to be implemented on UNIX systems supporting TCP/IP and it has enjoyed widespread acceptance although complete implementations are rare. Some elements of DCE have experienced success as commercial products. Examples include the Motif GUI and, to a lesser extent, ANDF.

Using an ANDF *producer* on a system from which software is to be distributed, software is compiled from source-code into an intermediate form in which it is distributed. The target system further converts the distributed program image into its executable form using an ANDF *installer*. ANDF allows shrink-wrapped software to be distributed for systems of different architectures in a way which hitherto had only been possible for IBM-compatible PCs.

The RPC is the most important mechanism in the DCE. It is used to present APIs to application programs on distributed systems in a network and thereby distribute DCE services around the network. The major components of DCE are shown in pictorial form and are described below:

Structure of OSF Distributed Computing Environment

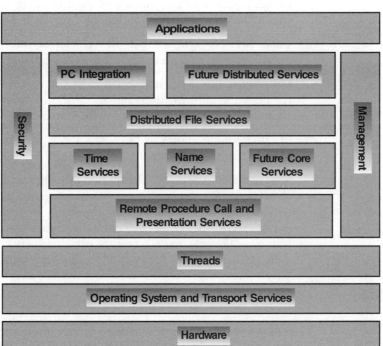

The main components of DCE are:

▸ *RPC and Presentation Services:* interface definition languages and RPCs provide programmers with the ability to transfer control and data across a network in a transparent manner

▸ *Name Services:* also known as *directory services*, allows users of the distributed system to find resources and services which have been distributed. Directory services supply a mapping between user-friendly names and resources and services

▸ *Security Services:* One of the first commercially-available implementations of security for distributed computing, DCE security is effected by the Kerberos Security System which originated in MIT's Project Athena. It provides encryption services for secure file transfer; checksums on data transfers to detect tampering; access control lists to control access to resources; and authentication of the identities of clients and servers

▸ *Threads:* a method of supporting parallel execution of programs by managing multiple threads of control (perhaps on different systems) within a process running in a distributed environment

▸ *Time Service:* synchronises the clocks of all the distributed systems so that executing applications can operate properly

▸ *Distributed File System:* extension of the local file system over the network, allowing users full access to files on remote systems. DCE uses the Andrew distributed file system

▸ *PC Integration:* allows DOS PCs to access file and print services outside the PC environment

▸ *Management:* the OSF Distributed Management Environment (DME) is for management of heterogeneous systems and networks in a distributed environment. It includes software management, including packaging, distribution and installation; software licence management; printing services; and host management services such as adding and removing users

UI ATLAS

The ATLAS specification was made by UNIX International, a consortium of system vendors using UNIX System V from UNIX System

Laboratories (USL), formerly owned by AT&T. ATLAS is a model for distributed computing which addresses three main areas:

► Desktop computing

► Distributed computing

► Corporate hub computing, providing security and administration features suitable for a business context

ATLAS overlaps significantly with OSF DCE while providing some extra features. ATLAS provides the RPC mechanism used in DCE as well as the Sun (Sun Microsystems Inc.) RPC. It uses a federated naming scheme which allows a single name to be used to identify objects in a directory of names of several formats representing distributed systems and resources. ATLAS also adds Object Management Group (OMG) ORB specifications, transaction processing with USL's Tuxedo On-Line Transaction Processing (OLTP), and OSI applications and services. The structure of ATLAS is best explained by a diagram:

Structure of UI
ATLAS
architecture

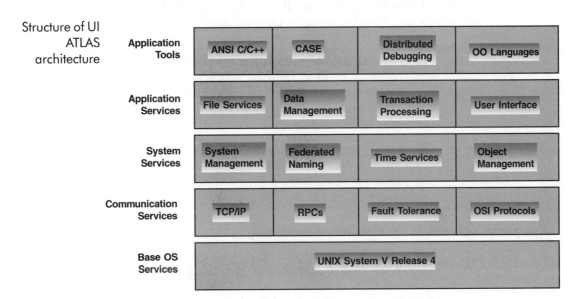

Sun Open Network Computing (ONC+)

The SunSoft system software subsidiary of Sun Microsystems Inc. defined the ONC model which is now encompassed by the Solaris 2.0 product offering. Solaris includes SunOS as its base operating system component.

ONC supports the NFS (Network File System) distributed file system; a directory service for supporting enterprise networks; the transport-independent RPC (TI-RPC) facility for distributed applications and the same Kerberos security system as has been incorporated into OSF DCE.

Source code for ONC+ can be licensed from SunSoft. The product has been implemented in the environments of many vendors and is not restricted to those running UNIX or UNIX-like operating systems.

Major components of ONC+ are:

▸ *Transport-Independent Remote Procedure Call (TI-RPC):* allows a distributed application program using RPC to run independent of the underlying transport protocol

▸ *External Data Representation (XDR):* provides a system-independent method of data representation, resolving differences in byte ordering, alignment and data type size. Applications using XDR may exchange data between distributed systems of different architectures

▸ *Transport Layer Interface (TLI):* the communications layer underlying ONC+ in Solaris allows procedures executed by RPC to run using the transport layers of multiple protocol sets, for example TCP/IP and the OSI protocols

Comparison of models for distributed computing

The following diagram summarises the characteristics of the DCE, ATLAS and ONC+ models, showing the technologies which they incorporate and the extent to which they are common.

Relationship of
models for
distributed
computing

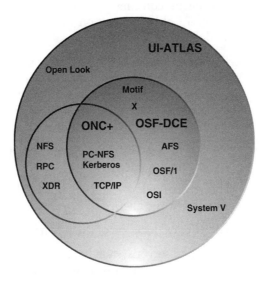

The client–server model

Definition and characteristics of client–server

A client–server system is an arrangement of networked computing devices which uses distributed intelligence to treat both the server (often a minicomputer or mainframe) and the clients (usually PCs or workstations) as intelligent programmable devices, thus exploiting the full computing power of both. Computer systems and networks running client–server applications embody some or all of the following characteristics:

► Client–server application software is generally partitioned into back-end (server) and front-end (client) components

► The client is a PC or workstation providing its own processing facilities; traditional timesharing systems use dumb terminals instead with all processing taking place on the central system

► The client offers all its power and facilities for running applications; the client portion of an application is usually optimised for user interaction

- The client consumes services provided by the server; there is therefore clean separation of software function with attendant modularity of software

- The server can be a PC, minicomputer or mainframe. It provides traditional strengths: data management; information-sharing between clients; network administration; and security. The server is typically optimised for providing centralised services in a manner transparent to the user

- The server handles many clients and controls their access to the server's resources

- The server is passive and responds only to transactions which are initiated by the client

- The physical location of the server(s) is transparent to the clients

- Client and server system hardware and software are connected on a mix and match basis; hardware includes PC clients and *super-servers*, minicomputers and mainframes

- Client and server application software should be independent of hardware and operating-system software (*platform-independent*)

- Clients and servers are loosely coupled and interact by means of messages

- Servers encapsulate services by providing a public message interface

- Clients and servers are scalable: client systems can easily be added or removed (*horizontal scaling*); servers can be replaced with larger, faster systems (*vertical scaling*)

- The client–server model protects the integrity of data stored on the server

- Centralised (server) facilities often include databases such as Oracle, Ingres and Sybase, accessible at will by users from their networked workstations

- On-Line Transaction Processing (OLTP) systems, such as AT&T Tuxedo, synchronise data updates across the network by maintaining several concurrently running processes on different data repositories

- A typical client–server system includes one or more server-based database management systems (DBMSs) connected by LAN

(Ethernet backbone with Novell NetWare) and/or WAN (TCP/IP and X.25) to many workstations and other peripherals

- Clients, from their workstations, run GUI-based applications which interactively generate database queries

- Increasingly, server systems run the UNIX operating system to support large databases

Rationale

The reasons-for-being of the client–server model are:

- To cut enterprise computing costs by customising powerful low-cost computer systems for specific application programs rather than having an expensive centralised mainframe

- To improve the flexibility, ease of use and quality of the services provided by the computer system, encouraging end-user acceptance and reducing the workload on MIS resources

Factors influencing migration to client–server

The term client–server is often used interchangeably with open systems because the implementation of client–server systems is so heavily influenced by open technologies. The forces driving migration to the client–server model include (in the jargon) *downsizing*, *rightsizing*, *upsizing*, and *re-engineering*.

- *Downsizing:* This can be defined as downward migration of application software from minicomputers and mainframes to low-cost standardised hardware, including PC-based clients and servers. Minicomputer and mainframe applications are split into modules running on networked servers and client workstations, while GUI-based front-end software runs on the client systems. Centralised processors, with their timesharing dumb terminals, are gradually replaced, giving local MIS managers greater autonomy but resulting in substantial software and hardware conversion efforts

- *Rightsizing:* Applications are moved to the most appropriate server platform in an *enterprise network* within which heterogeneous servers co-exist. Interoperability of enterprise network clients and servers is made possible by open communications protocols and standards described in previous sections.

The benefit of rightsizing is that services are distributed across different types of computer depending on required price-performance, availability and specialisation

▸ *Upsizing:* PCs were first attached to LANs so that they might share peripheral devices. Now, they are more commonly networked to use e-mail and share databases. The requirements of these applications have led to upsizing: networking hitherto standalone PCs or internetworking standalone LANs with a corporate database server

▸ *Re-engineering:* A vogue term which refers to the changing organisation of large companies and enterprises from the very structured and hierarchical model prevalent in the mid-20th century to arrangements with fewer layers and more autonomous groups

An example of the contrast might be a company such as General Motors as organised in 1960 on the one hand and Apple Computer Inc. in 1990 on the other. In the car company, there were many layers of management between the chief executive officer and the assembly-line operative; the job of the latter was very specifically and narrowly defined. Computer systems applied to such a business tended also to be hierarchical along the IBM mainframe/SNA model (see *Systems Network Architecture (SNA)* on page 222).

In the more modern organisation, the structure is relatively flat with few middle-management layers and autonomous project teams may report directly to the Chief Executive or an immediate subordinate. This kind of structure both demands and is more suitable for the application of distributed client–server computing.

The following diagram depicts the migration from the traditional centralised approach to the client–server model under the influences of downsizing, rightsizing, upsizing and re-engineering. This migration in turn is made possible by advances in hardware and software technologies and the standardisation brought about by open systems.

Forces
influencing
migration to
client–server

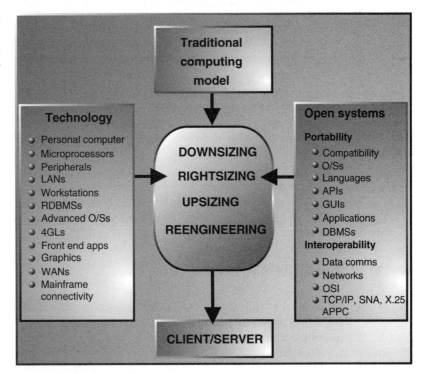

Types of client and server

Client/Server systems involve more than just PC LANs or the notion of a server as a database repository. Client/Server technology is often (wrongly) equated only with file servers or database servers. In fact, there are at least four different kinds of server:

▶   *File Server:* Application software on the client system retrieves a number of file records from the server. There is no selectivity in the request for data, resulting in correspondingly heavy network traffic due to the size of reply transmissions

▶   *Database Server:* Requests on the server are made as intelligent selective queries in the form of SQL requests. Network traffic is less than when using a file server because only results matching selection criteria are returned over the network. The SQL processor and the database reside on the same server. The clients must run front-end software to generate the SQL queries

▶ *Transaction Server:* Groups of SQL statements, called transactions, reside on the server.

These transactions are executed as remote procedures from a client system, often responding to *trigger* messages. Remote execution requires that the client and server be connected by a peer-to-peer protocol allowing remote procedure call (RPC). Application software implementing a transaction server is referred to as *on-line transaction-processing* (OLTP) software. Traffic on the network is even less than that generated by a database server

▶ *Application Server:* This is similar in concept to the transaction server, but not necessarily centred on a database. In principle, any application can be on the server side. An example is Lotus Notes

Balance of client and server software

One of the major bottlenecks in client–server network performance is the size of database queries and the replies to them. It can be difficult to distribute database access intelligence without overloading the network.

Most current client–server software concentrates the intelligence on the client side. This is the simpler and more traditional approach, and it encourages development of GUI-based front-end client software to generate queries.

Client-centred applications include those which implement file-server and database-server systems. *Server-centred* applications minimise network traffic because most of the code runs on servers providing a relatively abstract level of service.

Server-centred applications include those which implement transaction-server and application-server systems. Object-oriented technology has particular potential for moving the processing load away from the client to the server: requests are encapsulated in the database with the data.

Benefits and disadvantages of client–server

Benefits

- Client–server systems cooperate in application processing, using their combined power more efficiently than in the timesharing model. If one component of the networked client–server system fails, the rest of the system (and the business) stays in operation

- Because of the distribution of computing power, end-users are encouraged to work locally on their workstations. This reduces demands on central processing resources and allows the end-user to work in the way he/she wants instead of by the MIS department's rules

- Productivity of users can be expected to increase

- The cost to the enterprise of developing and maintaining a client–server system should be lower than the equivalent costs for a traditional system

- With the exception (sometimes) of server systems, the components of a client–server system are open, modular and interchangeable, allowing the enterprise to pick and choose its equipment and software from among many competing vendors, with clear cost benefits

- The openness and modularity of the client–server system facilitate later modernisation and expansion

- It is possible to implement as part of the system a range of platforms to suit individual users' needs and preferences. For example:

  - Apple Macintosh for a graphic designer
  - UNIX workstation for an engineer
  - PC with spreadsheet for an accountant

- These systems may all be able to take advantage of the centralised data repository

- Openness of hardware and software components of client–server systems tends to lead to those components becoming commodities, which increases competition and lowers prices. Currently, PC hardware and operating-system software including DOS, Windows and OS/2 can be regarded as commodities

Disadvantages

► One of the main problems associated with adoption of client–server systems is the diversity of equipment and the need for versatility on the part of those managing them. The enterprise (not a paternal single supplier!) must diagnose component failures and must therefore have a better understanding than heretofore of how all the system components work and interact

► Increased maintenance/administration costs because of the proliferation of hardware and software components of different types

► It may be difficult to get components from different suppliers working together; as an example, data may be lost at the interfaces between software subsystems

► Cost: a database server (for example) usually requires a separate computer system

► There may be a lack of software tools for management of the client–server system and the enterprise may have to fund development of these tools. Examples include network management software and multi-platform software debuggers

► Client application software is typically fronted by a graphical user interface (GUI) which requires programming of a very different type from that familiar to traditional COBOL or C programmers. The event-driven paradigm can require much effort and expense to master

► Programmers and software developers working in a client–server environment need to be more versatile than those from the traditional background. Skills required include:

  ► LAN management
  ► Transaction processing
  ► Database design and programming
  ► Communications programming
  ► GUI programming

► Different client system architectures, for example: Sun workstation running UNIX; a PC running OS/2 or Windows; and Macintosh, make necessary tools which allow development of application software portable across them all

► The existence of many different client applications increases the cost of programming support and increases the impact of change

- Moving to client–server from the traditional environment requires a significant amount of relearning and retraining

- At first sight, moving to open client–server systems from a traditional system seems attractive on a cost basis. In practice, the balance of less-obvious advantages and disadvantages given may make the move cost-neutral at best. The actual benefit may be the business gain of improved service by means of a distributed system.

Database applications of client–server

Although the majority of current client–server implementations run database applications the client–server model is not restricted to such applications. In general, a database system is of two parts: a DBMS and a database application program to access and update information stored by the DBMS. It is common for both parts to reside on one computer, but the client–server model separates them.

In the client–server model, the database application program runs on one or more client workstations (usually PCs) and communicates with one or more DBMSs over a network. Under the relational database model, applications only see a logical view of the data, unlike in the hierarchical and network models. This encourages the separation of the DBMS from the accessing application in a client–server arrangement.

The front-end application program querying the RDBMS asks for data by means of an SQL request. The RDBMS does the necessary searching in a manner completely transparent to the front-end and returns the matching records.

This separation of function makes the RDBMS ideal for application in transaction processing and client–server databases. With other models, the application must make changes directly to the data. This can cause trouble if simultaneous access is attempted by more than one application. With an RDBMS, each change is a transaction done on a temporary copy of the table being changed. The changes are only applied at predefined intervals or when the user application commits them to the database. It is possible to maintain a transaction log of all changes, insertions and deletions which can be applied retrospectively to restore the database if it is corrupted.

Transactions on an RDBMS are usually (but not necessarily) expressed in SQL. General-purpose DBMSs use four language interfaces between the procedural programming language of the application and the DBMS.

These four languages are:

- ► Data Definition Language (DDL)
- ► Data Manipulation Language (DML)
- ► Query Language
- ► Report-Writer Language

SQL incorporates the first three; the report-writer must be separately provided by the DBMS or the client application.

Client–server DBMS architectures

There are four principal DBMS architectures (ways in which the constituent computers, peripheral devices and software comprising the database system are organised). They are these:

- ► Centralised DBMS
- ► Database on PC LAN
- ► Client–Server Database on PC LAN
- ► Distributed Database

Centralised DBMS

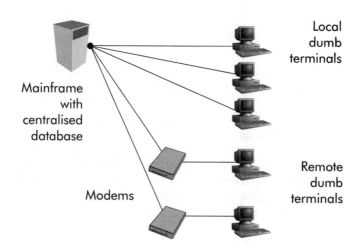

Traditional centralised mainframe-based database system

Mainframe with centralised database

Modems

Local dumb terminals

Remote dumb terminals

The centralised system is usually a mainframe or large minicomputer on which all processing takes place, including the DBMS, its applications, communications and terminal handling.

Users access the database by means of locally connected or remote dial-up terminals. In traditional implementations, the terminal are dumb and the central system must do all processing for them.

With the wide availability of microprocessors, even centralised systems now use smart terminals, which offload from the mainframe or minicomputer functions such as screen painting and handling of user input.

PCs can also be connected to centralised systems provided they are running appropriate communications software and can emulate the (typically 3270) terminal. The main advantages of the centralised database architecture are its security and reliability; the principal disadvantages are expense, total system failure if the central system fails, and lack of user flexibility.

Database on PC LAN

Conventional
database
arrangement
on a PC LAN

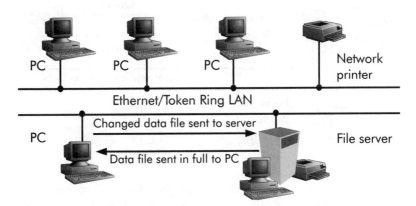

When a database is implemented on a PC LAN, one of the networked PCs is designated the file server: this PC supplies files on request to the other PCs on the network. The file server is usually a powerful PC which can respond quickly to the file requests. Typically, it also runs the network operating systems and stores all data and applications used by the other PCs.

The DBMS runs on the individual user PCs. When the DBMS wants a file, it makes a request on the file server, which sends back the whole file. The DBMS must then do the searching on the returned file and extract the data required.

LAN-based DBMSs such as this are really no more than multi-user versions of stand-alone PC database systems.

The performance of the DBMS is limited by the speed of the PC on which it runs, regardless of the performance of the file server. Because whole files are returned from the file server, network traffic can get very heavy when a number of users are simultaneously requesting data. Additionally, a scheme of record locking is required to ensure that simultaneous update operations do not corrupt the database. The problems of performance and network loading encountered with LAN-based DBMSs are addressed by the next DBMS architecture: the client–server model.

Client–server database on PC LAN

Client–server database arrangement on a PC LAN

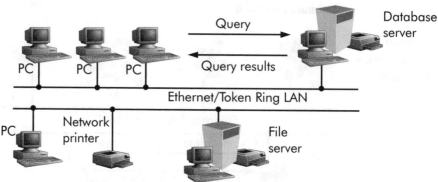

In the client–server model, the database processing is split (in the simplest case) between two systems: the client, usually a PC, running the database front-end application program and the server running the DBMS. The LAN file server continues to provide shared resources to the other PCs on the network, including print facilities and disk space.

The database server can be the same system as the file server but, for reasons of performance of performance and data integrity, the database server usually occupies a separate computer, which can range in power from PC to mainframe.

The database application – the front-end – runs on the client PC and handles all screen and I/O processing, including creation of queries on the DBMS. The DBMS back-end runs on the database server and handles all queries on the database.

Traffic on the network is reduced because the processing load is distributed between client and server. Database performance is improved by the fact that the DBMS engine is running on a powerful, dedicated system, not on a local PC.

The disadvantage of this arrangement is that the database must reside in full on one computer.

Distributed database

Distributed database arrangement on a LAN/WAN internetwork

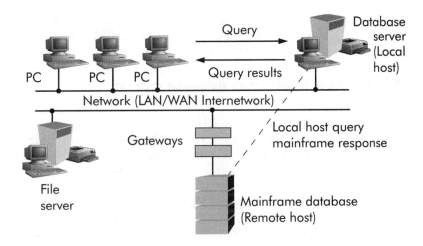

In the simplest form of distributed database, data is shared among many hosts, so-called *local hosts*. The database application program runs on some or all of the local hosts and, at a predefined interval, sends changed data to the other hosts which then update the other databases. In this arrangement, the central host is usually a mainframe and the databases across the network are synchronised after the end of a working day.

This scheme does not address the problem of how a user gets data which is not on the local host. The user has to change connections and to know which host is where. It is also difficult to combine, on the user's system, data retrieved from different hosts.

The local hosts cause a great deal of duplication of data.

The solution is the full distributed database architecture, in which the user requests data from the local host and that data is returned from somewhere on the network, without the user having to be aware of where it originated.

When the user issues the query, the local host may have the required data; if it does, it returns it. If the local host does not have the data, it issues a request over the network (which is likely to be a WAN connecting disparate systems using gateways, bridges and routers), gets the data from the system which has it and returns the data to the user who requested it. Users connected to another host can, in the same way, get data from this local host.

Keeping updates synchronised is difficult. If an application updates several databases then all the DBMSs have to ensure that all the updates worked on all the databases before finally committing them.

Advantages of client–server database systems

In a client–server database system, processing is split between the client and the database server. The speed of the DBMS server is not tied to that of the workstation. This fact allows PCs which are too slow to run database engines to be used as clients running a front-end application.

The fact that the DBMS is remote and the user is limited to making enquiries and updates on it through a front-end application means that the *integrity* of the data is safeguarded. It is possible for the DBMS, while handling queries, to:

- ▸ Do encrypted file storage
- ▸ Take database backups in real time
- ▸ Do disk mirroring (duplicate database information on the same disk)
- ▸ Do disk duplexing (duplicate information on a different disk)
- ▸ Take a log of transactions for possible future restoration of the database

Future directions for client–server databases

Multimedia technology is growing increasingly important in applications including catalogue shopping, banking and stock trading. To accommodate transfer of multimedia files, increased network bandwidth is required and SQL-type character-based tabular structures are not well suited to storing multimedia data.

Increasingly, hybrid relational/object-oriented databases will be developed in which the data is treated as an integrated object containing all necessary information about its own structure and retrieval strategy. With object-orientation, user queries are shortened – and network loading reduced – because the access operations are encapsulated in the database objects themselves.

On-line Transaction Processing (OLTP)

OLTP is one of the most important of all applications of distributed computing and database technology. It is a specialised form of distributed database processing offering a high degree of system reliability, data accuracy and fast recovery from failure.

Prominent applications of OLTP include fields such as airline reservation, financial and retail systems. The critical requirement is that a transaction on a data resource stored in part at a number of distributed locations will either be correctly completed in all its parts or will not be applied at all. Given the complexity of distributed databases and the diversity of hardware and software components they comprise, this is not a trivial requirement.

One of the classic OLTP applications is to bank Automated Teller Machines (ATMs). A simple example of an ATM transaction illustrates the required characteristics of the OLTP system managing it. A customer of the bank has two accounts, both of which are accessible from an ATM. The accounts are at separate branches and the account details in each case are stored on separate transaction processing systems connected as part of a WAN. The customer uses an ATM to transfer money between the two accounts. Both systems must record the transaction correctly and in full. If there is a failure or the transaction otherwise does not complete, the accounts must both be returned to the state they were in before the transaction was initiated.

An order-entry application presents similar requirements. The transaction is started by a telephone call from a customer to a retail outlet. The customer wants to make a purchase using a credit card. First, the credit card number is entered to an order-entry workstation. A credit check is requested and must be carried out using customer credit data held on one or more remote systems. If the check is successful, the card may be debited and the retail account credited. Then, from the workstation, order placement and shipping instructions must be dispatched to a warehouse system. Again, the whole purchase transaction must be done fully or not at all.

OLTP systems are characterised by the requirements of ACID: atomicity, consistency, isolation and durability. These are described as follows:

▸ *Atomicity:* any transaction started must be correctly completed in all parts at all distributed locations. If there is a failure, the whole distributed system must be returned to its state before the transaction

▸ *Consistency:* a transaction can only change a distributed database from one valid state to another valid state; it must not leave the database in an intermediate invalid condition

▸ *Isolation:* until it is complete, no transaction is visible to or affects any other transaction

▸ *Durability:* the effect of a completed transaction will continue to be reflected in the database unaltered by any later processing failures

The critical part of most OLTP systems is the transaction processing monitor, often called the TP monitor. The TPM ensures completion of a sequence of steps needed to process a client transaction. To do so, it must perform services such as message queueing, network routing, load balancing and application of the transaction to the different distributed systems involved. The transactions are often applied using the *two-phase commit* technique: only when it is ascertained that the transaction can be carried out on all participating systems is it applied to any of them.

The pre-eminent OLTP package currently available remains IBM's Customer Information Control System (CICS), with up to 30,000 installations worldwide. It was originally released in the 1970s for the hierarchical mainframe SNA environment (see *Systems Network*

Architecture (SNA) on page 222). CICS has been updated repeatedly since, to the point where it is now available in distributed computing environments incorporating IBM mainframes, AS/400, OS/2 and RS/6000 AIX (UNIX) systems. Additionally CICS OS/2 can be installed under OS/2 as either a server, allowing a PC to act as a full transaction monitor, or as a CICS client to a mainframe-based CICS server. The following is an idealised diagram of a distributed CICS environment of heterogeneous systems:

Distributed CICS
environment

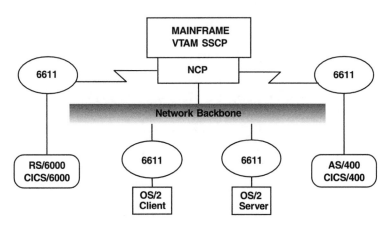

Refer to *Systems Network Architecture (SNA)* on page 222 for explanation of IBM terms and acronyms. The IBM 6611 is an APPN router.

CICS is a proprietary product of IBM and 20 years in existence, it is far more established than any open, standards-conforming competitor. The ISO 10026 series of standards specifies the necessary components of a distributed transaction processing (DTP) system as well as APIs for development of OLTP applications. The ACID characteristics are supported in full. A number of OLTP products now exist which claim to be open. The most prominent of these are:

▸ Tuxedo (Novell/USL)

▸ Top End (NCR)

▸ Encina, ENterprise Computing In a New Age (Transarc): a set of transaction-processing products, based on the Distributed Computing Environment (DCE) and announced by IBM to work with CICS/6000.

Afterword

The foregoing text has dealt with a very wide range of disparate subjects, many of them only loosely connected but all of them necessary to the construction of open, distributed, client/server computer systems. The technologies are advancing at such a pace that, during the time it has taken to write this book, revisions have been necessary 'on the fly' to take account of advances including Windows 95, OS/2 Warp, high-speed Ethernet, ATM and second-generation middleware, to name but a few. Keeping it up to date is rather like painting an ocean liner: upon reaching the propellers, you know that you will have to start again or at least patch rusty bits.

Predicting technology is a dangerous pastime, but a few glimpses into the future are attempted here.

At, or shortly after, the turn of the millennium, the distinctions between operating systems which today are still rather sharply evident will have largely disappeared. There will be a generic operating system (called, let us say, ACME or Advanced Computing and Media Environment) incorporating most of the facilities of historical UNIX, heavily influenced by Microsoft Windows derivatives and their application software and employing an object-oriented graphical interface descended from today's Apple Macintosh and OS/2 Workplace Shell products. ACME will be the base operating system layer underlying a distributed processing software framework of a type foreshadowed by today's Distributed Computing Environment, UI ATLAS and IBM Open Blueprint. ACME will run on all of the multi-BIP (billion instruction per second) RISC processors available; these will likely be descendants of the current DEC Alpha and PowerPC microprocessors. The dominance of the current Intel CISC processors, and that of the IBM PC standard, will fade but the new chips will provide options to emulate their operation.

In much the same way as few people today bother to look under the bonnet of their car, all users save a very few specialists will have only the dimmest awareness of the existence, never mind the operation, of their standard operating environment. The need for corporate product differentiation accepted, the forces demanding homogeneity will be overwhelming.

The predominant programming languages for development of business application software will remain COBOL and RPG, but with extensions implementing object-orientation and graphical interfaces. Successors of Visual Basic, adapted to run on ACME, will also be important. For technical software development, C++ (having completely subsumed C) will be predominant. Extensions to the C++ environment now on the horizon will be augmented and the language's originators may be prompted finally to take the plunge and call it D. Improved CASE tools will be produced as an antidote to the increasingly daunting complexity of D.

Multimedia and voice technologies will be ubiquitous. Integration of text, graphics, sound and prolonged television-quality presentations will be taken for granted. The keyboard will go the way of the punched card, as voice recognition reaches a state of refinement that makes typed input irrelevant.

Multimedia will require high-speed networking, ensuring the dominance of high-bandwidth network protocols derived from ATM, FDDI and B-ISDN. Few users will care though; they will see only the advanced mail, messaging, groupware and network management facilities that (quietly) use the underlying protocols. One hardy annual will remain: TCP/IP will not have been supplanted by OSI protocols.

Relational database technology will still be with us, but enhanced by integration with text data of all kinds of multimedia information. Fully distributed database networks will be common and middleware will be predominantly message- and object-oriented. Pure object-oriented databases will be important but will not have supplanted the relational workhorse.

So much for the crystal-ball gazing. If we are fortunate enough that this book requires further editions, I hope that not too many words will have to be eaten.

Appendix A

Glossary

Abstract data type: A programmer-defined type of a higher level of abstraction than the basic types provided by a programming language.

Abstract Syntax Notation 1 (ASN.1): In a network management system based on SNMP, a hierarchical naming sequence used to name network objects for which references are stored in the Management Information Base (MIB).

ACID: Set of requirements which characterise OLTP systems: they are atomicity, consistency, isolation and durability.

Ada: A procedural programming language, named after Augusta Ada Byron, an associate of Charles Babbage, designed under the direction of the United States DoD. The language is derived from Pascal but is also designed to support additional features such as data hiding, concurrent processing, operator overloading and modules.

Address: A name which identifies a location on a computer network, on a peripheral device or in computer memory. A network address identifies the location of a computer so that other machines can communicate with it.

Address Resolution Protocol (ARP): A set of addressing rules used to map network access layer addresses (such as Ethernet) to Internet addresses.

AIX: Advanced Interactive eXecutive; IBM's version of UNIX is based on UNIX System V and the Carnegie-Mellon Mach kernel.

Andrew File System: A distributed filesystem developed at Carnegie Mellon University.

Anonymous 'ftp': An 'ftp' login which accepts any password; it is often used on the Internet to access systems with publicly readable files.

ANSI: American National Standards Institute, proposes US standards to the International Standards Organisation (ISO) for adoption internationally.

ANSI C: The standardised generic version of the C language; the standard was devised by the American National Standards Institute committee X3J11 and adopted by ANSI in 1989 as American National Standard X3.159-1989 or "ANSI C". ANSI C was superseded in 1990 by the identical ISO (International Standards Organisation) C. The effect of these standards is that any C program conforming strictly to the ANSI/ISO specifications will, without change, compile and link correctly into an executable program on any computer system which supports an ANSI/ISO C compiler.

ANSI C++: The standardised version of C++, due to be completed in 1995; the ANSI C++ standardisation effort is based on the Annotated Reference Manual (Stroustrup & Ellis). The syntax of some language features, including templates and exception handling, is still not completely finalised.

APPC: The LU6.2 API (called a verb set by IBM). LU6.2 runs in a PU2.1 and using its own API allows programs running in distributed systems to communicate and share data directly.

APPN: A set of session and routing functions of which LU6.2 and APPC present the programmatic interface; used in modern distributed SNA systems to carry out functions equivalent to the Network and Transport layers of the OSI Reference Model.

Application Binary Interface (ABI): A specification that defines how executable programs are stored and how they interface with hardware on which they run. Given a common ABI, conforming programs can run on any system with the same processor architecture.

Application Program Interface (API): A definition of an interface comprising a number of function specifications which may be called by application programs. The calling programs do not have to know the internal details of the facility for which the API is the interface. Well-known APIs include the functions provided by Microsoft Windows for messaging and graphical display, and the Oracle DBMS API which provides database services.

Architecture: The way in which a computer system's microprocessor handles its internal data and commands. Architectures differ sharply from processor to processor. This inhibits binary compatibility of application programs.

Architecture Neutral Distribution Format (ANDF): A standard specifying an intermediate code format which allows shrink-wrapped software to be distributed for systems of different architectures in a way which hitherto had only been possible for IBM-compatible PCs. Using an ANDF producer on a system from which software is to be distributed, software is compiled from source-code into an intermediate form in which it is distributed. The target system further converts the distributed program image into its executable form using an ANDF installer.

Arithmetic and Logic Unit (ALU): The component of a computer's processor which does the actual computation and processing.

ARPANET: A network created by the US Department of Defense (DoD) Advanced Projects Research Agency which connected universities and corporations doing research for the US Government. ARPANET was part of the Internet until its recent disconnection and used the TCP/IP networking protocols.

ASCII: American Standard Code for Information Interchange; a standard 128-member character set encoding most the control, numeric, alphabetic and punctuation characters used in U.S. English.

Assembler Language: A mnemonic computer language of a higher level then machine code but lower than high-level languages such as COBOL and C. One assembler command typically corresponds to a single machine operation.

Asynchronous Terminal: A device which sends and receives data one character at a time, with each character being independently clocked out on transmission and clocked in on reception. An asynchronous terminal is also referred to as a serial terminal.

Asynchronous Transmission: Typically, character-by-character transmission, where the characters are clocked in at the receiving end of the communications medium.

Asynchronous Transfer Mode (ATM): A high-speed packet-switching LAN architecture based on fixed length frames, called cells, each of 53 bytes, including five bytes for header and address (virtual path) information. The cells are fixed in size to reduce the complexity of switches in the network. The cells are small, as well as fixed length, in order to be quickly transmitted and to meet requirements for short delays when transferring audio or video data.

AT&T: The company which originated UNIX through its research laboratory, Bell Laboratories.

B-ISDN: Broadband ISDN: integrates video, voice and data services over a public network using ATM as the underlying transfer protocol.

Berkeley Software Distribution (BSD): A series of UNIX system implementations developed at the University of California. The current version is BSD4.4; features of BSD4.2 are included in UNIX System V, Release 4.

Binary Synchronous Communication (BSC): Character-oriented data link protocol; encapsulates the data to be transmitted in sequences of non-printable character codes the interpretation of which governs the half-duplex transmission and reply.

Bit-mapped: (Of terminals) Where system memory is mapped onto a grid of bits rather than a grid of characters; usually used to refer to high-resolution (as opposed to character) terminals.

Bourne Shell: A command processor or shell, on which the standard UNIX System V shell is based; it is named after its author.

Bridge: A device used to connect networks; transmissions in one network destined for a computer on another are passed between the networks via the bridge. A bridge generally does not route the data to its destination; it only guarantees to get it to the right network.

Bus: A parallel set of electrical connections between the computer's processor and the main memory; can be used to transfer data or to specify a memory address.

C: A programming language of the 'ALGOL' algebraic class providing both high-level and low-level operations; the original definition of C was based on B and BCPL and is sometimes called 'Classic C'. Classic C is still widely used although it is being superseded by ANSI C.

C++: See ANSI C++.

C Shell: An alternative shell to the Bourne shell, developed at the University of California at Berkeley; the C shell has many syntactic similarities with the C language.

Cache: A special memory unit provided on a microprocessor in which commonly-executed instructions are temporarily stored and quickly retrieved.

Carrier Sense Multiple Access/Collision Detect (CSMA/CD): The transmission protocol on which Ethernet is based. A node needing to transmit a frame first checks to see if another node is transmitting. If not, it begins its own transmission. There is a delay before all the other nodes become aware that a transmission is in progress. During this delay, called acquisition time, another node may transmit and a collision results. The originating node listens to its own transmission and, if it detects a collision, aborts the transmission, which is scheduled for retry after a randomly-generated time interval.

CCITT: Consultative Committee for International Telephones and Telegraphs; European body which specifies standards for connection of equipment to public communication networks including the PSTN (the 'V' standards), PSDN (the 'X' standards) and ISDN (the 'I' standards).

CDIF: CASE Data Interchange Format, a set of standards which specifies formats for exchange of data between diverse CASE tools. These formats include entity descriptions, process logic and data flow diagrams.

Character: An entity represented by most small computer systems as an ASCII character code. Some characters are printable (for example, the letter 'A'); others, such as the newline, and carriage return are not displayed or printed; and some graphical characters are defined in extensions to the ASCII code set.

Character-based: (Of terminals) Opposite of bit-mapped.

Character set: A numeric encoding of a group of characters such that they can be represented in a computer's memory. In the ASCII character set, for example, the numbers 0 through 9 have the numeric encodings 48-57.

Class: An abstract data type which encapsulates declarations of data objects of more-basic types and declarations of functions that are allowed to operate on those data objects. In C++, the data objects are data members of the class, while the functions are member functions.

Class inheritance. The property of a derived class that allows it to take on all the characteristics of a base class and optionally add more.

Client: Generally, a workstation or PC that requests services from a larger and more powerful computer acting as the server. In the context of X Windows, the terms mean the opposite.

Client-server (X): X Windows is a client-server model in which the client – an application program running on a computer connected to an X-terminal – requests services of the software running on the terminal.

COBOL: Common Business-Oriented Language, a high-level third-generation language originated by the CODASYL (Committee on Data Systems Languages) in the 1950s. It is particularly suitable for use in business applications. COBOL has been codified as a standard a number of times, the most recent of which is the 1985 ANSI standard.

Command Interpreter: A program that parses and evaluates user input. The UNIX shells are examples.

Command Line: A line consisting of one or more commands, options and arguments, parsed, and submitted to the operating system for execution, by the shell.

The UNIX example:

```
ls -l -a -s *dat
```

lists all files with names ending in the characters 'dat' with size and long-listing information.

Command Line Interface (CLI): A user interface presenting a character-based command line. The original interfaces offered by the DOS, UNIX and OS/2 systems were command-line interfaces.

Common Application Environment (CAE): An environment specified by the X/Open organisation including not just standardised operating system interfaces based on UNIX but also applications such as languages and database systems.

Common Management Information Protocol (CMIP): A network management protocol that provides facilities for management by a network administrator of configuration, faults, performance, security and accounting within an ISO-conforming network.

Common Object Request Broker Architecture (CORBA): The first OO standard proposed by OMG, a specification which defines ORB implementations, services and interfaces.

Common Programming Interface-Communications (CPI-C): An API provided by IBM which allows application software can be written without regard for the underlying network protocol stacks. The abstraction provided by CPI-C is referred to by IBM as common transport semantics, meaning that the method used by applications to access the low-level network protocols, of whatever stack, is consistent.

Common User Access (CUA): A GUI usability standard proposed by IBM which guarantees consistent look-and-feel of interface software.

Compatibility (binary): Exists between two computer systems if a given executable program may be run without change on either; depends on the two systems' having the same processor architecture as, for example, have all IBM and compatible PCs.

Compatibility (source code): Exists between two computer systems if the source code of a given application program may be moved from one system to the other and, without change to the program or the target system's software environment, may be compiled and rendered executable on the target system.

Compatibility Package: A software package used to enable programs that were designed to run on a variant of the UNIX system, such as BSD or XENIX, to run on UNIX System V, Release 4.

Compiler: A program that parses a program written in a high-level language into tokens, performs grammatical analysis on the tokens and produces as its output an object code file.

Complex Instruction Set Computer (CISC): Microprocessors which implement an extensive set of low-level machine instructions, many of which have several operands and perform indirect memory addressing.

Computer-Aided Software Engineering (CASE): Software products that provide software engineers with tools to help them specify functional requirements and designs for software development projects. These tools include methodologies as well as computer programs for design and for automatic generation of code. CASE separates the design of a suite of application software from its coded implementation and automates the generation of software based on the design built with CASE tools.

COSE: An open systems profile defining standard approaches to implementing desktop, networking graphics, multimedia, object technology and system services;

promoted by a consortium including IBM and Hewlett-Packard.

Customer Information Control System (CICS): IBM's industrial-strength OLTP system; although originally mainframe-based, versions now exist for AIX and OS/2 platforms.

DARPA: Defense Advanced Research Projects Agency; an agency of the U.S. Department of Defense, responsible, in 1975, for promoting development of the TCP/IP set of network communications protocols and the resultant Internet connection of many computer networks throughout North America and Europe.

Datagram: A packet, transmitted across the Internet, which contains data and addressing information.

Derived class: A class derived from a base class and inheriting its characteristics; also sometimes called a 'subclass'.

Device Driver: A program that controls transfer of data between a peripheral device and the application via the operating system.

Directory Service (DS): Naming service used in a network to provide a directory of users who can be reached over the network.

Distributed Computing Environment (DCE): A set of standards and products implementing distributed computing based on the OSF/1 version of UNIX.

Distributed File System (DFS): A filesystem in which programs and data files are physically distributed across more than one computer system connected by a network but which can be used in much the same way as a local file by any local or remote user who has access to them.

Distributed Queue Dual Bus (DQDB): The standard protocol for Metropolitan Area Networks; specifies two parallel fibre-optic cables connecting network nodes. The parallel cables offer redundancy and good reliability, while the realistic throughput is 80Mbps, a rate sufficient for a backbone connecting LANs, or almost any other application. DQDB offers connection-oriented, connectionless and isochronous (transmission of equal time segments).

Domain Name Service (DNS): The domain name service for the Internet providing node name translations.

Domain: In the Internet, part of the naming hierarchy consisting of a sequence of names followed by dots.

DOS: Disk Operating System, the original operating system of the IBM PC, also referred to as MS-DOS and PC-DOS.

E1: A PSDN transmission medium providing leased, point-to-point fixed-bandwidth services operating at 2.048Mbps, capable of carrying 29 64Kbps B channels using the ISDN standard.

EBCDIC: Extended Binary Coded Decimal Interchange Code. A character set alternative to ASCII that is mainly used by IBM computers.

ECMA: The European Computer Manufacturers' Association.

E-Mail: A facility which allows users on remote computer systems to exchange messages. Under UNIX, e-mail is implemented using 'uucp' and TCP/IP.

Encina: Encina, ENterprise Computing In a New Age (Transarc): a set of transaction-processing products, based on the Distributed Computing Environment (DCE) and announced by IBM to work with CICS/6000.

Encryption: Encoding of the contents of a file, using a key, to produce cipher text. After encryption, the contents of the file must first be decrypted using the same key before it can be read.

Ethernet: A set of data transmission rules governing the passing of packets of data over a network of computers and other devices typically connected by a coaxial cable. Ethernet is a contention protocol, relying on data being re-transmitted if it fails to reach its destination. Maximum speed of transmission is 10MB/sec.

Executable File: In UNIX, a text or binary file which has permissions set to allow execution by typing the name of the file.

External Data Representation (XDR): A data format used in an NFS network to provide a common representation of data on different machines running different operating systems.

Fibre Distributed Data Interface (FDDI): A standard specified by ANSI for high-speed fibre-optic LANs. It provides specifications for transfer rates of 100Mbps over Token Ring-based networks.

File: A collection of characters or binary data, perhaps resident on an external storage device such as a disk.

File Server: A computer system on a network acting as a central repository for files and application programs which are accessible by other machines on the network.

File Sharing: The process of allowing files on one system to be accessed by users on another. UNIX file sharing environments include RFS and NFS.

Filesystem: A hierarchical structure of directories and files, organised in UNIX as a collection of linked blocks, which may be mounted and unmounted under the name of a directory.

File Transfer: The process of moving or transmitting a file from one location to another, as between two programs or between one computer and another.

File Transfer Access Method (FTAM): A protocol according to which distributed client application programs can access a remote file server, possibly with a different operating system and filesystem from those of the clients. FTAM also allows transparent transfer of files between systems differing in these characteristics.

File Transfer Protocol (FTP): A scheme available within the Internet which permits authorised users to log in to a remote system, identify themselves, list directories and send and receive files.

Fortran: Formula Translation, originated at IBM in the mid-1950s. One of the first high-level algebraic programming languages, particularly suited to use in mathematical and computational applications.

Fourth-Generation Language (4GL): High-level programming languages with syntax of a level of abstraction from computer hardware higher than third-generation languages such as COBOL and Fortran. They are easier to program but carry a consequent performance cost.

Frame Relay: The Frame Relay protocol is a derivative of X.25 which is simpler and does relatively little error-checking. It assumes the availability of high-quality digital and fibre-optic physical media. The protocol functions at Layer 2 of the OSI Reference Model, providing a connection-oriented service called the permanent virtual circuit (PVC).

Front-End Processor: In an IBM mainframe environment, communications controllers which serve to offload responsibility for terminal handling from the mainframe processor.

Gateway: A device for storing and forwarding packets between networks. More powerful than a bridge, a gateway can be used to connect networks with incompatible addressing formats.

GUI: Graphical User Interface providing a uniform graphical interface allowing easy use of application programs by means of icons, menus, scroll bars and other controls. UNIX GUIs include Motif and Open Look.

HDLC: A standard bit-oriented data link control protocol which is the basis for all modern network data link protocols.

HP-UX: UNIX variant produced by Hewlett-Packard Corp.

IEEE: Institute of Electrical and Electronic Engineers; a U.S. standards body, responsible for the POSIX family, which refers its agreed standards to ANSI for ratification.

IEEE 802 Standards: A set of layer 1 and 2 communications protocols defining transmission rules for various network types. 802.2 defines the uniform interface presented at the Logical Link Control (LLC) layer; 802.3 specifies rules for transmission in an Ethernet network; 802.4 Token Bus; 802.5 Token Ring; and 802.6 the Metropolitan Area Network.

Integrated Services Digital Network (ISDN): A world-wide digital communications network which is an outgrowth of existing telephone services. Its goal is to replace current telephone lines, which require digital to analogue conversion, with digital switching and transmission facilities capable of supporting a variety of digital services including transmission of voice, data, music and video. The ISDN uses two channels, the B channel and the D channel. The latter carries control information; the B channel carries data at a rate of 64Kbps. Many B channels can be multiplexed onto higher-capacity trunk lines.

Internet: The DARPA network using the Internet communication protocol suite; the Internet connects many different networks and is used to share information and resources among its sites.

Internet Activities Board (IAB): The body appointed by ISOC to be responsible for setting the technical direction and defining the standards to be used on the Internet.

Internet Address: An address consisting of four fields of eight bits each that uniquely identifies a machine to the Internet and allows TCP/IP communications to occur.

Internet Control Message Protocol (ICMP): An Internet protocol which records error and control information generated by TCP/IP software and notifies concerned parties about errors which occur in transmission. ICMP enables hosts and routers to exchange information about the state of the network so that, for example, the most efficient route can be used. ICMP data is transmitted within IP datagrams.

Internet Protocol (IP): An internetworking protocol which provides connectionless communication service across multiple packet-switched networks.

IRDS: Information Resource Dictionary System, an entity-relationship model defining the contents of a CASE object repository, the way information is stored in the repository and how CASE tools should access this information

ISO: International Standards Organisation, responsible for definition of the Reference Model and many related standards; ratifies national standards such as those adopted by ANSI.

ISO C: ISO C standard 9899:1990, includes ANSI standard C, reference X3.159-1989.

ISO Standards: The standards populating the seven-layer Reference Model; for a partial summary, see page 215.

Kernel: The part of an operating system which controls process scheduling, file and other I/O operations and which interfaces to the system hardware.

Korn Shell: A command line processor, or shell, named after its author and designed to run with UNIX System V, Release 4. It is a superset of the standard shell, 'sh'.

LAN Manager: Network operating system jointly developed in the late 1980s by Microsoft and 3Com as a potential competitor to NetWare. Many other companies, including DEC, IBM, HP and AT&T back the product and supply their own version.

LAP-B: A subset of HDLC used at the data-link level within X.25 to transmit frames between DTE and DCE.

LAP-D: The data-link protocol used by Frame Relay; LAP-D is the Link Access Protocol - D Channel signalling standard developed for

ISDN.

Linear Addressing: Non-segmented memory addressing, characterised by the 4GB addressability made possible by the 32-bit 80386 processor and contrasting with the 16-bit addressing used by the 80286 and earlier chips.

Linkage Editor: Referred to in UNIX as the loader; combines object-code files produced by a compiler with library files to produce as output an executable program.

LLC: Logical Link Control; in LAN and MAN protocols, the upper sublayer of layer 2. It provides a level of abstraction to the network protocol, hiding the underlying protocol details at the MAC layer.

Loader: *See Linkage Editor.*

Locale: A set of conventions governing style and formats of data representation for a given national environment or culture.

Logical Unit (LU): In an IBM SNA environment, software corresponding to an end-user terminal.

LU2.0: In an IBM SNA environment, a type of program running on a networked PC that causes the PC to emulate a dumb terminal.

LU6.2: In an IBM SNA environment, communications software which supports sessions between application programs running on different computers in a distributed data processing environment.

MAC: Media Access Control; in LANs and MANs, the lower sublayer of layer 2. The MAC layer encapsulates the principles on which the different LAN types operate, including CSMA/CD for Ethernet and token-passing for Token Ring.

Mach Kernel: A streamlined UNIX kernel, developed at Carnegie-Mellon University, and used in a number of UNIX variants, including AIX and OSF/1.

Macro: A group of instructions combined into one instruction and referenced by a name. UNIX contains a macro package for writing memorandums and the 'vi' editor contains macros to speed editing.

Message-Oriented Middleware (MOM): Middleware using messaging, as opposed to RPC, for communication between software modules distributed over a network.

Message Handling System: The X.400 messaging protocol.

Message Transfer Agent (MTA): An intermediate system within an X.400 network; used to transfer messages on a store-and-forward basis.

Microkernel: A UNIX kernel made as small as possible, relegating all unnecessary facilities to the user area and controlling communication between them by means of messaging.

Motif: A GUI, similar in some respects to Microsoft Windows, introduced by the Open Software Foundation (OSF) and since adopted in many variants of UNIX.

Mount: The act of making a filesystem available for use by associating the filesystem with an existing directory. To use the mounted filesystem, the user changes to that directory.

Mount Point: The directory name where a filesystem is mounted.

Multiple inheritance: Class inheritance where a derived class has more than one base class.

Multistation Access Unit (MAU): In a Token Ring LAN, the MAU contains circuits that cause the physical star topology to be treated as a logical ring. Individual stations can be up to 150 feet distant from their MAU, by which they are in turn connected to the ring network.

Multitasking: UNIX is characterised as a multitasking operating system; it can run more than one process concurrently.

NetWare: LAN network operating system supplied by Novell Inc.

NetWare Loadable Module (NLM): In NetWare systems, the way in which network applications, which run on the server and can be used from client systems, are built and loaded on the network. Applications written as NLMs can be considered in two categories: application facilities provided by the NetWare environment; and popular third-party application software ported to NetWare.

Network Addressable Unit (NAU): IBM terminology used to describe elements, logical and physical, of SNA networks.

Network Control Program (NCP): In IBM SNA networks, software running on a front-end processor controlling connected terminals.

Network File System (NFS): A protocol set and associated programs, developed by Sun Microsystems, which allows file transfer to be carried out over heterogeneous (including UNIX-system) networks.

Network Information Center (NIC): The authorising agency that issues TCP/IP network addresses.

Network Information Service (NIS): A distributed database lookup service that maintains a set of databases and propagates databases among systems on the IP network ensuring consistency.

Network Operating System (NOS): A program that controls the operation of a LAN, in particular redirecting requests for resources from a local system connected to the LAN to the system actually possessing those resources.

NextStep: An object-oriented variant of UNIX provided by Next Inc., which provides a uniform graphical interface, superior mail facilities and integrates voice and video as well as text data.

Node: A computer on a network; it may be a gateway on an internetwork.

Object: In C++, an instantiation, or definition, of a class declaration.

Object Management Group (OMG): A non-profit consortium of information system companies; the main body concerned with establishment of OO standards. OMG is responsible for the CORBA specification.

Object-Oriented Programming (OOP): The programming method that uses the object-oriented approach: rather than concentrating on function and defining data later, or vice-versa, data and functions are defined concurrently in classes.

Object Request Broker (ORB): A mechanism for messaging between objects. ORB specifies, among other things: object naming and location; invocation of object methods (to pass a message to an object is to call one of its methods); and encoding of parameters accepted by those methods.

On-Line Transaction Processing (OLTP): Distributed database software that synchronises data updates across a network by maintaining several concurrently running processes on different data repositories.

Open Database Connectivity (ODBC): A body of software, supplied by Microsoft, which allows a number of database front-ends to issue SQL-type requests on different database engines, in the process resolving differences in the various products' SQL implementations.

Open Desktop (ODT): UNIX and GUI environment supplied by the Santa Cruz Operation (SCO).

Open Look: A GUI developed by UNIX System Laboratories (USL) and Sun Microsystems, designed to run with UNIX System V, Release 4 and based on X Windows system.

Open Network Computing+ (ONC+): A distributed computing model specified by Sun Microsystems Inc. and encompassed by the Solaris 2.0 product offering. ONC supports the NFS (Network File System) distributed file system; a directory service for supporting enterprise networks; the transport-independent RPC (TI-RPC) facility for distributed applications and the Kerberos security system.

Open Systems: The concept of implementing non-proprietary operating systems, typically based on UNIX, for easy transfer of software between systems and independence of the software from any particular vendor.

Open Windows: UNIX desktop GUI environment supplied by Sun Microsystems, marketed as part of the Solaris operating system (based on UNIX System V, Release 4); incorporates Open Look and competes with Motif.

Open Software Foundation (OSF): A consortium of system vendors, including IBM, DEC and Hewlett-Packard, which supplies the OSF/1 UNIX variant.

OS/2: The single-user, multitasking operating system supplied by IBM for use with Intel-based PCs.

P1003.n: The working groups dealing with the various topics covered by POSIX are called P1003.n, in the case of the operating system interface, P1003.1. The name of a project dealt with by a working group drops the leading 'P', so the operating system interface project is 1003.1. The approved standard based on the conclusions of P1003.1 is called IEEE Std 1003.1-1990. This is also called simply 1003.1 or, synonymously, POSIX.1.

Packet Assembler/Disassembler (PAD): The process, and the software, used to break into packets messages transmitted over an X.25 network and to reassemble them on reception.

PCTE: Portable Common Tools Environment, an initiative of the European Computer Manufacturers' Association (ECMA) to provide a reference model for software engineering environments, into which various CASE development tools can be plugged. PCTE is being considered for adoption as an ISO standard. It specifies methods of data integration, data modelling and data sharing across different CASE tools.

Peer-to-peer: A network node in peer-to-peer communication with other nodes operates at the same protocol layer as those nodes, and contributes resources to the network while at the same time running autonomously and executing its own application programs.

Physical Unit: In an IBM SNA environment, different physical devices on the network: PU5 is a large computer; PU4 a front-end processor and PU2 is a terminal controller. The physical units all run software programs, called LUs, which implement different aspects of network communication.

PU2.0: In an IBM SNA network, the least capable type of physical unit, serving as a terminal concentrator supporting dumb terminals, or PCs emulating dumb terminals, which run LU2.0.

PU2.1: In an IBM SNA network, PU2.1 are intelligent, do not require SSCP to establish network sessions and can maintain peer-to-peer (LU-LU) communication with each other. They are sometimes referred to as Low Entry Networking (LEN) End Nodes and are usually implemented with PCs or other computers.

Point-to-point: Direct communications connection between two computer systems: the simplest type of network.

Polymorphism: Processing of 'many forms'; in C++ implemented with virtual functions. Under polymorphism, an operation is defined for all members of a class hierarchy. The operations in the various members of the hierarchy differ in detail. Depending on the type of the class object in use, the language system guarantees that the appropriate overriding definition of the virtual function will be called without the programmer having to be aware of the type of object in use.

Port: A connection point from a system processor to an external device such as a terminal, printer or modem.

Portable Operating System Interface (POSIX): A set of existing and emerging standards defined by the Institute of Electrical and Electronic Engineers (IEEE) to specify the characteristics of an operating system between which application programs are generally portable, and utilities associated with such an operating system.

Pre-emptive: An operating-system characteristic, not generally embodied in UNIX, which means that the kernel has the power to terminate execution of a process running under the control of the kernel. Real-time operating systems have pre-emptive kernel scheduling.

Presentation Manager (PM): The software controlling operation of the GUI (Workplace Shell) presented as the interface of the OS/2 operating system. PM also has an API that can be used to program the GUI.

Process: A transient image in memory of a program in execution.

Project Athena (X): The MIT research project that did the original definition of the X Window system, in 1984.

PSDN: Public Switched Data Network, a digital transmission service provided by a data communications carrier and designed to carry binary data over long distances at high speeds.

PSTN: Public Switched Telephone Network (the telephone system), an analogue transmission service designed to carry voice messages over long distances at low speeds. The PSTN can be used for data transmission if the data is converted before transmission to analogue form (modulation) and afterward back to digital (demodulation).

Real-time: A process is real-time if it can be guaranteed that it will terminate before a definite time-limit.

Reduced Instruction Set Computer (RISC): Contrasts with CISC. RISC processors use relatively few simple instructions which are then combined the more-complex instructions of their RISC counterparts. All I/O is done with high-speed registers. RISC chips are always faster than equivalent CISC devices but need software to be tailored to take advantage of their capabilities.

Reference Model: The ISO Seven-layer Reference Model for Open Systems Interconnection; specifies a large number of layered protocols for networking of hetero-geneous computer systems.

Remote Execution: A mechanism to execute a process on a system other than the local one, without having to log in at the remote machine.

Remote File Sharing (RFS): In UNIX System V Release 4, a networking facility which allows processors to share file systems across the network.

Remote Procedure Call (RPC): A network system call which allows execution of a procedure on a remote networked machine also running RPC; used by NFS.

Request For Comment (RFC): The first stage in the procedure under which Internet protocols and standards are implemented. RFCs that are submitted to the IAB and the Internet community for examination and approval. RFCs are published by the IAB and may be obtained from the Network Information Center (NIC), which also administers and issues Internet addresses.

Repeater: An electrical device acting as a signal booster; connects two LAN segments and passes on all data it receives in both directions. Extends the normal transmission range from 500 m to 2 km.

Resource (device): A system's devices and filesystems are resources that can be shared by other systems on the network.

Resource (Window): In the context of a GUI, resources include such things as bitmaps, dialog box specifications and message text.

Router: A device which interconnects LANs, enabling messages to be sent from one to another. A router receives messages transmitted from one computer and forwards them to their destination over the most efficient available route.

RS-232C: A device interface standard used to control interconnection of DTE and DCE (modem) equipment over short (typically less than 100 metres) distances. RS-232C defines a set of signals numbered from 101 to 125 which are used to control orderly flow of data between DTEs or between DTE and DCE.

r* Commands: A set of networking

commands which allow operations to be started from a local computer on a remote networked system. The commands include 'rsh', which executes a shell on the remote system, and 'rlogin'.

Santa Cruz Operation (SCO): The company which combined XENIX and UNIX System V to produce SCO UNIX System V/386 Release 3.2; now markets its version of UNIX with the ODT graphical environment.

Server: A computer in a networked environment which provides resources for clients on the network. In the context of X Windows, the server is the program controlling display on the X Terminal and the client is the program whose results are displayed.

Share: The act of allowing other users of a distributed file system access to resources, such as files, on a local system.

Shell: A process that handles and controls the execution of commands input by a UNIX user; shell programs include 'csh', 'ksh', and 'sh'.

Simple Mail Transfer Protocol (SMTP): The standard electronic-mail system used within the Internet.

Simple Network Management Protocol (SNMP): The standard network-management procedure used within the Internet, SNMP exchanges data between the computer being managed and the network management station. SNMP may be used for queries relating to entries in the routing table, the state of network interfaces and

protocol statistics.

SMDS: A data transmission service based on IEEE 802.6 and DQDB, SMDS is offered in a number of cities in the U.S.A. by the Bell companies. SMDS is suitable for transmission of traffic in concentrated bursts of the type common with many LAN architectures, including Ethernet. Consequently, SMDS is useful for linking conventional LANs within a metropolitan area.

Sockets: A means in BSD4.3 by which a process can access the Internet. A process opens a socket, specifies the service desired, such as reliable stream delivery, and then sends or receives data.

Solaris: The UNIX software environment developed by Sun Microsystems; it consists of SunOS (Sun's System V Release 4-compatible operating system), X Windows, Open Windows and the Deskset Tools.

SONET: An alternative to FDDI for implementation of fibre-optic LANs; it was adopted by ANSI in 1990. SONET allows transmission products from different vendors to be connected on the same link. It provides extremely high bandwidths, in the range 51.84Mbps to 2,488.32Mbps.

SPEC 1170: The set of APIs specified by the COSE consortium for its open computing environment; the name arises from the number of function calls supposedly contained in the APIs.

SPX/IPX: The transport and network layer protocols underlying Novell's NetWare network operating system.

SSCP: In an IBM SNA environment, the main control point, implemented by VTAM which, in older systems, entirely controls the network's operation.

Structured Query Language (SQL): A database sublanguage used for querying, updating and managing relational databases. SQL is used in formulating interactive queries to be applied to a database, and for embedding in application programs (written in other languages) as instructions for handling data.

Subnet Address: An Internet address of which part is used to represent other networks; a given address can then refer to several networks.

SunOS: Sun Microsystems' System V Release 4-compatible version of the UNIX operating system. Solaris in turn incorporates SunOS.

System Application Architecture (SAA): A strategy to tie together IBM's multiple system architectures in a manner that ensures consistent operation of application programs across them all. SAA is a set of software interfaces, conventions and communication protocols that provides a framework for developing integrated applications for all the architectures. In principle, a program that complies with the specifications of SAA is independent of the underlying IBM hardware and operating system: it will run unchanged on any IBM SAA system.

System Call: A call made by a process on an operating system kernel to request a service (such as reading data from a file) of the kernel.

System Network Architecture (SNA): IBM data network architecture, SNA is capable of linking all the computing devices used by an enterprise and of allowing them to share and transfer data. Traditional hierarchical SNA is being supplanted by APPC/APPN allowing peer-to-peer communication by terminals connected to the network.

System V: The version of UNIX released by AT&T in 1983, which was based on UNIX version 7 and System III, and which guaranteed forward compatibility: any program capable of running on System V Release 1 would also run on all later System V Releases. System V and its derivatives are the most common versions of UNIX. The current Release is System V Release 4.2.

System V Interface Definition (SVID): A document first released in 1985 specifying, among other things, the system call interface to which programs must adhere in order to be compatible with UNIX System V.

System V Verification Suite (SVVS): A set of test programs that can be used by system developers to verify that the SVID specifications have been met on a new port or version of UNIX System V.

T1: A PSDN transmission medium providing leased, point-to-point fixed-bandwidth services operating at 1.544Mbps, capable of carrying 23 64Kbps B channels using the ISDN standard.

Thread: A part of a process that can execute largely independently of other parts of the process. Threads are effectively sub-processes. OS/2 and recent Windows products support threads but most versions of UNIX do not.

TCP/IP: Transmission Control Protocol/Internet Protocol. A set of network communications protocols developed by the Advanced Projects Research Agency (ARPA) of the U.S. Department of Defense (DoD) and now supplied as standard with most versions of UNIX. TCP/IP provides for reliable transmission of packets over networks and internetworks and is the basis of the Internet public network.

'telnet': A process which allows users remotely to log in to computers on a TCP/IP network.

Token Ring: The LAN protocol originated by IBM and codified by the IEEE as standard 802.5

Transmission Control Protocol (TCP): The protocol implementing the reliable stream service provided by the Internet. In contrast to the underlying IP protocol, TCP ensures correct, orderly, delivery of messages transmitted.

Transport Layer Interface (TLI): The interface to the Transport Layer of the Open Systems Interconnection Reference Model; it has been implemented for UNIX and allows programs to use the TLI library to get services from the network without having to be aware of the implementation details.

Trivial File Transfer Protocol (TFTP): A simple communications protocol for transferring files across a TCP/IP network.

Tuxedo: The open OLTP software product supplied by Novell Inc.

UI ATLAS: A model for distributed computing, similar to OSF DCE, which specifies standards to be used in desktop, distributed and corporate hub computing

UniForum: An international organisation of UNIX system users formerly known as /usr/group. UniForum is active in defining and promoting standard for Open Systems.

UNIX: The multi-user, multitasking operating system, originated by Bell Laboratories in 1969, now supplied by Novell Inc. as UnixWare; UNIX is at the heart of all specifications of open systems.

UNIX International (UI): Disbanded in 1994, a consortium of system vendors that was set up to advise the UNIX Software Laboratories on the development and marketing of UNIX System V Release 4.

UNIX Software Laboratories (USL): The body set up as an independent operation by AT&T to develop the UNIX system according to the specifications and direction provided by UI.

UnixWare: The version of UNIX, based on System V Release 4.2 and supplied by Novell Inc; Novell now owns the UNIX trademark. UnixWare features very tight integration with the company's NetWare LAN communication products.

User Agent (UA): The end-user system in an X.400 message handling system.

User Datagram Protocol (UDP): A simpler alternative to TCP, UDP uses the underlying IP protocols to carry datagrams – simple packets of data – between network addresses on a so-called unreliable basis. The message will probably get to its destination but very little verification is done to see that it does.

'uucp': A system of commands used for communication between computers running UNIX, including file transfer, remote execution and terminal emulation.

V Standards (CCITT): A set of standards specifying characteristics of low-level device interfaces; V.24 and V.28 are collectively equivalent to the RS-232C standard.

VINES: A network operating system based on a modified version of UNIX, SVR3.2.1, supplied by Banyan Systems.

Virtual Filesystem: A filesystem architecture incorporated in System V Release 4 from BSD which allows multiple types of filesystem to reside on the same machine.

Virtual Memory: A scheme of memory management, involving paging of parts of processes to disk when there is insufficient real memory available to accommodate them. Virtual memory is available in many versions of UNIX.

Virtual Terminal Access Method (VTAM): Program in an IBM SNA network that controls the SSCP and access by connected terminals to a central computer system.

Windows: The GUI and operating environment supplied for PC systems by Microsoft; the term can now be taken to mean any of Windows 3.X, Windows 95 or Windows NT.

Widget (X): In X Windows, a function which implements a graphical display such as a scroll-bar, push button or pop-up menu.

X Network Protocol: The set of rules governing communication between X clients and X servers. The protocol consists of two types of messages, requests and events. Requests implement actions such as drawing screen objects and events report to the software things that happen at a hardware level, for example a mouse-click.

X Server: The terminal part of the X Windows system, it services display requests generated by application programs running on the X client.

X Standards: A set of standards for data communication over PSDNs, published by the CCITT. Examples include X.3, X.28, X.29, X.25 and X.400. Many of the X standards have ISO equivalents in the Reference Model. See page 215 for a partial summary.

X Windows: A networked, device independent system for windowing on bit-mapped displays. It originated at MIT in 1984 and has since been included in most UNIX versions as the software on which their GUIs are based.

X/Open: A consortium of system vendors which promotes Open System standards and confers brandings for conforming products, but which does not develop any standards of its own.

X/Open Portability Guide (XPG): A specification of requirements for software portability published by the X/Open Organization. Programs which conform to the XPG should be portable at the source-code level between all conforming systems.

X3J11: The ANSI technical subcommittee responsible for drafting the ANSI C standard.

XDR (External Data Representation): A machine-independent standard for the description and encoding of data used by RPC to transfer arbitrary data between networked systems of different internal architectures.

XENIX: The version of UNIX originally introduced by Microsoft in 1982 for IBM-compatible PCs. It has since been taken over by SCO and has merged with UNIX System V Release 3.2.

Yellow Pages: *– See Network Information Service (NIS).*

Index

A